Laws, Outlaws, and Terrorists

The Belfer Center Studies in International Security book series is edited at the Belfer Center for Science and International Affairs at Harvard University's John F. Kennedy School of Government and published by the MIT Press. The series publishes books on contemporary issues in international security policy, as well as their conceptual and historical foundations. Topics of particular interest to the series include the spread of weapons of mass destruction, internal conflict, the international effects of democracy and democratization, and U.S. defense policy.

A complete list of Belfer Center Studies in International Security appears at the back of this book.

Laws, Outlaws, and Terrorists

Lessons from the War on Terrorism

Gabriella Blum and Philip B. Heymann

Belfer Center Studies in International Security

The MIT Press
Cambridge, Massachusetts
London, England

For information about special quantity discounts, please email special_sales@ mitpress.mit.edu

This book was set in Sabon 10/14 by Toppan Best-set Premedia Limited. Printed and bound in the United States of America.

Library of Congress Cataloging-in-Publication Data
Blum, Gabriella.
Laws, outlaws, and terrorists : lessons from the War on Terrorism / Gabriella Blum and Philip B. Heymann.
    p.   cm. — (Belfer Center studies in international security)
Includes bibliographical references and index.
ISBN 978-0-262-01475-5 (hardcover : alk. paper) 1. War on Terrorism, 2001–2009. 2. Terrorism—United States—Prevention. 3. Terrorism—Government policy—United States. I. Heymann, Philip B. II. Title.
HV6432.B58 2010
363.325'15610973—dc22
                                                                    2010005427

10   9   8   7   6   5   4   3   2   1

Contents

Preface

The motivation to coauthor this book was sparked when we began teaching together first a reading group, then a course, on the Law and Policy of Counterterrorism at Harvard Law School. With different professional and academic backgrounds, we each brought our own training and inclinations to the subject. Gabriella Blum specializes in public international law with a particular focus on the laws of armed conflict; this, and her experience as a lawyer for the Israel Defense Forces, shapes her approach to the challenges of dealing with international terrorism. Philip Heymann has a long career of both practice and teaching in domestic law enforcement and pre-9/11 terrorism, subjects on which he has also written several books. His own experience likewise shapes his approach to addressing the threat of international terrorism.

Given our divergent experiences and perspectives, we expected to find ourselves on opposite sides of the familiar debates. In fact, this was mostly not the case. Even where we disagreed, for instance, over whether terrorism was essentially a crime or an act of war, our disagreement did not have significant consequences. We might also have found ourselves on opposite sides of the Cheney/Obama argument about how beneficial or costly it would be to depart from liberal-democratic values as embodied in domestic and international law. On this count, however, disagreement never materialized. We found that we had very similar views of what history, comparative practice, and common sense instruct about the issues America faces in dealing with terrorism. More important, we discovered a common underlying approach. Blum relied on the protections of the laws of war as limits that should not be breached absent extraordinarily compelling circumstances. Heymann naturally turned to the protections of civil liberties in the United States and its allies; for him, it was this body of law that staked out the bounds of acceptable action, which were not to be crossed unnecessarily or based only on an assertion—rejected by most of our friends—that we were in some sort of war. Ultimately, these two different paradigms led us to nearly the same place: when debating particular issues, we found that our boundaries were very similar.

From there, we considered how we could employ our legal instincts to approach the all-too-real threat of international terrorism without destroying values that mattered deeply to both of us: respect for human dignity and the rule of law. In order to design a sound counterterrorism strategy for the United States, we started with the axiom that there were certain principles to which a rule-of-law democracy, embedded within a larger community of nations, must adhere. We also both believed that in weighing the burdens and dangers that a government should expect its citizens or others to accept, any departure from international or domestic commitments must be reserved for the most exceptional cases and employed to the most limited extent possible. This proposition held true whether we approached terror attacks as acts of war, warranting a response governed by the laws of war, or as a crime, requiring a law enforcement approach. We discovered that many of the practices of the previous administration, and some of the current one, were not truly faithful to either body of law, and we were unconvinced by the justifications proffered for such departures from legal protections. The key, for us, is that any deviation from legal rules must still respect the underlying values and principles that animate the law to begin with. This standard was frequently met.

We did sometimes disagree on particular measures or on particular instances of accommodating law and necessity. These occasional debates usually arose because the laws of war, as a general matter, permit a country to use more aggressive means against external threats than the laws of peace do. Legitimate disagreements can arise over measures that a law enforcement model (which has been favored by many of our allies) would preclude, but that a war model would permit. Pushing the boundaries of the law enforcement model was sometimes necessary and allowed those entrusted with our security some bounded leeway to exceed the limits of criminal law when confronted with the unique dangers of transnational terrorism. From both a moral and strategic perspective, however, it remains much harder to justify those measures that go even beyond the principles that animate the war model.

It is for the most part a fallacy—although an oft-repeated one—that adherence to the rule of law and individual rights necessarily comes at the expense of security needs. A commitment to certain liberal-democratic traditions *is* part of our security. Moreover, experience time and again has shown that the most aggressive and hotly contested means (such as torture, detention without protections, or overwhelming fire-power), some of which required a departure from preexisting legal understandings, may backfire and actually undermine our security.

The threat of transnational terrorism is here to stay for the foreseeable future. The most recent events in Fort Hood and on the Northwest air-liner bound for Detroit prove that the threat remains, and that it doesn't take one particular form or emanate from one identifiable enemy. Going forward, we would be wise to legislate the precincts of permissible action when the United States faces violent attacks by terrorists abroad; we need also to find agreement with our closest allies on this issue. Only the dangers posed by the largest and most lethal of drug cartels come close to the threats of terrorism, and neither menace is easily accommodated by domestic law. Neither, however, yields readily to the definition of conventional war; the heterogeneity of actors, the clandestine nature of operations, and the lack of a coherent geographic "battlefield" can deify a straightforvard application of either paradigm. Modern terrorism presents a different problem from those that were in mind when the laws of war or peacetime were created.

Perhaps a third legal regime, one that would accommodate the necessities of counterterrorism as well as the need to protect individual rights, is warranted, but reaching a consensus over such an intermediate regime will be a lengthy process. Today's governments must decide how to act in between the existing paradigms and without the clear guidance of a third. To make the law that is required now, they must consider the application of statutory and constitutional powers, the relevance of international commitments, the role of the legislature and domestic courts, and the way domestic and international audiences will perceive any chosen strategy.

In facing these challenges, a government must begin by asking what, if any, departures from the normal rules of national behavior are actually necessary or truly important for security purposes. We can find no evidence for the intuition of some in the Bush administration that more coercion is necessarily safer. Having identified what departure from the law of peacetime or the law of war a sensible and effective strategy may require, the decision maker must examine whether the proposed strategy is still compatible with our common values and the principles animating the law. If a departure from law is inevitable, the chosen course must still respect the values the law embodies. Not all answers may be found within the limits of existing legal rules, nor are they found in the boldest defiance of our laws and values. In this book, we strive to offer some insights as to how law, strategy, and morality should shape the hardest questions about counterterrorism.

Our thinking about these issues was greatly advanced by discussing them with our students, American and foreign, who have shared with us their own perspectives, insights, and experiences, for all of which we are deeply thankful. We have also benefited from a wonderful group of research assistants, including Taylor Lane, Sarah Miller, Rachel Murphy, Neha Sheth, and Anne Siders, and particularly Natalie Lockwood and Whitney May.

Several commentators who are renowned experts in their field have shared with us their insightful comments and suggestions on the manuscript as it developed: John Bellinger, Robert Fein, Jack Goldsmith, and Robert Mnookin. All remaining errors are ours.

We are grateful for the support we have received from Harvard Law School, under the leadership of, first, Dean Elena Kagan, and then Dean Martha Minow, in the process of writing this book

Finally, we are indebted to Sean Lynn-Jones for the invitation to publish the book with the MIT Press, to Clay Morgan for dealing with us on behalf of the MIT Press, and to the editors, Kathleen Caruso and Julia Collins, who have worked hard to make our work more coherent and readable.

Introduction: The War on Terrorism—Lessons from the Past Nine Years

In *A Man for All Seasons*, playwright Robert Bolt depicts an imaginary, yet entirely plausible dialogue between Sir Thomas More, the Renaissance humanist who refused to succumb to a direct order from King Henry VIII, and More's son-in-law, William Roper, who warns More against Richard Rich. Rich was the solicitor general who would later give false testimony against More, leading to the latter's conviction and execution. "Arrest him," pleads Roper. "For what?" asks More, forever a lawyer. "That man's bad," a courtier intervenes. "There is no law against that," says More. A frustrated Roper then protests that if the laws could be imagined to be trees in a forest, and the devil were hiding behind one of them, "I'd cut down every law in England" to get him. To that, More queries: "Oh? And when the last law was down, and the Devil turned round on you—where would you hide, Roper, the laws all being flat?" He then concludes by stating, "Yes, I give the Devil benefit of law, for my own safety's sake!"[1]

The past nine years' "war on terrorism" has been a formative time in U.S. history and, indeed, global history, no less than the 9/11 attacks themselves. It has influenced and reshaped relationships between East and West, North and South, the Christian and Muslim worlds, democratic and nondemocratic regimes. Wave after wave of historically rooted fears as well as new fears, real and exaggerated, have generated demands for government action that would thwart this new threat; three broad sets of interest were to be maintained in unison while taking into account three broad sets of interests: the safety of the United States and that of its allies; adherence to American traditional liberal democratic values; and the global status of the United States.

It is common to hold, as the Bush administration did, that these interests are necessarily in tension, if not in direct conflict, with one another, especially when it comes to reconciling security needs with liberal democratic values. And further, that in the name of national security, traditional American values as embodied in domestic and international law and institutional arrangements must be set aside, far aside. As we will argue in this book, more often than not this tension is contrived or misconceived.

We often think about law as a tool for accommodating various sets of interests and for striking the balance between and among interests that are in conflict. This is true for peacetime law as it is for wartime law, although each system of law operates on the basis of different assumptions and is guided by different principles of accommodation. Peacetime laws apply to the quotidian life with a modicum of peril and assign the meeting of threats to law enforcement operations with the judiciary playing a central role. Although constrained to some degree by international law, each country chooses its domestic law enforcement regime. Wartime laws, which are largely international in origin, define a model in which danger is heightened—no longer an everyday sort of danger, but one that appears in the shape of war and that assigns the meeting of threats to military and intelligence agencies. Judicial involvement is minimal. These two sets of laws in combination constitute our existing legal paradigms for dealing with danger.

The September 11 attacks threw a wrench into the works—rattling, then redefining, not only our critical distinctions of law between peace and war but also our very conception of the role of law when we are in danger at home. Citizens and government alike stood aghast at the enormity and novelty of the events. As President Bush described the attacks a few days later, "Americans have known wars, but for the past 136 years they have been wars on foreign soil, except for one Sunday in 1941. Americans have known the casualties of war, but not at the center of a great city on a peaceful morning. Americans have known surprise attacks, but never before on thousands of civilians. All of this was brought upon us in a single day, and night fell on a different world, a world where freedom itself is under attack." The new type of attacks did not resemble any threat that law enforcement was intended to handle, nor did it resemble any of those wars that the laws of war were designed to address. The challenge, then, was for law to serve its purpose of accommodating the interests of national security, traditional American values—especially a commitment to human dignity and the rights of the individual—and the global status of the United States when confronted by this new, unnamed danger.

Neither of the main paradigms—peace or war—seemed to apply. Indeed, the Bush administration determined that law, essentially, had failed to address the new threat. In coining and declaring a new *global war on terror*, the administration found peacetime domestic law to be irrelevant. This was "war" but a new kind of war with a new kind of enemy, to whom traditional wartime international law was also largely inapplicable. With domestic law irrelevant and international law inapplicable, the war on terrorism was thus to be conducted within what we have termed here a No-Law Zone.

We do not doubt that the threat of modern international terrorism poses new challenges for governments of liberal democracies, challenges that our existing legal paradigms might not suffice to meet. But we believe that conducting a war on terrorism within a No-Law Zone was neither warranted nor useful. In fact, we believe it ultimately frustrated all three sets of U.S. interests: security, liberty, and international leadership.

The Choice of the War Paradigm

So why was this approach chosen? The war paradigm promoted three major goals: First, it allowed the employment of warlike measures—military strikes, invasion, battlefield detention, to name some—alongside the traditional law enforcement measures of arrest, extradition, trials, and imprisonment. Second, the executive branch could concentrate and exercise wide-ranging powers under the commander-in-chief constitutional authority. Indeed, the debates over the scope of executive power and the autonomous power of the president to act without congressional approval or oversight reached new levels of intensity during this period. And third, once a "war" was declared, the government could demand—and get—an almost unlimited pool of resources, supported by both Congress and the American people; after all, who wants to stand in the way of America's winning the war?

But the declaration of war was also fraught with obvious problems. First, there was a definitional problem in declaring war against a nonstate actor, which was difficult to identify and was not confined to any particular territory. While the Taliban regime still ruled Afghanistan, supporters of Al-Qaeda could appear anywhere, and they have. Moreover, the goals of the war, as defined by the 2001 Authorization for Use of Military Force (granted by Congress and signed by President Bush), were "to prevent any future acts of international terrorism against the United States [by those responsible for the 9/11 attacks]." However, prevention of a measure available to millions is an ill-defined purpose. How do we know when that goal has been attained and the war can be declared over, victory won, and the danger done with? What should we learn, if anything, from the fact that some of our allies have been successfully attacked over the last nine years, but we have not? In all probability, the threat is still there. And if we cannot tell when the threat is eliminated, how—or when—can the war ever be over?

Another problem with the war paradigm is that *war* is a highly charged term, on the most basic human psychological level, as well as politically, morally, and legally. A declaration of war against a human enemy, unlike the more metaphorical wars declared on disease, poverty, drugs, and global warming, naturally exacerbates the sense of suspicion, hostility, and defensive-offensive posturing on all sides to the conflict. Every move is a threat, every response—a counterattack. To the extent the enemy is motivated by a belief that he or she is defending the land and culture, declaring war only heightens that fear.

Crucially, too, for our considerations here, *war* is also a legal concept, especially but not only in international law. Not all is fair in love, and not all is fair in war. The international community has long come to realize that if humanity is to have any chance at survival, it must assume some limitations on how it fights. This is the impetus behind the body of international humanitarian law, also known as the Laws of War, developed through centuries of bloodshed and cruelty that were nonetheless oftentimes tempered by unwritten laws limiting warfare. But the established limitations were not designed for the new battlefield, one that had no identifiable borders, armies, or even enemy. This state of affairs allowed the Bush administration to take a more aggressive approach, and left it free, in its own mind, to jettison all limitations and commit, instead, to a much narrower, self-chosen set of restrictions. These legal acrobatics further weakened domestic and international support and in fact strengthened opposition to the United States worldwide.

Finally, a truism that applies to all wars is that there are no clean wars. All wars inflict unintended harms on the innocent as well as the guilty. Long-term effects, both domestic and international, are impossible to assess accurately in advance. Decision makers, so psychological studies tell us, tend to be overoptimistic and overconfident about their ability to affect and control the course of events once the match has been lit. The wars in Afghanistan and Iraq are not over. We did not capture Bin Laden. Alongside harming Al-Qaeda and its support network, we have harmed a great many innocent civilians; alongside building infrastructure and introducing democracy and human rights, we have, directly or indirectly, ruined entire neighborhoods and ripped apart social groups and communities. These often unavoidable effects of war create new recruits to terrorism.

At this point in time, any cost-benefit analysis of the Bush administration's war strategy is contestable. In particular, it is impossible to offer any definitive causal explanation for the absence of another successful terrorist attack on U.S. soil since 9/11, as it is always hard to explain why an event has not occurred. The fewness of attacks may be due to the administration's aggressive posture. The greater ease of attacking in Europe, as our enemies have been doing, may also be a contributing factor. Alternately, relative safety at home may stem from the more benign defensive measures taken, such as watch lists, airport and border security, more effective cooperation among the intelligence communities, and general safety and protective means. It may even mean that the level of threat was never as high as we thought.

A Third Paradigm: Neither War nor Peace

The struggle against international terrorism has not been won. Allegiance to the goals and means of Al-Qaeda has not been ended. To the contrary, we believe that the phenomenon of terrorism, in one form or another, is here to stay, in America and worldwide. Since 9/11, terrorists have struck repeatedly in the Middle East, as well as in London, Madrid, Bali, Colombia, Russia, and elsewhere (albeit in different forms and driven by different motivations). What we have learned from both the successes and the failures of U.S. strategy over the past nine years should provide an invaluable guide—domestically and internationally—on how to devise an effective, legal, legitimate, and politically viable counterterrorism strategy for years to come.

While post-factum assessments of successes and failures involve counterfactual calculations, and although it is always near impossible to determine with certainty why something—in this context, another major terrorist attack on U.S. soil—has not happened, we believe this much can be asserted with a high degree of confidence: the conduct of a "war on terror" outside clear legal boundaries was unnecessary if not downright harmful to U.S. goals. The costs this war has inflicted on the rule of law, traditional American values, and America's position as world leader are evident; the benefits to national security are doubtful, especially since much if not all that was achieved might well have been achieved by taking a different path.

How, then, should an administration react to this new type of threat? To begin, we must, like our most successful allies, learn to manage the fears that terrorism is designed to create. The real danger from terrorist attacks is hard to predict; the level of fear has long seemed detached from reality. Even before 9/11, when the scale of terrorism involved for the United States was generally less than ten victims in any single event and less than a score in a year, a terrorist attack (especially in a Western country) was capable of capturing the attention and fear of an entire nation—indeed of anyone with access to media. Hijacking, hostage taking, explosions, and suicide bombings all breed vicarious fear and a sense of universal danger, often out of proportion to the actual threat they pose. Judging by the sheer allocation of resources before September 11, we already cared more about a phenomenon whose very worst and rarest case, prior to that point, was a bombing of an Air India plane in 1985 that killed 329 people, than we did about cancer or car accidents. Post 9/11, our fears have multiplied tenfold. They now involve dirty bombs, chemical and biological warfare, and nuclear devices.

If internal law as it stands will not conform, then we must develop a new paradigm, for international terrorism will not fit comfortably into either the paradigm of war or that of law enforcement in peacetime. We had thought the two existing paradigms fit nearly seamlessly together, but they do not when terrorism becomes a major international threat falling in the gap between the two familiar bodies of law. In the long run, we will need a new body of domestic and international law providing a set of powers and protections falling somewhere between those now available in traditional war and those available in domestic law enforcement. But what about the decades before we have such new, internationally sanctioned laws?

The interim, third paradigm we propose in this book recognizes that values and principles lie, relatively obviously, beneath the explicit rules protecting individuals in the two traditional paradigms. It is as if one were confronted with defining the rules for a new sale/loan arrangement for automobiles when only the rules for sales and those for loans had been established. The new rules will obviously fit between the two established sets of rules. Indeed, here, the two sets of values and principles are, although different, often closely related as they deal with such matters as interrogation, detention, collective sanctions, and permissible killing.

The Bush alternative was to note the gap between the coverage of the two systems of rules and to deny any binding effect to the values and principles they shared and that motivated both paradigms. Seeing the costs of such a policy, we urge and demonstrate the benefits of a strong presumption that whatever is done to and about international terrorists should be consistent with either the principles behind the law of war or the principles reflected in domestic law. Policy may strongly suggest imitating law enforcement or armed conflict, but a state of near-law should require a clear, principled justification for any departure from the established rules.

The U.S. Supreme Court has come to insist that the threat of modern terrorism cannot be dealt with outside the law. The novelty of the threat may require a degree of adaptation of existing laws, but not the jettisoning of all legal arrangements. Our argument is that, in devising an effective counterterrorism strategy, one should begin with either of the two paradigms: law enforcement or war (imperfectly corresponding to the paradigms of peacetime law and wartime law). The choice of which of the two paradigms to begin with would depend on the nature and scale of the threat, who it emanates from, whether it has a distinct territorial space, and more. More important, however, is that both paradigms have their own internal logic of how to accommodate the interests of national security and human dignity. While a departure from familiar, traditional law might borrow from either paradigm, what is borrowed must preserve that accommodation. Only the minimal necessary departures should be contemplated. And when departures or adaptations are deemed unavoidable, they must still remain loyal to the underlying logic of each paradigm and to the set of values it protects.

The point is simple. Nations that are protective of liberties conscientiously limit and balance those powers that could readily be abused. That is of course what drove the demand for our Bill of Rights. In international warfare, government powers seem dangerously absolute, yet they are restrained by protective international agreements like the Hague and Geneva Conventions.

The granting of dangerous powers is rendered safer when we give them with strong protective limitations. That terrorism, which demands new powers, falls somewhere between the law of war and the law of peace does not mean that the protections found in traditional legal constraints in each of these areas suddenly disappear into a gaping black hole somewhere between law's two separate realms.

The constraints on powers are often very similar in war and in peace. There may be room for debate about which set of powers—military or law enforcement, each with its accompanying protections—should be applied; but we should never be left in a dark new realm of no law, where the powers of killing, interrogating, detaining without trial, or departing from due process procedures are exercised without protections. The same rationale that ensures checks on the use of power, both in peacetime and in war, must restrain governments' powers in dealing with new threats, until new statutes, treaties, or judicial decisions fill remaining gaps.

The Structure of Our Argument

We divided this book into three parts. The first, "On Law and Terrorism," concerns the relationship between law and counterterrorism strategies and, more generally, the function of law in times of dire emergency—a subject that occupied Thomas Jefferson and Alexander Hamilton two centuries ago as it does us today. The second, "On Coercion," explores the promise and limitation of various coercive strategies in counterterrorism and the need to place these strategies within a plausible legal framework that would ensure the accommodation of our various interests. The third part, "Beyond Coercion," considers noncoercive means that do not require any departure from or adaptation of existing law, and that may be effective in countering the threat of terrorism.

In part I, which describes the relationship between law and counterterrorism, we address the value of both domestic law and international law as the frameworks for what should guide our counterterrorism strategies. We highlight the function of domestic law as a protection against abuse by executive power; at the same time, we acknowledge that it may sometimes be necessary to depart from familiar legal constraints to protect the gravest of national interests; and we weigh the various options and consequences of doing so. In response to what seems an ideological battle waged by the Bush administration against international law, we reject the idea that terrorists' disregard for the rules can justify—much less require—a symmetrical lawlessness on the part of governments that resist terrorists. In particular, we show that as a matter of principle, leaving aside some exceptional cases, complying with international law serves America's interests. Finally, we address what that rare necessity—departure from the law—means for government lawyers when it comes to providing legal counsel to the executive, specifically in the context of the war on terrorism.

In part II we demonstrate that the nation loses when *either* national security *or* the rule of law wholly vanquishes the other at a time of emergency. The health of our democracy depends on our capacity to fashion principled compromises between these powerful ideologies in light of the political and security needs of a democratic state. We apply the themes drawn from part I, on the role of law in counterterrorism operations, to evaluate a set of coercive measures employed by the Bush administration. We address the limits that should be placed on the practice of targeted killings, the lessons to be learned from coercive and noncoercive interrogations, and the appropriate model for detaining terrorists.

Coercive power is a necessary tool in combating international terrorism. But it is also a dangerous tool; it tends to be overused or indeed abused. Frequently, its effects are overinclusive, affecting more people than necessary, and backfiring by arousing resentment and hostility. The battle against terrorism is as much over allegiance as it is over physical control. It is certainly *not* the case that the government should strive to employ as much coercive power toward local populations as it possibly can. With regard to three of the coercive measures—targeted killing, detention, and interrogations—we argue that they were authorized far too broadly, used excessively, resulted in too much harm, and often proved to be counterproductive on all three fronts of counterterrorism policy: national defense, protection of American law and values, and U.S. world standing. Particularly, we claim that the national security benefits that accrued from using these methods were often outweighed by their costs and that the war paradigm was neither always necessary nor always useful in promoting these benefits.

Part III highlights the need to consider the community base of terrorism and the collective effects of counterterrorism measures. In discussing the collective face of terrorism, we start off by rejecting the "good vs. evil" archetype, adopted by the Bush administration shortly after the 9/11 attacks, along with the paradigm "Axis of Evil"—designed to resonate with the label for the enemy in World War II. Both labels suggested a danger far greater than the immediate phenomenon at hand and, in reliance on the symbolism of "evil," led to an ultimatum that "you're either with us or against us." This framing, a derivative of the war paradigm, may have had positive effects, at least at first, in garnering domestic enthusiasm and international support for the war on terrorism and in sating feelings of unquenched anger and pain after the 9/11 attacks. But it soon became clear that it was neither helpful descriptively, in identifying who was good and who was evil, nor prescriptively, in providing a strategy for diminishing the community support on which terrorist groups like Al-Qaeda depend. Just as it became apparent that the unconstrained use of force may be counterproductive when dealing with those fitting neither label, it was also possible that there could be non-coercive means—such as negotiations or, indeed, cooperation—that would sometimes help abate the threat of terrorism by making far more difficult the creation by the Bin Ladens of the world, of dangerous, new enemies, hateful of the West.

We begin in chapter 7 by challenging the claimed policy of the U.S. government and other democracies to refuse absolutely to negotiate with terrorists or their sympathizers. We show that the policy is neither followed in practice nor warranted in principle. In some cases, negotiations with any party regardless of its ethics or methods may prove a more effective tool than the employment of military force or other coercive means. We take seriously the risks of encouraging further acts of terrorism, but we see distinctions in this regard.

The second issue we address, in chapter 8, is the measures we should take to reduce moral support for terrorism, often dubbed "the war to win hearts and minds." Polling data has shown that about 7 percent of the world's Muslim population, roughly ninety million people, express support for the attacks of 9/11 and thus for using terrorism more broadly against the United States and its allies. While devising a plausible strategy for changing the attitudes of those ninety million people is an enormously complicated task, surely it begins with recognition that we are fighting to diminish the allegiance and support of groups now sympathetic to terrorism. Our aim therefore cannot be to incapacitate this immense group or even to ignore its sympathies on the ground that it is entirely evil.

We conclude the book by turning to the future and exploring what an American government should do now to anticipate public reaction to and devise a sensible reaction to a successful new terrorist attack on U.S. soil. Finding a fitting response to terrorism is still a learning process. In the conclusion we discuss how to manage that process, responsibly and sanely.

Learning from mistakes, failures, and successes is not only paramount in devising a U.S. and global counterterrorism strategy, but also valuable when thinking about other contemporary transboundary threats to safety and security, such as piracy or drug cartels. All of these demand the same effort at integrating safety, commitment to our laws and values, and consideration of our international standing. A successful model for detention, interrogation, negotiation, reducing tacit support, and so on, in the counterterrorism arena could lend itself, with some modification, to fighting other threats of the twenty-first century. And we believe that in meeting all these threats, law, as the mediator of the various democratic interests, must play a crucial—if not a definitive—role. We hope this book, which assesses the strategies of the eight years of the Bush administration and the first year of the Obama administration, will speed the learning process in the years to come.

Part I

On Law and Terrorism

In peacetime, there is no stronger commitment among democratic citizens than to the rule of law, even—perhaps especially—as it serves to limit the authority of those who govern. The commitment to law applies most rigorously to citizens and activities within the state, but it is also powerful as an international force regulating relationships among nations and across borders. In wartime, by contrast, citizens' highest commitment is to protect the nation and its independence, territory, and powers. Terrorism exists in the uncertain realm between peace and war, dividing us between our deep commitments to law and to security. The relationship between these responsibilities, and among the ideals that animate them, is the subject we address in part I.

Governments have certain legitimate powers to confront enemies in war; they have other legal instruments to enforce the law against violators in peacetime. Accompanying each of these sets of powers are certain constraints—protective provisions like the Geneva Conventions for war, or the Fourth Amendment or the Law of Extradition in the case of law enforcement.

The law of war and the law authorizing domestic law enforcement both describe what can be done by government forces to deal with a human danger, under what conditions any set of options may be used, and in what way. Each body of law also describes what is forbidden in the interest of common humanity. Scholarship and legislative history spell out in each case the purpose of these directives. Neither the law of war nor international human rights law specifies when a government power must or should be exercised. In common-law countries, most explicitly, there are many accepted reasons for deciding not to exercise a domestic power such as the authority to arrest or to shoot a fleeing suspect or to charge with a specific crime. The same discretion is universally available and necessary with regard to acts that are especially permitted in times of war. The difficulty is that international dangers such as terrorism, piracy, and drug cartels do not fit comfortably into either category. They do not seem to warrant the full applicability of the wartime regime, but, depending on their scale, the advantage they take of foreign havens, and the threat they pose, they might also require going beyond the capacities of domestic law, tailored to address ordinary crimes at home. If the government therefore chooses to supplement domestic powers with wartime powers, it must also accept the protections that generally accompany war powers to guard against abuse of power and excessive harm. Indeed, President Bush initially proposed to do this with regard to terrorist detainees, promising detainees much the same protections as they would have under the Geneva Conventions if these had been fully applicable. Conversely, if the government chooses to rely on the peacetime powers of law enforcement, but finds them inadequate to meet the threat even with the cooperation of other countries, it might seek to enhance these powers directly, without recourse to the laws of war; but only while honoring the protections that accompany them. Starting from either legal regime, one ought to include as many of the accompanying protections as security concerns can reasonably accommodate.

The Bush administration soon chose a different path. It reasoned that the dangers of terrorism required and justified the powers that come with war. Thus, it saw no reason to include the protections of peacetime law enforcement. At the same time, however, it also found that the protections of the law of war were inapplicable, for the dangers did not emanate from a traditional "enemy" that bore allegiance to a state or wore a uniform. In other words, it accepted neither the possibility of preserving the protections of wartime law as fully as this new situation would permit, nor of expanding the powers of peacetime law only as far as was necessary to accomplish its aims and with their accompanying limits. The result was a black hole where little of the law of war and none of the law of human rights or domestic law applied.

We recognize that acts of terrorism, piracy, and violent drug cartels are not effortlessly accommodated by the present legal regimes of war or law enforcement. But the consequence should not be the establishment of a law-free zone. The protective values that are reflected in the limitations both regimes impose on the authorized use of violence are too important to disregard. One alternative, as we have suggested, is to expand domestic criminal law to more effectively address the threat posed by international forms of terrorism; another, often equally advantageous, is to adjust the law of war, ensuring that its standard protections will be accorded even to those who do not meet the traditional conditions for receiving them. What is not an option is to claim the powers of both regimes but deny the accompanying constraints that make those powers acceptable.

Attacks planned and mounted abroad by large and well-armed terrorist groups signify dangers that are different from those of familiar wars and no less different from ordinary criminal events, generally falling somewhere "between" these realms. It would therefore make sense to regard the outer bounds of governmental power to be whatever harms are permitted to be imposed on individuals by *either* the law of war *or* the law of peace (including both domestic law and binding international treaties on human rights). Anything that would be prohibited by both bodies of law—if the terrorist suspect were either a uniformed soldier or someone within the peacetime jurisdiction of domestic law—would not be permissible but for the most extreme and exceptional cases, and even then—only temporarily and to the most limited extent possible. This choice would be sensible at least until new treaties and statutes come to regulate the unfamiliar dangers of international terrorism. Of course, a governmental action permissible within these broad legal boundaries will not, by reason of that, necessarily be desirable. Strategic, political, and moral considerations might further constrain the powers of the government, even within legal boundaries.

Some argue that by merging anonymously into a civilian population a suspected terrorist might be more dangerous—more likely to succeed in carrying out an attack—than a soldier in a uniform and thus not warrant even the protections of the law of war. But our experience has shown that, without markings indicating membership in a hostile army, the suspect would also be far more likely to be no danger at all—to be mistakenly suspected—than would be a uniformed soldier of a hostile government. Nor is a suspected terrorist necessarily more likely to be dangerous than a suspected member of a Mexican drug cartel who would be entitled to the normal protections of law enforcement. In both cases, articulatable suspicions of planning extraordinary grave harms might, if demonstrated, warrant extraordinary powers under a legitimate, broadly accepted interpretation of the law. In both cases, harsher treatment for failure to signal one's dangerous activity is highly unlikely to be a useful incentive to change these practices of hostile groups.

It is true that providing a state with an option of using the law of war or the law of peacetime creates a degree of freedom—a choice—that is not generally considered consistent with legality. It would be preferable to develop rules that were more determinate for any particular situation. Moreover, it is far from clear at what level of danger a terrorist threat becomes potentially subject to the laws of war and whether that danger must be international or could be solely domestic, by analogy to a civil war. But this discretion and these uncertainties are manageably limited compared to the risks of a completely law-free zone such as that for which the Bush administration argued, leaving its fears to operate freely in a policy realm unconstrained by either the law of war or the law of peace.

In the chapters that follow, we address various aspects of the relationship between law and national security. Chapter 1 explores the difficult choices the president must make in reconciling his duty to obey the law with his obligation to protect the country. We recognize that it is the president's prerogative—perhaps even his moral duty—to overstep the bounds of legality, but only in times of dire emergency. Nevertheless, the *manner* in which he deviates from the law will have profound consequences. We examine several possible options for exercising this presidential prerogative, each accompanied by varying degrees of external review and political risk, and finally argue that a "civil disobedience" model offers the best compromise between the demands of law and emergency decision making.

Chapter 2 focuses on international law and the so-called War on Terror. We argue that the perceived tension or outright incompatibility between the two concepts—that is, the notion that international law places impossible constraints upon U.S. counterterrorism efforts—is misguided, and that to disregard international law is ultimately self-defeating. The interests of the United States, which has long been a champion of the values embedded in international norms, are plainly served by widespread compliance. If we properly broaden the horizons of our cost–benefit analysis, international law operates mostly in America's favor.

In the final chapter of part I, we set out a case study that examines the role of government lawyers in the context of counterterrorism. Specifically, we discuss the Bush administration's 2001 decision to undertake electronic surveillance in violation of the Foreign Intelligence Surveillance Act. We then review the approaches taken by various government counsels in the months that followed. The challenges posed by the concurrent demands of legality and national security are thus brought into focus through the lens of actual events that took place in the immediate aftermath of September 11. FISA offers a particularly poignant case study, as its legitimate legislative scope is now being reviewed and debated by the Obama administration.

1

The Complicated Relationship between Counterterrorism and Legality

Introduction

Steps that appear useful for fighting terrorism will sometimes be constrained, either unauthorized or forbidden by domestic law. There are generally very good reasons for such constraints, just as there may be very good reasons for wanting to bypass a constraint to take particular steps to counter the threat of terrorism. The reason for imposing these legal constraints may be moral; the law is often a distillation of, and a way of emphasizing the importance of, certain values central to human dignity. It may be political, reflecting historic American fears or suspicions of executive power that go far to explain the presence in our Constitution of both the Bill of Rights and the principle of separation of powers.

Law has a generality that puts it at a disadvantage in dealing with competing demands in the face of the danger of terrorism or any other unforeseen emergency. A normal reading of the words constituting a law will almost always reach some extreme and unusual situations where the moral, policy, or political concerns it reflects are barely present or some extreme situation where the threat to the lives of individuals is far more acute than the drafters of the law imagined. These are situations in which most people would like to be without a constrained executive *if* they agreed with that description of the situation. But the people concerned about the moral and political policies behind the law will reasonably fear the consequences if the leaders of their country are free to decide for themselves whether the benefits of the constraint are greater than the costs in a particular situation.

If we were prepared to always trust the individual judgment of our leaders to make exceptions to the law when they thought it wise, no statute or treaty or clearly limited authorization constraining government powers would be necessary. But the law is intended to guard against executive misjudgment of individual cases as well as the various biases that can affect decisions. Moreover, even if in a particular instance it would seem right to deviate from a carefully designed rule, insistence on compliance with the law would often yield better results in the long run. Still, when the reasons for limiting government powers seem to apply as mere technicalities, or are being invoked in the face of a danger far beyond the contemplation of the law's authors, the "rule of law" as a limit on executive powers is likely to fall under grave political pressure.

The problem is inherent in law; it is not necessarily a result of some historic oversight by earlier drafters. Enabling citizens to prevent certain government actions, by imposing limits on executive powers, presupposes a wide range of conditions in which those limitations make sense. When an extraordinary situation outside the assumed range creates a very different and unforeseen type of condition, the new reality almost demands a reconsideration of the established allocation of governmental powers. When the condition is a risk far greater than those within the range the drafters had contemplated, the pressure is particularly acute. International human rights laws recognize this, and allow governments to derogate from certain commitments to individual rights and freedoms in times of great emergency.

Domestically, every nation must find a way to mediate internally the emergency situation and the constraints law imposes on government powers. Most Western nations have allocated emergency powers either in very general terms or by listing specific powers only available when it is legitimately determined that an emergency of a defined sort exists. Such provisions are generally incorporated in the nation's constitution, as in the case of France and Germany, with care given to the question of who can determine the existence of such an emergency and by what criteria and for how long. But even states that do not recognize emergency powers, like the United States, have to find a way to deal with the same problem. The traditional American way has been to use interpretation to stretch ordinary powers of the executive. But there are limits to how far law can be stretched without losing public credibility and respect. Moreover, the interpretation itself creates new powers that may persist even after the emergency ends, as Justice Jackson cautioned in the case of *Korematsu*, where a majority of the Supreme Court authorized the mass internment of Japanese Americans during World War II.[1]

That is the situation we are presently addressing.

The Moral Question that Logically Precedes Any Legal Issue

Assume for a minute that you must choose between two presidential candidates. One announces unequivocally that he will not, under *any* circumstances, knowingly violate a statute forbidding the executive branch to take certain actions. The other candidate is unwilling to take that pledge. She says that she understands the importance of lawfulness but will not promise that no danger can be so dire, no emergency so urgent, that she would violate the law. She turns to her opponent and asks, "What if the violation is of a minor law regulating some ordinary activity, or, more dramatically, a traffic offense?" Would her opponent never violate such a law, no matter what the risks to the lives of citizens by complying in a particular situation? Many of us would want to be sure that the second candidate did recognize the importance we attach to the executive not deciding, casually or comfortably, that a law should be ignored. We would be concerned if her answer did not promise that she would depart from the law only in extraordinary circumstances—if, for example, she said something much more sweeping, such as "It is the role of the executive to weigh risks and offer responses that at times must be in violation of existing laws." But many of us would also feel uncomfortable with the thought that the executive in charge of our national military and civilian institutions would really tie his hands completely in situations of dire emergency. For those of us who are made nervous by the absoluteness of the commitment of the first candidate, legality remains a hugely important condition of acceptable executive action but it is not as absolute as the first candidate would make it.

The issue is not obvious. The first candidate has important reasons to pledge absolute allegiance to legality. The moral and political claims of law that control the decisions of all of us, including the president, are based on the notion that we have an obligation to honor agreements we arrived at in the past about our social and political arrangements and structure. That obligation to past agreements or understandings creates predictability for our present actions. Predictability allows us to have confidence that we can use new agreements to shape the future. It makes investment sensible, and—most important for our present purposes— allows us to accept and cooperate with organizational structures that create vast, hierarchical power in governmental, business, or social organizations without fearing the dangers they would create if their powers were unchecked by such prior understandings. In the final analysis, we have only laws, elections, and the threat of rebellion to guarantee our liberties and only the first is always there. Our commitment to the formality that we call *the rule of law* is our acceptance of prior agreements, limiting freedom of action in the present, and, unless modified, the future. This healthy respect for the importance of honoring past understandings turns out to be an immense advantage in the politics and economy of the modern state.

The second candidate has reasons at least as strong for not making that absolute pledge. We honor the rule of law because of the hugely important benefits we can see that it bestows, not as a fetish. In our daily lives, we recognize that the binding power of prior understandings sometimes confronts inconsistent and powerful counterclaims. In governance, the major rival claim is that we must be able to rely on the leaders—to whom we must look for unified direction in times of natural catastrophe or extreme danger—to take the steps necessary to save lives and to preserve our national institutions. There may be rare situations where (1) refraining from actions forbidden by past understandings would threaten many lives or national survival, (2) there is no time to take the steps that would be required to modify the previous understandings by new legislation or a constitutional amendment, and (3) the costs of departure from the valuable practice of giving prescriptive priority to any earlier understandings formally adopted as law seem containable. In the presence of these three circumstances, it seems unwise to insist on the moral superiority of complying with the prior understanding. Its framers may not have even contemplated the danger we now face.

At least this much seemed clear to Thomas Jefferson and Alexander Hamilton, both of whom saw the need for executive prerogative in such emergencies. Jefferson drew upon John Locke's *Second Treatise of*

Government, in which Locke made the argument that a sovereign must act in situations "which the law can by no means provide for" and which demand swift action to protect the public good. For Jefferson, the executive must then seek post-hoc approval of his actions from the people. Hamilton, in contrast, saw the same need for emergency powers, free from judicial review, but found those powers implicit in Article II of the Constitution and therefore not requiring post-hoc public acceptance of their exercise.[2] Presidents Lincoln and Roosevelt both acted in times of national emergency as if they possessed this prerogative to go beyond the law: Lincoln suspending the writ of habeas corpus during the Civil War, Roosevelt sending torpedo boats to Britain in 1940 in defiance of contemporary American neutrality laws.

The president's moral claim to defy prior understandings—in the case of President Bush, in ordering the detention of Americans as well as others, authorizing highly coercive interrogation methods, and expanding electronic surveillance—depends on more than his view that these steps are necessary. He must in addition be able to argue that the situation was not considered by legislators or judges, that it is qualitatively different in the danger it presents, that he will respect the separation of powers by taking the matter to Congress as soon as possible, and that the costs of inaction so plainly exceed the costs of action that Congress and the American people would likely have agreed that he should act. But, with all these conditions met, many would want as president someone who would on rare occasions accept the responsibility and the political costs of violating the law to save lives or the nation.

Even with all these conditions, the political risks to the president of acting without authority or in defiance of legitimate constraints will remain great; we should want it that way to discourage illegality. Those are the risks that Deputy Assistant Attorney General John Yoo, Attorney General Alberto Gonzales, and others tried to eliminate for President Bush by choosing the path of construing the law broadly enough to "find" authorization for what had never been authorized. The Office of Legal Counsel in the Department of Justice assured the president that the powers he was granted as commander in chief under Article II of the Constitution were encompassing of almost any measures he felt necessary and were sufficient to override statutory prohibitions in time of "war"; that there was indeed a global war against terrorism; and that

Congress did not have competing powers that might limit the power of the president as commander in chief in various areas where his actions were challenged as outside the "rule of law."

But this effort is badly misconceived, legally and politically. Legally, it is too narrow an answer, for there are grave emergencies wholly unrelated to war, as the emergency provisions in the constitutions of most democracies indicate. To deal with natural disasters, the president may be justified in taking temporary steps that require the use of powers nowhere authorized, whether the disaster is a smallpox epidemic, a collapsed dam, an earthquake, a hurricane, or any of a number of grave emergencies having nothing to do with war and thus with his powers as commander in chief.

The argument is also too broad legally if it is the president who decides when he is to assume the wartime powers of the commander in chief. It is simply not possible that the writers of the U.S. Constitution, who carefully and conscientiously separated powers among three branches of government and added a Bill of Rights needed to get the Constitution ratified, would allow the president to suspend those two absolutely core protections whenever *he* decided we were at war.

We should *want* the president to be at political risk if he acts without apparent authority or apparently in violation of congressional or constitutional constraints. Presidents Lincoln and Roosevelt were—and should have been—at this risk. It is this danger of a political sanction that, as Jefferson saw, provides a critical guarantee that any exceptions to the president's obligations to obey the law will be rare and in a context not dangerous to our democracy and our freedoms.[3]

The Scope of Public Tolerance for a President Claiming the Moral Authority to Ignore Prior Understandings in Emergency Situations

With Judicial Review

The political demand for the American president to comply with prior understandings that are embodied formally in law is at its strongest if the courts have declared an executive action illegal and yet it is taken anyway. The influence of the courts on presidential willingness to bypass legality in a time of emergency has, with rare exceptions, been an unquestioned result of our history from *Marbury v. Madison* (1803) to *U.S. v. Nixon* (1974). President Bush, like most of his predecessors, accepted the legal conclusiveness of any Supreme Court decision. He therefore sought to avoid judicial review. A claim of ultimate presidential authority to bypass legality in the name of saving lives or protecting the country might be tenable in some circumstances; however, for reasons that are peculiarly American, such claims are nearly always doomed to fail if they directly challenge that aspect of the rule of law that we identify with the finality of Supreme Court decisions. Lincoln's refusal to honor habeas corpus during the Civil War, despite the Court's order, was a rare, if notable, exception.

The critical question for the courts is how to exercise the power they have to deny presidential authority to violate the law in a context where the law dictates restraining the president but the possible dangers of the situation may make the president's actions appear morally justified to the American public, Congress, and the Supreme Court.

The Supreme Court could, at one extreme, apply normal statutory and constitutional modes of interpretation to the facts without any adjustment for the extreme dangers the government asserts and without any review of the usefulness of the proposed executive action to deal with those dangers. Only if it found, with a normal reading of the law, that the framers of the Constitution or the writers of a statute had contemplated an applicable emergency authorization or an exception to a constraint would the Court sustain the president's actions. For other cases, whatever the emergency, it would force the president to proceed, if he so chooses, at his own peril, facing the political response to his unauthorized action and, perhaps, the imposition of legal sanctions including impeachment.

At the other extreme, the Court could assume that, in the face of claims of grave, unanticipated dangers and assertions of the importance of the steps the president proposes, the framers of the Constitution or the writers of statutes would have wanted an emergency exception allowing what they had written to be bypassed. The Court might not even decide the threshold questions of who can find and declare such an emergency. As to judging the action the government in fact takes, the Court might well follow Justice Jackson's suggestions in *Korematsu* and, recognizing its own lack of competence to judge the danger, decline to decide for fear of providing continuing legal authority for what is really a rare necessity.

Between these two extremes there are many possibilities, which vary by the degree of deference the Court grants to the executive. As to the factual issues claimed to constitute a dire emergency, the Court might make its deference turn on some limited showing by the executive branch of the danger, some limited defense of the proposed remedy, and some limited argument as to what form of risk is relevant to the final determination of legality. Or it might take the view that an assertion of dire emergency should not be made solely by the executive, who is empowered by this claim of extraordinary need, but should require congressional resolution of these questions. The former option risks abuses of executive power while the latter harbors dangerous forms of delay, publicity, and divided authority. In assessing the administration's otherwise forbidden actions, the Court could give more, less, or no weight to the public's current fear of terrorism, its longer-lasting commitment to traditional American values, and the impact of the intended action on either one.

None of these alternatives is a congenial one to our courts. With these hard choices before it, our Supreme Court has recently taken a fourth path. Recognizing that Congress has the power to declare war or to explicitly authorize extraordinary actions by the executive, enjoys a greater capacity than courts do to get at facts and assess risk, and is sensitive to popular commitment to traditional American values, our Supreme Court has repeatedly used interpretive devices to force Congress to decide what powers the president should have in an emergency. Much as a court in a country with an unwritten constitution protecting liberties would be likely to do, the Supreme Court has time and again concluded that, without legislative action, the steps the executive was proposing were not legal. At the same time, it has left Congress largely, but not entirely, free to define what is and what is not permitted. This active use of Justice Jackson's opinion in the *Steel Seizure Case*—discussing the lawfulness of the seizure by President Truman of the steel mills during the Korean War and describing the president's wartime powers as being far greater when supported by legislation—substitutes decision in terms of grand legislative design for judicial second-guessing of necessity in a concrete case.

Without Judicial Review

We have so far discussed the powerful claims of legality as if without technical illegality a president need not fear a political sanction for "being lawless." That is not an adequate conception: it is also the principle behind the law—the values and understandings we have used law to express—that leads us to object when law is cast aside. Besides setting important legal boundaries to the field of authorized presidential action, the laws that limit measures of counterterrorism also crystallize, in a form that gives them additional weight and status, the moral values of, and the principles and relationships accepted by, a very large number of citizens. For these, it is not a distantly technical, expert understanding of the law that matters; what matters is a wider set of public beliefs, even ones that a court might consider unspecified by any legislative text or judicial precedent, about the values and principles that are settled and can be taken for granted.

Let us begin with a nonemergency example. In 1981, President Reagan's Department of Justice announced that, after a decade of contrary tax practice and in the wake of twenty-five years of national commitment to desegregation, the Internal Revenue Service would resume giving the tax benefits of a charitable status to private schools that practice racial discrimination. The Reagan Administration's argument was, as a technical matter, quite defensible legally—that is, it was within the bounds where interpretation does not raise fears of lawlessness. It was, however, directly contrary to deeply held American beliefs and principles about what was impermissible and relied on technical distinctions understood only by lawyers. The public, the media, and Congress exploded in bipartisan outrage at what was taken to be not only immoral but also illegal. (The Supreme Court then stretched to find the administration's decision illegal.[4])

Much the same thing happened after the pictures from Abu Ghraib were linked to the legal memos prepared by Deputy Assistant Attorney General John Yoo. Americans' (and foreign spectators') widespread and deeply held expectation that the United States would not be involved in the mistreatment of prisoners could no longer be preserved by hiding facts to the contrary as a national security secret. Nor could it be handled by a technical argument about what the law did or did not require. Once the facts surfaced, Congress voted overwhelmingly to reject the legal positions of the Department of Justice that no binding constraints could limit the president's power to interrogate for "wartime" intelligence and also that certain provisions of the UN Convention against Torture did not apply to aliens abroad. The same thing happened with regard to President Bush's proposed rules for trying suspected terrorists before military commissions. First, the Supreme Court rejected the claim of presidential authority that would have justified the executive's planned departure from familiar expectations as to fair trials; second, Congress imposed more familiar understandings by statute.

In a very real sense, the power of demands for lawfulness goes beyond what has been formally declared by framers, legislators, or courts. The demands include widely and long-held expectations—principles—with regard to the propriety of governmental behavior—expectations that the public believes its officials understand. In times of emergency, particularly involving physical danger, the public may, for a time, not want to know whether its leaders' choices are consistent with those expectations. But once triggered by an inescapable display of sharp departure from those expectations, there is a very likely prospect of a large and focused public and legislative reaction. The threat to liberty sensed in the legal but "line-crossing" firing of Archibald Cox, a special prosecutor investigating President Nixon during the Watergate era, was such a case. So was the perceived threat to fairness when President Bush fired a number of U.S. Attorneys who were considered disloyal. Besides a felt danger to liberty or fairness, other politically charged motivations are the perceived threats to feelings of national decency and respectability, and to the desire to maintain pride in one's country. A president can no more ignore such expectations than he can disregard legal rules.

Explaining the operations of the Israeli Supreme Court in dealing with terrorism, Chief Justice Aharon Barak described a responsibility to make sure that government actions remain within reasonable bounds set by notions of human rights, decency, and tradition. The bounds are themselves frequently defined by the court. But they are not made up of whole cloth; they express public attitudes that the court recognizes and the public refuses to have ignored. For the United States, defiance of widely valued expectations may be more likely to generate congressional than judicial action. Claiming that formal legality alone is enough to authorize actions, and ignoring the importance of even unfocused prior understandings of the population about highly valued traditions, is almost as much a path to public rejection of the executive as is a court-declared violation of the law.

How a President Can Deal with the Political Risks of Violating the Law

From the time of Thomas Jefferson to now, a president's decision to ignore the limits of his constitutional powers, or to disregard Congress's checks on his authority, has prompted deep and broad concerns over the potential risks to democratic values. However, to those concerned, the *way* in which the president ignores the limits of his power may make a great deal of difference.

The president has at least eight major options. He could

1. act in secret, not acknowledging in any way what he has authorized;
2. rely on the security agencies of other countries to engage in the activity at our secret request;
3. seek from his lawyers a broad constitutional interpretation of his powers—one that overrides inconsistent treaties and statutes;
4. seek from his lawyers a narrow interpretation of the statutory and treaty prohibition, stretching the legal boundaries on his authority;
5. rely on an after-the-fact prosecutorial or judicial determination that there was a legal justification (e.g., a defense of necessity) for taking the action;
6. operate on the understanding that prosecutorial discretion or the vast discretion of the president to pardon offenders will be used to defend the perpetrators of the action;
7. adopt an open form of civil disobedience, such as Jefferson urged, relying on the American people to decide on the propriety of the departure from law; or
8. go to the Congress for new authority (which, even if not sufficient to override international commitments to other nations, may allow the president to act domestically).

From the limited point of view of effectiveness, the various options differ in the speed with which they can be accomplished; in their capacities to keep the activity secret from our enemies; and in the certainty that there will be no adverse consequences to executive officials. From the perspective of protecting democratic values, the options vary in the breadth of the president's claim to ignore the rule of law; in the extent to which they allow a review of the seriousness of the need to engage in illegality; and in the judicial or political accountability of the use of the power and practice that they provide. All these strategies also differ in their short- and long-term effects on separation of powers and the rule of law more broadly.

To demonstrate what may be at stake in following one or another option, we will consider the prohibition on torture and of cruel, inhuman, and degrading treatment found in the Convention against Torture and the Geneva Conventions (including Common Article III that applies to all detainees) and in domestic criminal statutes enacted to give effect to these international obligations. Many of those most determined to maintain these prohibitions in U.S. law and international law recognize that treatment that would be legally prohibited in almost any circumstance could be justified in the rare event of a ticking-bomb scenario. To justify harsh, prohibited forms of interrogation, such a ticking-bomb scenario would have to combine an imminent and highly lethal attack; a suspect whom we have good reason to believe has concrete and verifiable information about that attack; and no other feasible way to protect innocent citizens from the attack.

The Choices of the Bush Administration

President Bush used the five methods that are least protective of the rule of law and the democratic values of the United States. First, he secretly authorized highly abusive interrogation to be carried out under the most secret circumstances by the CIA. For years, the activity was not acknowledged; its details only emerged slowly half a dozen years later. Second, President Bush used extraordinary renditions to cooperative countries that would torture largely on our behalf. Again, this was done in the deepest secrecy that the CIA could manage. Third, he bolstered the protection provided him by secrecy as to the relevant facts with secret, extremely broad, authorizations of these activities furnished by the Department of Justice's Office of Legal Counsel (OLC). Fourth, unavailable for legal criticism, because of the secrecy in which its opinions were held, the OLC also claimed inherent presidential powers in the "war on terrorism" that broadly overrode the U.S. Congress and, fifth, and again secretly, found that reliance on OLC's definition of the defenses of necessity or self-defense protected those violating the legal prohibition on torture.

While enjoying the somewhat questionable national security advantage of keeping our interrogation techniques secret from our enemies, the Bush administration intentionally hid its claims and actions from any public scrutiny. By doing so, President Bush's choice, among the methods available to him, put at greatest risk the applicable rule-of-law values. His claim of power was extremely broad. It was made without any independent review of the actual necessity of prisoner abuse as a matter of security tactics. His steps to assure secrecy were unnecessary except in so far as it temporarily fooled and thus calmed the American people and our allies. He created a system of minimal accountability for how the broad power he was secretly claiming was in fact exercised by hundreds of subordinates.

So abuse spread, unchecked, from the CIA to military detention facilities in Guantanamo, Bagram, and Abu Ghraib. Bush further managed to provide guarantees against after-the-fact prosecutorial or judicial evaluation of OLC's actions, promising immunity for those who relied on OLC's opinions even if they were later deemed erroneous or implausible. In any event, there would be little evidence. The CIA destroyed tapes that would vividly document what had happened. The administration invoked the very broad notion of "state secrets" to block judicial review in the form of actions for damages brought by those individuals claiming they had undergone torture.

The two strategies the president notably did not use to find exemptions from the absolute prohibitions of torture and cruel and inhuman degrading treatment were (1) going to Congress to seek authority to bypass the prohibition; and (2) the civil disobedience strategy—admitting to violating the law and facing the consequences.

Going to Congress: The Most Protective System

Presidential departure from the law is rarely if ever appropriate if it is reasonably possible to seek legislative authority for what is thought necessary. Congress can often legalize, and therefore bring within the protective umbrella of "separation of powers," an activity that is otherwise dangerously lawless. Yet the Bush administration purposely foreswore this route to legitimacy.

It could not have believed that it was obtaining authorization when it, first, informed eight congressional leaders who were sworn to take the information no further and, second, in the ensuing years, also informed other selected members and their staffs presumably under the same conditions. Sworn to secrecy and thus powerless to initiate a legislative response, the members of Congress who were informed were also powerless to legitimate the actions described. The risk that terrorists might successfully train to resist such techniques as waterboarding when our military had not been able to accomplish that through training is too small to explain the secrecy from Congress. As we shall argue, the case for secrecy was much stronger when President Bush ignored the statutes regulating electronic surveillance for intelligence purposes. Here there was a real fear that revealing the action might help our enemies. A far more likely explanation for not going to Congress was the fear of an adverse action by Congress. Indeed, it overwhelmingly rejected the highly coercive interrogation techniques when Congress finally addressed them in 2005.

The unlikelihood of obtaining congressional authorization was hardly a justification for the administration to ignore Congress. Nor is a claim that Congress would be indifferent to our safety. Congress is no less anxious to protect our national security than is the president. The fact that Congress overwhelmingly rejected the highly coercive interrogation techniques when legislators finally addressed them in 2005 surely is not an indication that it was appropriate to bypass Congress in the earlier years; it suggests the opposite.

To whatever extent it is critical to keep such activities secret from U.S. citizens and our allies, seeking legislation may be impossible. Urgency might sometimes justify executive action before legislative approval is obtained. Yet these arguments, as applied to illegal, highly coercive interrogation method are factually weak. Reluctance to go to Congress instead seems to have been largely based on fear that the proposals would be met with abhorrence in Congress, among the American people, and by our allies.

Had the president gone to Congress, and had Congress been more sympathetic than it later proved to be, we would have had a system of accountability that provided a check on the necessity of the illegality as well as on the scope of the exercise of whatever powers were authorized when times of necessity were found. We would have had, in other words, something like the system for searches that requires a judicial verification of the need and judicial control of the practices used.

The Israeli Answer: A Necessity Defense without Prior Authorization

An alternative strategy could have been provided by accepting account-ability to the powers of courts and prosecutors rather than to the powers of Congress. This would be the result of a transparent use of the neces-sity defense after the actions were taken. The Model Penal Code, as well as the criminal laws of most U.S. and foreign states, recognizes the defense of "necessity," justifying breaking the law in an emergency in an effort to cause less harm than would result from following the law. The necessity defense does not change the law, nor does it create an obliga-tion to break it; it only exempts the violator from criminal liability if, in fact, she chose the lesser evil in a situation the legislature had not contemplated.

Reliance on the necessity defense to enable even torture in extraordi-nary cases was upheld by the Israeli Supreme Court (sitting as the High Court of Justice [HCJ]) in a landmark decision from 1999.[5] In that deci-sion, the HCJ ruled that Israeli law did not authorize the use of torture in any type of interrogation. Nonetheless, if the security agencies encoun-tered a "ticking bomb" case, and used necessary coercive means to deal with it, they could rely on an ex-post justification of necessity if prose-cuted. The necessity framework leaves wide room for prosecutorial dis-cretion in deciding whether to press charges against any individual interrogator. If an individual is prosecuted, it is then up to judges (or juries or both) to decide whether the circumstances were such that the interrogator had reason to rely on a choice-of-evils defense and break the law.

Under the necessity framework the law does not authorize torture as a practice; it simply acknowledges that some otherwise forbidden actions may be justified under unexpected and extreme circumstances. By keeping cruel interrogation outside the law, merely exempting the evildoer from criminal liability in a particular case, the necessity defense is more respectful of the idea of a rule of law and of the values reflected in the law's commitment to view torture as an illegal act.

Moreover, by subjecting the torture to a choice-of-evils test, the legitimacy of the act of torture in any particular case must be tested against the degree of danger or harm: The nature of the threat (WMD [weapons of mass destruction] or conventional), its imminence, likelihood, and the availability of alternative ways of obtaining the information must all be examined. In this way, the test provides a measure of prosecutorial and judicial accountability as a safeguard against increasing and excessive use of torture.

But the necessity framework is not without its own difficulties. First, unlike a well-defined congressional authorization, a presidential determination, or judicial approval, reliance on the necessity defense reduces high-level accountability and spreads authority vastly by shifting the burden of decision making onto the individual interrogator. Second, this is not entirely fair to the interrogator. The evaluation of his choice is ex-post factum, with the benefit of hindsight, whereas the decision whether to torture or not is made under extreme conditions of uncertainty and risk. The interrogator's fate may ultimately be determined by the value of information produced through the interrogation, rather than by any objective assessment of the decision to employ harsh techniques in the first places.

Beyond the question of the fairness of this form of individual accountability, it is not at all clear that reliance on the necessity defense actually safeguards against the excessive use of torture. According to Israeli human rights non-governmental organizations (NGOs), since the 1999 decision was rendered, legally forbidden coercion and abuse have still been practiced in a large number of interrogations without any single interrogator ever facing trial. Even more problematic is the fact that the possibility of invoking the justification of necessity has been translated by the Israeli Security Agency into an elaborate system of permits and authorizations, largely by prosecutorial authorities, which are employed before coercive measures are used in the interrogation. In other words, the post-factum exemption has turned into an ex-ante authorization to use torture.

For these reasons, both the German courts and the European Court of Human Rights have rejected a plea of necessity as a defense for torture. In 2002, a young German man, Gäfgen, kidnapped an eleven-year-old boy and demanded ransom for his release. The ransom was paid, and Gäfgen was caught collecting it. In his interrogation, Gäfgen refused to disclose where he had hidden the boy. The deputy police chief in Frankfurt ordered his subordinates to extract the information from Gäfgen by threatening to torture him. Under the threat of torture (torture was not in fact practiced), Gäfgen disclosed the information; but when the police arrived at the hiding place, they found the boy already dead.

Even though the German law recognizes the defense of necessity, a German judge ruled that any information obtained from Gäfgen under the threat of torture was inadmissible in his trial. Gäfgen confessed again, in court, and was convicted of kidnapping and murder. In parallel, the two police officers who were involved in threatening the kidnapper with torture were convicted of coercion and incitement to coercion and were given suspended fines (a light punishment, by any standards). Commenting on these events, German Interior Minister Otto Schily said in an interview that there could be no relaxing of the rule against torture: "If we begin to relativize the ban on torture, then we are putting ourselves back in the darkest Middle Ages and risk putting all of our values into question."

Gäfgen then took his case to the European Court of Human Rights, which found that, even in the event of a public emergency threatening the life of a nation, no exceptions or derogations from the prohibition on torture are permissible (although also finding that Gäfgen's right to a fair trial had not been violated).[6]

Professor Oren Gross of the University of Minnesota Law School has proposed a "civil disobedience" model closely related to the necessity defense. Under the civil disobedience model, an official actor decides to break the law but is open about what she has done and is willing to face the consequences of her actions. This is essentially the model adopted by Germany in the Gäfgen case. Punishment can be mitigated (as in the German case), but the message of an illegal act remains intact. The civil disobedience model may seem less fair in that, as in the case of the necessity defense, it shifts the burden of risk onto the individual actor; and unlike the necessity defense, the individual actor must then rely on prosecutorial and judicial discretion (and, perhaps, the pardoning power of the president), in making the decision to engage in torture to thwart an imminent attack. Moreover, in not being restrained by the contours of the necessity defense, this model runs the risk of inviting violations of law by individuals engaging in conscientious defiance of rules that were intended to have few if any exceptions.

The Jefferson Proposal: Politically Accountable Civil Disobedience by the President Alone

The advantages of tolerating transparent lawlessness in a dire emergency would be very great if the president alone were given the choice to ignore the laws and accept the attendant political risks. He could, within reasonably short limits, decide when he would make public the action he has ordered. Delay may reduce substantially the risks, such as they may be, of important revelations to enemies. Within limits he could also decide on the level of generality of the revelation, subject to the demands of Congress and the press. At the same time, the risk of an angry response from an American public deeply committed to the rule of law will operate as a significant check on the president's willingness to act illegally. His need to justify the action will mean that the public will be able to decide in light of the facts that he has put forward or has not put forward about the emergency. The claim of extraordinary powers is case-specific, so that it does not spread into other areas, as would a broad determination of presidential powers in "wartime," or authorize too broadly, as would a defense of necessity that would be available to every agent and soldier.

Jefferson knew that civil disobedience should not be undertaken lightly by government officials. One of the central purposes of having laws that distinguish the prohibited from the permissible is to do away with permission for individuals to weigh the costs and benefits of actions. We assume, instead, that the law has already taken into account these costs and benefits and has struck the right balance. This is particularly important in the area of responses to terrorism, for history shows that, in times of emergency, people tend to overestimate the threat and underestimate the costs of extraordinary security measures. The mass internment of Japanese Americans during World War II, the inhibition of unfettered speech during the Cold War, and the detentions immediately after 9/11 of numerous "suspected terrorists," none of whom was ever indicted, were all security measures believed necessary at the time, but revealed by hindsight to be superfluous and even counterproductive.

Nonetheless, we agree with Jefferson, Hamilton, and Lincoln that there may be instances in the life of a nation in which a president may need to take some exceptional measures—measures that would be extraordinary, probably unlawful, but nonetheless necessary to limit a lethal threat. For this rare situation, we believe that Jefferson's civil disobedience model, in which the law remains intact and the president faces the political consequences, offers the best compromise between the demands of law and the needs of an emergency response. The president not only is likely to be in the best position to assess the justification for breaking the law, he also is most clearly subject to law, thus assuring political accountability. And concentration of emergency responsibility in a single, elected official reduces by orders of magnitude the risk of an unintended spread of extremely dangerous powers.

In chapter 6, we demonstrate how the Jeffersonian civil disobedience model would work in the context of coercive interrogations, requiring the president himself to decide to violate the law.

2

International Law, the President, and the War on Terrorism

Introduction

In the 2005 National Defense Strategy (NDS), under the heading "Our Vulnerabilities," the Bush administration made the following assessment of the dangers we face: "Our strength as a nation state will continue to be challenged by those who employ a strategy of the weak using international fora, judicial processes, and terrorism." The bizarre grouping of law, diplomacy, and terrorism articulated the prevalent thinking at that point, which was that the national interest required the use of overwhelming force. Further, the NDS implied that the constraints on the use of overwhelming force, whether in the war on terrorism, Afghanistan, or Iraq were "imposed" on the United States by international law and diplomacy, or more implicitly, by European liberal obstructionism. At best, international law and institutions were dismissed among administration officials as irrelevant or a nuisance; at worst, they were lined up alongside Bin Laden and Saddam Hussein as enemies of the state. The underlying supposition of government and conservatives alike was that, for America to be effective, it needed to "go Bismarck," and that what prevented President Bush from exercising a fuller measure of "iron and blood," beyond resource constraints, were international law and diplomacy as exploited by the enemies of America in order to curb its power.

But by treating national security and international law as inconsistent, the Bush administration misdiagnosed the American national interest. International law, as it currently stands, fundamentally reflects America's enduring interests as well as its values. The real threat to America's interests does not derive from European internationalism but instead from Chinese competition, Russian defiance, Latin American reactionism, the volatility of African governance, Islamic jihadism, and the rise of dangerous nonstate networks. Other dangers to American power are escalating economic instability, environmental degradation, natural disasters, and health crises. On all these fronts, international law generally serves, not hampers, American concerns. Sacrificing international law for the war on terrorism is not squaring international law with the national interest; it is sacrificing the national interest for constricted and erroneous perceptions of security.

In chapter 1 we outlined the potential necessities and implications of a president's decision to deviate from domestic legal arrangements and understandings in the face of supreme emergencies. At the heart of the question of how to manage the tension between the rule of law and the necessities of emergency action lie political understandings of democratic structures and the allocation of powers among the various branches of government. In chapter 2 we address the considerations that should inform the decision to depart from *international* law in responding to national security threats and focus on those considerations that are unique to the legal and political implications of breaching international law.

International Law and the War on Terrorism

Although the United States had suffered from terrorist attacks long before the events of September 11, 2001, the magnitude of Al-Qaeda's attacks on American soil prompted the first American declaration of a "war" on global terrorism. The United States was not the first country to describe its counterterrorism operations as *war*, but it was the first country to characterize the war as global. Unlike other campaigns colloquially labeled *war*, such as the war on drugs, on crime, or on poverty, the war on terrorism included the use of warlike means, such as land invasion, airstrikes, commando operations, and mass detention of enemy combatants.

War is not only a political or strategic concept; it is also a legal construct that carries with it a host of international rules regarding the permissible and impermissible use of force. The exact terms of these rules as they pertain to the war on terrorism are unclear, in part because the exact scope of the war itself is ill-defined. The nature of the enemy (nonstate, elusive), the location of hostilities (potentially, all over the globe), the type of tactics employed (a mix of law enforcement means and combat operations), and the ultimate aim of the relevant parties (the unclear terms of "victory") all make the war on terror different from more traditional wars—those that have historically provided the context for the promulgation of the international law of armed conflicts.

Even beyond the question of the laws of armed conflict, the means employed by traditional domestic law enforcement, such as arrests, interrogations, surveillance, extradition, and trials, are also regulated under international law, albeit under a different branch—the international law of human rights. The degree to which international human rights laws can or should constrain government power was hotly debated, even before the onslaught of the war on terrorism, in domestic contexts, such as the death penalty, abortions, or gay rights, and is particularly contested as applied to government actions outside U.S. territory, for instance, in Guantanamo Bay.

The freshly declared war on terrorism thus sparked a voluminous debate among lawyers, politicians, human rights activists, and academics about the extent to which international law regulates or should regulate U.S. actions both within and outside of its borders. The debate involves three types of questions. The first two are familiar: Are existing international rules relevant to the war on terrorism? And, if they are, has the United States violated them? We proceed on the assumption that, at least in some cases, the answers to the first two questions are "yes," meaning that there are at least some international legal rules that are relevant to the war on terrorism and that, at least in some instances, the Bush administration chose to violate these rules, as most international legal scholars understand them.

As these first two issues have been widely discussed by others, our focus is on a third question: To what extent, and why, should the executive feel bound by the same international rules it once characterized as the weapon of the weak against us?

Does International Law Bind the President as a Matter of U.S. Law?

As a matter of U.S. law, international law can constrain the president's actions in the war on terrorism in several ways. First, some international law is incorporated into congressional legislation, either explicitly or implicitly, thus turning the international obligation into U.S. law, as binding as every other U.S. law. For instance, the Uniform Code of Military Justice (UCMJ) makes several references to the law of war and provides that the executive can create military commissions to the extent permitted by the law of war.[1] The UCMJ thus explicitly makes the Geneva Conventions part of American law. In such cases, the president becomes bound by domestic law rather than by international law as such.

A second way in which international law may be binding on a president is under the Supremacy Clause of Article VI of the U.S. Constitution, which provides that "all treaties made, or which shall be made, under the authority of the United States, shall be the supreme law of the land."[2] Article II, Section 2 gives the president the authority, "with the advice and consent of the Senate, to make treaties, provided two thirds of the Senators present concur."[3] Furthermore, Article II, Section 3 requires that the president "take Care that the Laws be faithfully executed." Thus, treaties enacted with the support of at least two-thirds of the Senate as well as the president fall under the Take Care Clause and constrain executive decisions. Of course, not all treaties are judicially enforceable.[4] As a matter of political reality, the president may have considerable de facto interpretative latitude with respect to the constraints of international law wherever judicial enforcement of treaties is not available.

Customary international law is another source of obligations on the international plane that may carry over to domestic law, at least if neither the president himself nor Congress has rejected its application. It refers to those norms that have not been incorporated into treaties, but that the international community, through consistent practice and expression of commitment, has come to view as binding. The Constitution makes no explicit reference to customary international law (CIL), and there have been numerous legal debates surrounding the degree to which CIL is even part of American law, let alone binding on the president. To date, no federal court of appeals has ever held that the president is constrained by CIL.[5] CIL may, however, bind the actions of lower-level officials where neither the president nor Congress has spoken. In addition, the courts should employ relevant CIL in interpreting ambiguous domestic statutes, so as to avoid conflict to the extent possible.

In addition to the status of international law under the Constitution, the allocation of interpretative power and the scope of legislative power also shape the extent to which the president is bound by international law or statutes. The construct of the "war on terrorism" in general, and some of the actions of the Bush administration in particular, have prompted debates about both the scope of executive interpretive power and the degree to which the executive can act contrary to or altogether without authorization from Congress. The executive branch is generally thought to have more foreign relations power than the other branches of U.S. government. The Constitution makes the president the commander-in-chief, and empowers the president to appoint ambassadors and to make treaties, with the consent of two-thirds of the Senate.[6] Many lawyers argue that, in contrast to Congress, the executive also has various qualities that make it more suitable for handling foreign relations. For instance, the president can act in secret and quickly; the executive is always in session; it is a unified hierarchical branch so subordinates will follow decisions made at the top and the branch can speak with one voice; the president is accountable for the entire government and is politically accountable to all the American people; and last, but not least, the American people tend to hold the president responsible for foreign relations.[7]

The constitutional provisions do not make it overwhelmingly clear that the executive was intended to be the primary interpretive authority in the laws of foreign affairs. But, because the executive arguably has the primary responsibility for foreign relations, some commentators have argued it should be given great deference with respect to issues involving international law. Such deference could be either with regard to the president's interpretation of international obligations or with regard to statutes incorporating international obligations.[8]

These positions have been sharply criticized by other commentators, for threatening "to undermine the rule of law by radically increasing the executive branch's capacity to use interpretation to break the law under its foreign relations power."[9] Critics argued that, under the separation of powers doctrine, the judicial branch should retain the power to interpret international law, especially when the latter has become law through congressional action.

In the background of such differences on interpretive authority lie more fundamental differences in points of view on policy and structure—one aiming to increase executive power with respect to issues of international law and one wishing to constrain executive power in order to prevent abuse. Because the president rarely admits that he is acting contrary to international law and almost always tries to justify his actions either as based on congressional authorization to violate international law or as satisfying the law, courts have not often dealt explicitly with this question.

Should the President's Actions in the War on Terrorism Be Constrained by International Law as a Matter of National Policy?

From an international legal perspective, there is no doubt that the United States is constrained in the means and measures it chooses to apply in its war on terror. The exact scope of these constraints is often unclear, as it depends on the interpretation or adaptation of certain international legal rules in specific contexts. Is there a separate status of "unlawful combatants" or are there only "civilians" and "combatants"? Can combatants, lawful or unlawful, be detained until the end of hostilities even where the "end" may be indefinitely delayed and impossible to define? What is the line separating torture from cruel, inhuman, or degrading treatment? All of these questions are subject to heated debates among international law scholars, in much the same manner as questions about executive power or statutory interpretation are debated among domestic law experts.

But in the present context we wish to ask a more general question: Assuming that a widely accepted interpretation of international law constrains the president from acting in a particular way in fighting terrorism (or any other threat to national security), to what extent should the president see himself constrained accordingly, even though the U.S. courts are unlikely to enforce these constraints upon him and U.S. constituencies are likely to be far less fearful of the threat posed to their liberties by disregard of international law? In other words, should the president take international law seriously, and why?

Like the preceding discussion of the degree to which the president should be bound by domestic law, we think it is impossible to answer this question in absolute terms as a matter of law or morality. Instead, we address the considerations that any administration must take into account in deciding how to address issues of foreign policy. We then assess the effect of compliance with international legal constraints on these concerns—with an emphasis on those considerations that are unique to the international legal sphere.

In outlining these considerations we remain cognizant that international law and international politics are intertwined. The political perspective is wide ranging and encompasses concerns about what course of action will best protect the country, gain the most support from other nations, strengthen international alliances, and be most acceptable to U.S. citizens. While political considerations may often push the president to either ignore international law or use interpretive power to act up to, or beyond, the limits of what it would permit, they may as readily drive him to pursue a *more* cautious or tightly regulated path than international law authorizes. The particular content of the law, popular understanding of the law, and the nation's reputation for compliance with international law more generally all take part in shaping the political landscape.

International Law Reflects and Projects the Values We Have Chosen, Not the Dangerous Views of Strangers

Despite the Bush administration's skeptical view of international law and institutions as either irrelevant or harmful to U.S. interests (recall the remark by John Bolton, interim U.S. Representative to the United Nations, that if the UN headquarters in New York lost ten of its thirty-eight stories, nothing would be lost), it was, after all, the United States that sought to establish and bolster international law and institutions in the post World War II era. The United Nations, the General Agreement on Tariffs and Trade (the precursor to the World Trade Organization), the International Monetary Fund, and the World Bank, as well as the Non-Proliferation Treaty regime were all established under U.S. leadership with the belief that these institutions would enhance global stability, interdependence, and, where pertinent, America's competitive edge.

Our commitment to international law and institutions does not rest on the same procedural structures that endow domestic law with legitimacy. It is not about public participation, popular deliberation, universal voting, or any other domestic notion of democratic legitimacy. It is about the agreement of states on rules of engagement—in peacetime and conflict—among themselves, toward one another's citizens, and toward their own citizens.

Most important, international law is also about creating the foundations for a common language of moral choices, signifying the dos and don'ts for states, organized entities, and individuals across the globe. It is a language with a special purpose, of denoting worthy and unworthy behavior of states and other entities. Once accepted, even partially, this language begins to shape conduct. And, in part, this effort has been successful. The acquisition of territory by force, a colonial privilege, is no longer permitted and rarely practiced; war criminals face a greater risk of meeting with punishment; the global incidence of torture has decreased though it has not been eliminated; the world stockpile of chemical weapons has been reduced; discrimination on the basis of gender or race must be denied or else justified in other terms; some endangered species have been saved from extinction; and pollution is consensually understood as a common evil even if the right remedy for it is disputed.

The language that international law speaks is very close to American; much of the substantive international legal rules reflect American—and more broadly, Western—values. This is hardly surprising given that large parts of these rules were negotiated and created when the international community was dominated by Western states. The Universal Declaration on Human Rights was Eleanor Roosevelt's initiative following World War II. Woodrow Wilson envisioned the idea of a League of Nations, later replaced by a United Nations with American veto power. To this day, the United States is the largest contributor by far to the International Red Cross (donating twice as much as the European Commission).[10] The world's antidrug regime is largely of our creation. Democracy, secular government, the rule of law, the call for preserving human dignity and freedom, the regulation of the use of force, and promotion of open markets—all are "Western values," which underpin and drive the bulk of international law. So are a spate of treaties and UN Security Council resolutions addressing terrorism.

This is not to say that opinions on the right scope and reach of international law are homogenous throughout the West. Where the United States is concerned, disputes are rife; most urgently in the context of the war on terror, but also on the lawfulness of the death penalty, the response to climate change, the use of antipersonnel landmines, and the operation of the International Criminal Court. For other states, there are different points of contention. For Japan and Iceland, it is the prohibition on whaling. For Australia, Germany, and Norway, a major challenge is how to balance the pressure of immigration and the protection of refugees with state autonomy and national identity. France and Switzerland are grappling with mounting tensions surrounding the free exercise of faith and religious practices in a secularist society. Yet, so far, none of these disputes are conducted free of the language of international law, balancing different notions of human rights or freedom or liberties or social and economic interests. These are legitimate controversies, eliciting debates not very different from domestic deliberations within the United States regarding similar issues and with values very like ours playing a central role in the discussion. There is no threat to America when disputes arise with those who share underlying norms as espoused by current international law about how to reconcile competing values; the real threat emanates from those who reject those values altogether.

The obvious American interest should thus be to reinforce and disseminate the language of international law and make it more—not less— pervasive. The United States should make an effort to expand the norms that America has traditionally championed to include wide international publics and citizenries, thereby spurring domestic constituencies around the world to challenge totalitarian and fundamentalist regimes. Alongside the media and the Internet, international law has shown itself time and again to be a powerful vehicle for the propagation of values and for validating these values as the foundation of the international system. The United States should embrace this function, not fight it, even when, occasionally, it does not necessarily suit our particular set of immediate interests.

How Much of an Impediment Is International Law to America's War Powers?

International law does impose limitations on America's war tactics: it prohibits torture, regulates detention, and imposes limitations on the adverse treatment of foreign nationals. But those international rules are not arbitrary rules regulating interactions among nations; they also express and ratify commitments to values we share. The real constraint for the West on the modern battlefield is not the one posed by the formal international laws about wars. Rather, it is the full sway of public opinion, cultural sensibilities, and domestic preferences, which cannot be "interpreted away" through manipulation of the law. Law may have shaped these in the past, and has been shaped by them; today, however, law and public morality are sufficiently intertwined to make a change in one impossible without adapting the other. Hypocrisy becomes the surprisingly effective charge by our opponents when we pretend that we can comply with the words and yet ignore the values we have worked to embody in international law.

The laws of war have always been violated. Their strength is not, and never has been, in their immediate enforcement, which is often lacking, but rather in the values they stand for—minimizing the use and the brutality of armed force, ensuring some degree of human dignity even on the battlefield and curbing unnecessary cruelty—values that the United States has always declared it holds dear. Indeed, the first modern codification of the laws of war was not made at The Hague or in Geneva or in Paris but in Washington, D.C. It was the Lieber Code, promulgated by President Lincoln as Order 100 to the U.S. Armed Forces fighting the Civil War.

Moreover, some values have become so entrenched in public consciousness that they are more demanding than anything that the laws of war prescribe. A striking example is the norm obliging combatants to minimize civilian casualties on the enemy's side. Large audiences, far beyond the Western liberal constituencies, often express a false and unreasonable expectation of zero collateral damage as a claim under international law. The laws of war, in contrast, seek to minimize civilian casualties but operate with the understanding that no war can be fought without the infliction of some collateral damage. Nothing in the laws of war prescribes that no civilians may be hurt under any circumstances; the law only forbids the intentional, indiscriminate, or excessive harming of civilians.

But the law is almost irrelevant here; what matters in the conduct of counterterrorism is what the American, Muslim, and other international publics believe. If there has been any sea change occurring within the modern norms of war, it has been not so much in the shift from interstate wars to civil wars or even to the war on terrorism. To a much greater degree it is, in fact, the appreciation in value of—or at least a rhetorical commitment to—human life and dignity. "Enemy civilians" is a disappearing concept. Present-day Western governments regularly announce that their conflict is not with an adversary's people but only with its government; the unattributed and unbounded civilians, whose documented, communicated, and legally protected life is supposedly equal everywhere, must be shielded from any deliberate harm. When the United States, as the most powerful country in the world, is at war, there is a further expectation that it would not only spare civilians from harm, but also take active care of them, through humanitarian assistance and reconstruction programs.

This is not to say that the laws of war are always followed, or that civilian casualties are no longer inflicted, even illegally. It only means that the real constraint on U.S. war powers does not derive from international law, but instead from the values underlying the law, as they are understood and interpreted by the domestic and international publics. It then follows that the effects of violating the laws of war reach far beyond the legal arena; the violator runs the risk of generating at least four significant strategic problems for a country at war:

The first danger is that policies that seem overaggressive or unjust make it easier for enemies to garner support for their cause. The revised U.S. military counterinsurgency doctrine (*The U.S. Army/Marine Corps Counterinsurgency Field Manual,* or COIN) warns that collateral damage to enemy civilians makes it easier for insurgents to recruit more volunteers to join their fight.[11] COIN states that rather than using the maximum amount of force permitted in any given situation, counterinsurgency operations should use the minimum amount of force necessary to accomplish missions. According to the authors of the manual, General David Petreaus and General David Mattis, one of the "paradoxes of counterinsurgency" is that "sometimes, the more force is used, the less effective it is."[12] This is a strategic evaluation, not a legal one. In fact, what the doctrine seems to imply is that international law may be less relevant in counterinsurgency not because it is overly *restrictive*, but because it is overly *permissive*—that the U.S. military must constrain its power even beyond what international law mandates.

A second danger for a law-violating government is weakening the domestic support it needs for what it deems a necessary act of war and, indeed, for the conflict itself. As the relevant international rules reflect deeply held tenets of morality and decency among the domestic population, departure from these rules, especially when it is not perceived as absolutely essential, is liable to erode the support of the people for their government's action. In the age of uninhibited media, explaining pictures of dead civilians or tortured combatants is impossible. The Abu Ghraib debacle was the worst moment in the war on terror, in the words of President Bush, not only because of its repugnance to our self-perceived humanity, or even because of its exploitation by America's enemies, but mostly because of its effect on Americans' trust in the government handling of the war—not dissimilar to the detrimental effects of the My Lai crimes on domestic support for the war in Vietnam. Unless and until a catastrophic event fundamentally alters the norms and values espoused by the laws of war, violating them is bound to generate domestic opposition. Rightly or wrongly, international law serves as a compass for moral judgment.

A third danger is the erosion of the laws of war in their entirety. One need only ask the American military, which, unlike the Bush administration, abhorred the dismissal of parts of the laws of war as irrelevant in the war on terrorism. This was not—is not—simply a matter of indoctrination. The military's concerns for preserving the protections we enjoy under its laws of war reach beyond the current threat of terrorism; they encompass a range of possible future military engagements, ranging from classic interstate wars to humanitarian interventions à la Kosovo (e.g., Darfur). Wars of the twenty-first century, most likely, are not going to be limited to one form of warfare or another, but will involve a host of possible military confrontations. The laws of war as they currently stand are the best rule book a party in conflict can hope for or have any legitimate claim to. These laws may well need an adaptation to meet the challenges and complexities of the twenty-first-century battlefield, but jettisoning them on the terrorism front, without a coherent and shared design of other laws, pulls the rug from under any future claims we might make as to why these rules should be followed by other parties.

Finally, compliance with international law constitutes, for our allies, a crucial reassurance that we recognize that we are only one of a number of formally equal sovereign states, and not a lone superpower that can ignore the rules with which others must comply and disregard the values we have preached when they limit our discretion. Compliance generates the trust among allies on which cooperation depends. The indispensible value of international cooperation was not lost on the Bush administration in its more mature stages. In fact, the second Bush term was marked by a growing engagement with the international community on issues ranging from nonproliferation to the environment, and from health to the high seas. The Obama administration has greatly increased this commitment.

Critics of the Bush administration warned against its "pick and choose" policies of engagement and compliance with international law, cautioning against reputation loss abroad. This contention is hard to prove or disprove but quite beyond reputation, there are other very tangible costs to noncompliance with international law, especially in the military context. The war on terrorism, in particular, requires cooperation with other countries—in gathering intelligence, capturing terrorists, extraditing them for trial, mounting military operations, and so on. American violations of international law give rise to more than rhetorical rage elsewhere. They prompt even supposed friends, as well as foes, to mount obstacles to effective cooperation.

Some European governments, for example, now face private lawsuits for having cooperated with the United States in its extraordinary renditions program. No fewer than seven European countries have begun special investigations into their governments' cooperation with the United States in this practice. The United Kingdom stopped cooperating with the United States on interrogations as fully as it did before, once the coercive interrogations program became public. In February 2010, the U.K. Court of Appeal ordered the publication of a secret CIA memorandum that made it clear that the British intelligence community cooperated with its American counterpart even though it was aware of detainees being tortured or ill-treated by the CIA. This revelation sparked public outrage in Britain and demands for a public inquiry commission. On the other side of the Atlantic, the United States threatened that the court's ruling to make a secret CIA document public endangered the future of intelligence cooperation between the two countries. These fallouts make any future intelligence cooperation with the United States more difficult, or at least more cautious: The next time the United States invites others to join a "coalition of the willing" for an interstate military campaign it is likely to face serious questions and reservations regarding its commitment to handling the campaign within the law.

Should International Law Be Followed Even if Others Violate It?

The Bush administration's angry attack on international law did accurately locate the laws of war as one of the most important sites in which the war on terror takes place. The war on terror, sometimes referred to as Fourth Generation Warfare (4GW), is characterized by the blurred distinctions it exhibits between states and individuals, combatants and civilians, and indeed war and peace generally. It is also a war of asymmetries: in force formation, firepower, tactics, technological capabilities, and, not least, compliance with the laws of war. Much of the commonly heard frustration with the international laws of war stems from the fact that "the terrorists don't play by the rules," thereby giving themselves an unfair advantage.

Whoever violates any system of rules of behavior—of games, of domestic actions, or of international relations—enjoys an asymmetrical advantage, at least temporarily, in competition with those who abide by the rules. But this advantage is a source of resentment by all other players, of support for the efforts of the law-abiding, and of demands for punishment of the outlaws. The fact that the playing field is not level in respect to violations of the laws of war does not mean that the United States should feel free to ignore them. More than any improbably decisive military victory, the real struggle in 4GW is for a long-term victory in the realm of culture, beliefs, and perceptions. It is "a war of ideas," over competing definitions of justice, honor, right, and identity. The Western message of accepting legal restraints even in warfare cannot be reconciled with imitating terrorist tactics. It must stand in opposition to what the terrorists advocate, in action as much as in rhetoric.

This is as true for government compliance with the laws of war as it is, in the domestic arena, for government compliance with the rules of law enforcement. If the United States had refrained from calling terrorism "war" and continued, instead, to treat it as crime—as it had done for decades before—it would have had to operate within the constraints of domestic law enforcement. No one then would have thought to protest that the terrorists were "not playing by the rules," or drawn any conclusion from the claim as to what our own policies should be. Likewise, when David Parker Ray, Michael Swango, Ted Bundy, or Henry Lucas (each of whom is believed to have killed dozens of people) breached the most fundamental laws of our humanity, it was never seriously suggested that our domestic criminal system was entitled to break its own bonds in order to punish them adequately.

Moreover, there is no convincing empirical evidence that violating international law has been an effective tool in fighting terrorism. Even disregarding ethics, the practical benefits arising from torture, renditions, the denial of POW status for the Taliban combatants, or the invasion and long-term occupation of Iraq now seem to be daily outweighed by extreme costs.

But more fundamentally, there is a glaring tautology in the complaint that terrorists "don't play by the rules." The violation of basic laws of war *is* a common definition of terrorism: the direct targeting of civilians, the use of human shields, the absence of a distinguishing uniform, and the carrying of concealed arms are all practices that distinguish terrorism from all other types of conflict, including forms of guerilla warfare. No other form of warfare has ever been so clearly defined by its violations of the law. And it is this concept of lawlessness that in part explains why traditionally, and in large parts of Europe to the present day, terrorism has been condemned, though most often through a prism of crime rather than war.

What to do, then, about the uneven legal playing field? The legal playing field may have to be adapted to meet the new realities of modern war (and more on that later). As a general matter, however, violations by the enemy are a given challenge, just like bad weather conditions, threatening munitions, or resource constraints. To the extent possible, we must fight illegality with lawful means. In addition, we must use the asymmetry in compliance as a weapon in the war of ideas; not through reciprocal violations, but through persistent compliance and public demonstrations of the enemy's noncompliance, including by prosecutions.

International Lawfare and Appropriate Responses

The employment of law as a tool in social and political struggles is a common and wholly legitimate phenomenon; so is the response of making arguments for an opposing view of the law. International law can be used as rhetoric simply to criticize opponents and garner support for oneself, or in a more vigorous course of action, as an appeal to domestic courts, or to international fora. Domestic groups often resort to legal mechanisms in an attempt to promote policy agendas, ranging from the abolition of the death penalty to social and economic policies. Some have approached domestic courts in the United States to promote foreign or international agendas, bringing suits under the Alien Torts Claims Act for acts of torture by Paraguayan officials, abuse of human rights in Burma, terrorist activities in Colombia, and more.

When this strategy is employed against the policies in the war on terrorism of the United States and its allies, it has often been referred to, disparagingly, as "lawfare."[13] The National Defense Strategy, earlier quoted, warns against the dangers we face from others appealing to domestic and international judicial fora in an effort to curb U.S. actions in the war on terrorism. The NDS makes no distinction between cases in which this strategy is employed by the enemies of the United States, and cases in which it is employed by domestic actors within the United States seeking to uphold the rule of law.

Political use of international law is real enough. According to U.S. Air Force General Charles J. Dunlap, one tactic used frequently by opponents of the United States is "a cynical manipulation of the rule of law and the humanitarian values it represents."[14] David Kellogg, a war historian, adds that "in terrorist hands, the most commonly used tactic of lawfare has been to barrage the international news media with outrageous, often patently absurd, accusations of the illegality of coalition methods in prosecuting the [global war on terror] that invoke unrealistic norms."[15] Even U.S. Federal Judge Dennis Jacobs of the Second Circuit Court of Appeals argues that "international law and standards have become a tool of anti-Americanism, and it has become a culture in Europe and some U.S. law schools."[16] Other commentators point to the disproportionate criticism that the United States receives as compared to other countries that regularly violate human rights and international law.

While the threat of turning accusations of illegality, true or false, into instruments of politics is real, it is unclear why this should affect in any way the case for compliance with international law. Claims of illegality are part of the daily politics of democracies. That is one form of tribute politics pays to the rule of law. Unfortunately, false claims of illegality, whether malicious or merely mistaken, inevitably accompany true claims, as any public figure would attest. There is no excuse for malicious claims but they will occur. Mistaken claims are protected under the U.S. Constitution if made about a public figure or issue. Being the world's superpower naturally invites more criticism from more actors. So does being the leading advocate of the values embodied in that law. More contenders are likely to try legal channels to check America's power. We have come to accept all of this.

Prosecution on a false claim of illegality is a far more serious matter, but the United States is generally less vulnerable to international prosecutions or liability. When Belgium was pursuing a case against the then Israeli prime minister, Ariel Sharon, for his involvement in the 1982 Sabra and Shatila Massacre, there was little Israel could do other than issue diplomatic protests. When a lawsuit was filed against Donald Rumsfeld for war crimes in Iraq, under a similar Belgian law, the United States mentioned the possibility of moving the NATO headquarters from Brussels. The law was quickly changed.

Ultimately, however, lawfare, like other means used to influence the war of ideas, must be combated primarily by argument in the realm of ideas, not by abandoning its premises. If anything, the expression of greater respect for international law and the values it embodies would seem a better way of meeting the threat of lawfare than to dismiss international law as irrelevant. In fact, the Bush Administration lost as many points on rhetoric as it did on actions.

Reshaping International Law

While the Bush administration may have had an exaggerated estimate of the United States' power to single-handedly reinterpret or amend international law, international law is not immune to changes. True, historically, humanitarian provisions have been ratcheted up, not down, in terms of the protection accorded to individuals. Indeed, it would be hard to imagine a Fifth Geneva Convention on the laws of war that would reduce the basic humanitarian protections of combatants, much less expose them to torture or unregulated, indefinite detention. Nonetheless, it is not naive to think that the United States could form a "coalition of the willing" and reach some shared understanding on rules that would be applicable to counterterrorism or, more generally, to the modern battlefield, such as conditioning the prohibition of disguising oneself as a civilian on reciprocal compliance. This negotiation strategy may or may not work, but it would at least signal a willingness to engage with other countries on what the future laws of war should look like.

Nor should we rule out the possibility of negotiating some rules of engagement with nonstate actors, including our enemies. Forswearing the use of weapons of mass destruction would be an invaluable first step. In 1996, Israel and Hezbollah agreed (through the governments of Lebanon and Syria and by way of United States and French mediations) on rules for their war in South Lebanon between 1996 and the Israeli withdrawal from Lebanon in 2000. The "understanding" reached between the parties did not strive to put a stop to the conflict, nor did it change the Israeli perception of Hezbollah militants as terrorists (nor the image of Israel as an aggressor in the eyes of Lebanese civilians). But it did make for a more bearable existence for civilians in the region.

The idea of altering international law collectively is a fundamentally different strategy from a unilateral rewriting or an idiosyncratic reinterpretation of the laws of war. Engaging with international law on its own terms demands a psychological shift on our part; it requires us to go back to first principles, to negotiate with some people we don't like and said we never would talk to, even to forego ideals that are unattainable.

Conclusion

The United States is currently the strongest global power, but it is not omnipotent, nor is it unthreatened by contenders for that place. Its comparative advantage in military power, economic growth, and scientific and technological superiority is under constant challenge. America's hope for retaining its international leadership depends on spreading the values it stands for as widely as possible—on making democracy, individual autonomy, human rights, freedom, and pluralism the demands of almost every population around the world. It is a clear American interest that international agreements embodying these values be respected and abided by and that conflicts or disputes are fought or reconciled on the grounds set by international law and within the international regimes in whose design and operation the United States has had, and still has, unequal power.

This argument should not be misunderstood as a general prescription for a blinkered compliance with every rule of international law under any and all conditions. Preserving American power or protecting the vulnerable may at times require departure from others' understanding of what international law actually prescribes. Indeed, the fiercest European critics of American policies today once led the war in Kosovo without a United Nations Security Council authorization to use force (and rightly so). Some of these international rules were drafted in a different time, in a different political and strategic environment, with different types of armed conflicts in mind. They may be overly restrictive in facing new challenges and emergencies. But any short-term American departure from a principled commitment to international law has to be taken with a most careful assessment of enduring costs. In the war on terror, the departure from international law has proved itself largely counterproductive in terms of its effects on domestic support, the "war of ideas," international cooperation, and the possible ramifications for future military engagements. By this pragmatic measure alone, the view of international law as a threat to national security has been shown to be profoundly mistaken.

3

The Role of Government Lawyers in Counterterrorism

Introduction

Most of the very basic issues about the role of the government lawyer, particularly in dealing with matters that affect national security, were raised famously and dramatically when President Bush decided to conduct electronic surveillance in violation of the Foreign Intelligence Surveillance Act (FISA). Accordingly, that set of events, which dates from 2001, provides a useful framework for reviewing the impact on lawyers of the complicated relationship of law to national security concerns—a subject discussed two centuries earlier by the Founding Fathers, particularly Jefferson and Hamilton. Consider the following generally accepted version of events, drawn largely from the detailed account in *Angler: The Cheney Vice Presidency* by Barton Gellman and supplemented by the "Unclassified Report on the President's Surveillance Program" July 10, 2009, by the inspectors general of five federal departments.

The Basic Events

It is not necessary to know, and we do not know, the full nature of the President's Surveillance Program (the "PSP") approved by President Bush within three weeks of September 11. We do know that among its parts was an authorization of the interception of the content of communications into and out of the United States where there was a reasonable basis to conclude that one party to the communication was a member [or an affiliate] of Al-Qaeda—a part called the Terrorist Surveillance Program (the "TSP"). The latter did not follow the procedures required by FISA, which include certain emergency powers. That fact alone raises the central issues, although other, more intractable problems characterized different, still unrevealed, parts of the PSP. For purposes of examining the role of the government lawyer, we will divide the story into six stages.

First, at Vice President Cheney's urging, President Bush approved, inter alia, a proposal for electronic surveillance without compliance with FISA, to monitor phone calls and electronic transmissions between hotspots of terrorist activity and the United States or U.S. persons. Vice President Cheney had, immediately after September 11, asked the director of the National Security Agency (NSA), General Michael Hayden, to devise a surveillance plan without concerning himself about its legality or illegality. Significantly, if the Bush administration had taken the plan to Congress—where its nature might well have been revealed—the plan's purpose to secretly surveille possible terrorists might have been defeated, as the terrorists could have been tipped off to the presence of a form of surveillance they may have assumed was not used because it was illegal.

Second, the White House sought the approval—*after* making their decision—of the Office of Legal Counsel (OLC) in the Department of Justice, and in particular of its deputy, John Yoo, who alone knew of the president's plans. The nature of the required legal review meant that the plan had to be reauthorized periodically, perhaps in response to needed amendments in the program.

Third, the OLC's opinion, which held that the electronic surveillance plan was legal, was kept from all but a handful of people. It was not shown to the general counsel of the NSA, which carried out the surveillance, or to the head of OLC. When, at a later date, the NSA inspector general, accompanied by the acting general counsel, asked to see the OLC opinion under which his agency was operating, his request was sharply dismissed by the vice president's counsel, David Addington.

Fourth, John Yoo was not promoted to become assistant attorney general in charge of the OLC when his boss left. Resenting the secrecy—which excluded even the attorney general himself—that characterized dealings between the White House and John Yoo, Attorney General John Ashcroft objected to White House proposals to appoint Yoo as head of OLC. Instead, Jack Goldsmith was appointed to the position.

Upon his arrival to the OLC, Goldsmith reviewed Yoo's opinions and found them legally unacceptable. Addington's refusal to grant the NSA inspector general and general counsel access to the opinions only reinforced his concerns. The TSP, Goldsmith concluded, was based on a faulty interpretation of FISA. Some other parts of the PSP presented more difficult legal problems to remedy. Goldsmith obtained White House permission to show OLC opinions to the new deputy attorney general, James Comey. Goldsmith informed Comey of his own rejection of the opinions and Comey concurred in that judgment.

Addington pressed Goldsmith hard to reverse that result, telling Goldsmith that his decision would endanger many lives. Goldsmith held firm to his judgment, noting that President Bush was free either to reject his view of the law or to act in violation of the law on the basis of moral necessity as Jefferson and Hamilton recognized would sometimes be necessary and as Lincoln had done during the Civil War.

Fifth, when Attorney General Ashcroft refused, from his hospital bed, the entreaties of the president's chief of staff, Andrew Card, and his White House counsel, Alberto Gonzales, to reverse the judgment of Goldsmith and Comey on the illegality of the PSP program, including the TSP, Vice President Cheney and his counsel, Addington, turned to Gonzales to affirm the program's legality and thus enable its required periodic authorization. That approval was taken to the president, who initially planned to proceed on that new basis.

Finally, at that point, a threat of resignation by six or more of the top officials of the Department of Justice raised fears among the president's staff of a broad, Watergate-like, public repudiation of the president because of his apparent indifference to the law. President Bush quickly negotiated the changes that were necessary to avert the Department of Justice officials' mass resignation, and the program continued on that amended basis, as well as on a new, more defensible rationale for the violation of FISA posed by the PSP.

An Introductory Framework

For the sections that follow, it will be useful to lay out several premises to begin with.

Deputy Assistant Attorney General Yoo recognized, of course, that what the law requires or allows is not always clear. The realm between evident legality and obvious illegality is a continuous gradation; however, for our purposes, it can usefully be divided into three categories. Some aspects of the law will look very clear to the courts, which may therefore handle them summarily, and to a legal public at home or abroad. For convenience, we will call those parts *the core*. Outside the core, there is an area where a sizeable proportion of courts or legal publics would support each of two or more views of the law. This area of uncertainty, which remains even after much discussion, argument, and analysis, we will call *the penumbra*.

Outside the penumbra there is still room for making plausible arguments—although the great majority of lawyers and judges would consider them less than serious, responsible, or even respectable. Private lawyers are free to make such arguments before a court, although by doing so they may invite a reproach or disdain from the bench.

The government generally finds it advantageous not to press on courts those arguments that are outside both the core and the penumbra, because the government is a "repeat player" in court and derives a significant advantage from its reputation for only making arguments that a court could accept without fear of sharp legal criticism or reversal on review. Still, the executive branch and the president are entitled to the help of lawyers in litigating, negotiating, and defending government actions publicly. If the president wants his lawyers to zealously advocate opinions outside the penumbra, many would consider he may order this at the expense of reducing the credibility of the Department of Justice.

When the president asks, in good faith, for advice on the law, he is almost always asking his lawyers what the courts are likely to do, or, in the absence of judicial precedent, what has been the practice and precedent in the executive branch. He will also want to know what most lawyers would think and say and how the legality of the action would be understood by other important groups. He is interested in the repercussions for himself and for the executive branch of appearing to behave illegally or without regard for the law. It is hard to imagine why a president, in seeking advice, would ever be interested in the personal, idiosyncratic judgment of the lawyers he chose.

The president may seek a *written* opinion about the legality of a proposed action, to make clear to those concerned about legality that he is acting with great care to honor the law. Behind all this is the central role that law plays in American culture and the realization that the U.S. citizenry has been historically suspicious of governmental abuse and has relied on the executive's demonstrated commitment to the law for the reassurance necessary to maintain public trust in, and support of, its government.

Such reassurance is much less necessary when the public knows that courts can review the legality of any executive action, as they almost always can in some other countries. In the United States, notions of "standing" and of "case or controversy"—legal doctrines designed to limit who can invoke judicial review and what problems courts can resolve—render many executive actions unreviewable in court. When judicial review is unavailable, the choice for the public is between allowing the president complete freedom to do whatever he wants or looking outside the courts for reliable assurances that he is still acting within the law. Recognizing that appearing to ignore the law also entails dangers to trust in the office of the president, such as those suspicions Richard Nixon confronted, presidents since Nixon's downfall have sought to display their seriousness about legality. They have, for this purpose, often solicited the opinion of the Department of Justice and its Office of Legal Counsel for this purpose, hoping that the public and Congress believe in these institutions' independence and dedication to legality.

The First Three Stages of the FISA Story

Let us return to each of the six stages where lawyers had to decide between demands of law and national security and review these decisions. Note that in exploring the issue in this way we are departing from most discussions of what should be expected of a government lawyer. The tradition is to begin with a review of the ethical obligations of private lawyers, then move to the troublesome problem of identifying the client for a government lawyer, and finally conclude by wrestling with any modifications that seem necessary in a set of bar-imposed ethical obligations to a client, a court, and the law. Our assumption is different: in an executive restricted to the powers authorized by the U.S. Constitution and statutes, lawyers have obligations that cannot be cabined within the traditional paradigm of lawyer-client relations. Government lawyers play a critical constitutional role in certifying legality to a country jealous of the powers held by its leaders, suspicious of abuse, and fearful of tyranny.

The White House Asserts the Dominance of National Security over Law

Within three weeks of September 11, President Bush decided to disregard the apparent commands of the Foreign Intelligence Surveillance Act and the limits of its emergency exceptions, in order to increase the chance that we would know in advance of planned terrorist attacks. He was asserting either a power to go beyond the authority of statutes and the Constitution when necessity or emergency demanded his executive action, or else a broad interpretation of Article II of the Constitution as somehow vesting with him the powers he needed (free of any check by Congress).

The first justification might well have been accepted by Thomas Jefferson, who observed that during times of great necessity, "restrictive observance of the written laws is doubtless one of the highest duties of a good citizen . . . [but] laws of necessity, of self-preservation, of saving our country when in danger, are of higher obligation . . . In all these cases the unwritten laws of necessity . . . control the written laws." For Jefferson this moral authority of the president depended on his willingness to go to the people and explain why he felt it was essential to use extraconstitutional powers in the particular circumstance, subjecting himself to the people's judgment as to the necessity of his behavior. The second explanation or justification is closer to that adopted by Alexander Hamilton, who read Article II as implicitly giving the president powers to act that go beyond the authority *explicitly* granted him in the Constitution or statutes.

If going to Congress would compromise a plan that could be expected to save many lives, violating an existing statute on a particular occasion may, in appropriate circumstances, be morally justified—even conceding the illegality of the action. Thus, if Vice President Cheney and President Bush had only decided to act in violation of FISA on a single occasion, and had they considered all the possibilities for securing authority from Congress (as they eventually did) without compromising the program, and if the program was extraordinarily important (which it may have been), then Cheney's directive to NSA Director Hayden to ignore the law might have been morally justified in the minds of many Americans. That is ultimately a decision for the president and not one his lawyers can make for him. The people are the ultimate judges. As Jefferson argued, the American people should assess their government's actions in light of its deep concern about legality as well as the emergency that justified setting aside the demands of legality.

The moral justification, in this case, is weakened by two facts. First, Vice President Cheney had apparently expressed his readiness to disregard the law before knowing the usefulness of whatever surveillance Hayden would later propose, and without knowing whether violating the law would be necessary to accomplish it. Second, the proposal entailed a large number of violations to be carried out over a period of years—a reality that would magnify citizens' fears of a law-disdaining White House.

Even if the decision to repeatedly violate the FISA statute was morally justified, the president and vice president still had a choice as to the most morally justified *means* of setting aside legality on this occasion. They could have brought about the same end in any of several ways, including acting openly like Lincoln in suspending habeas corpus (or, in the international arena, like NATO in ignoring the United Nations Charter over the military operation in Kosovo). In this case, Jefferson's demands would emperil the secrecy required for the program's success. The same risk might preclude going to Congress for new legislation. The president could act in secret, hiding the fact that he was violating the law. He could find lawyers who would say that his action was legal in their own minds, and he could pretend that he understood this to be adequate assurance that he was not undermining the immense value of legality. All of this assumes he knew, just as Vice President Cheney knew, or suspected he was violating the FISA statute but considered that violation morally justified. In fact, he might not even have known the interpretations his lawyers offered differed dramatically from what the courts or legal publics could be expected to accept.

There is no indication that either Hayden or Cheney or Bush asked their lawyers about possible legal alternatives or an assessment of the real-world effects of ignoring the law. The legal rules binding the National Security Agency are notoriously complex; there is no practical possibility that any of the principals, including Hayden, fully understood them. The decision process, finalized within about three weeks of September 11, displayed an indifference to legality.

The Office of Legal Counsel

The most authoritative source of legal advice to a president and, when counsel to different departments or agencies disagree, to his subordinates, is the small Office of Legal Counsel in the Department of Justice. Considered far more independent than a president's White House counsel, its views of the law are assumed to be free of politics or favoritism. When John Yoo, as number two in the OLC, was asked to certify the legality of the new electronic surveillance program, he could have imagined his role in any of five ways. First, he might have thought of himself as a private lawyer charged with zealously supporting his client's desired position and certifying only that there was some plausible legal support for its legality. Second, he could have seen himself as a judge without the guidance of precedent or argument who must determine, in terms of his own beliefs and experience, what the law required or forbade. If he did this, his opinion might have included or excluded mention of his own uncertainties or the fact that his views were perhaps outside the penumbra of widely held views. Third, he could have seen that the president almost always wanted to know how his actions would be perceived in terms of the public's concern about abuse of power and the importance of legality in protecting its freedoms. As such, Yoo would see his role as describing mainstream views of the legal question—in particular, the views closest to those the courts would adopt. Fourth, only slightly differently, he might have considered his responsibility to be to predict the reactions of domestic and foreign publics to the assertion of domestic and international legality. Fifth, and finally, following American Bar Association guidance to private lawyers, he might have thought it was his job to draw the president's attention not only to the legal but also to the social, moral, economic, and political consequences of various actions.

In the "conversation" that takes place between the president, the OLC counsel, and the public over any formal and recorded opinion, the president wants to be able to tell the public that he has turned to OLC to be sure that those actions he felt were desirable were also legal, and therefore not show a dangerous contempt for the rule of law. Indeed, playing the role assigned in this conversation between the president and the public provides much of the enduring identity of the OLC and indeed of the Department of Justice over decades and administrations. In playing this role, OLC cannot simply assert any remotely plausible argument for legality or give the idiosyncratic views of its leaders on the law. Nor does this role necessarily call for social, moral, economic, and political judgments, although it might often be difficult to disentangle such judgments from the legal statement. OLC can only reassure the public of the president's commitment to lawfulness, as the public understands it, by finding that the president's actions are consistent with mainstream views of the law, in particular with the views the courts would be likely to adopt.

For our purposes, it is sufficient to note that the opinion by Yoo seems to have fallen outside not only the core but also the penumbra of mainstream interpretations of the FISA statute. Such a stance is inconsistent with the role the president wants to convey in "conversation" with the suspicious citizens of this nation—that OLC acts as guarantor of his good-faith intent to comply with the law.[1]

Depending on how clear Cheney's intent was when Yoo was asked for his advice, it should have been clear to him that the president was consulting him simply in order to provide a record of the president's concern to respect the law, whatever it might demand. In this situation, no matter how sincere Yoo was in believing his own idiosyncratic views, he hardly could have thought that providing them would satisfy the president's desire to reassure a public concerned about lawfulness. Only an opinion reflecting views within the core or the penumbra of familiar interpretations would do that. Nor could the president, seeking to convey that message of reassurance to the public, honestly ask Yoo to furnish whatever Yoo's idiosyncratic views might be, when describing the law; only mainstream views could reassure a suspicious public.

Even if the president chooses to ask for OLC's advice, he is not bound to follow it. As Jack Goldsmith later pointed out to Addington, the president can conclude on the basis of other advisors' judgments or his own that he has the authority that OLC believes he lacks. He can alternatively conclude with Jefferson and Lincoln that he is morally justified to do what he proposes, even if there is no legal authority, because there is no feasible option of going to Congress for authority.

Within the penumbra of lawfulness, there will be close questions about the president's authority—situations in which one could not readily predict the position of courts and in which informed legal opinion would be significantly divided. A clear and decisive legal answer is not necessary in that situation to preserve the president's reputation as law abiding and the public's confidence that he will not exceed his authority. OLC can say that responsible people will differ on the question of legal authority and that for the president to take one side or the other is not, and should not appear to be, lawless. The system is workable without deception or secrecy.

The Role of the NSA General Counsel

When General Hayden, Vice President Cheney, and President Bush decided to conduct a surveillance program outside the boundaries that Congress had set in the Foreign Intelligence Surveillance Act, they sought an OLC opinion from John Yoo. The opinion was not shared with the general counsel of the NSA. According to Hayden, he later "asked the three most senior and experienced lawyers at NSA" whether the program was lawful in light of the global threat. "They reported back to me. They supported the lawfulness of the program. Supported, not acquiesced."[2] It is impossible to tell from Hayden's account whether the general counsel of the NSA was consulted and whether Hayden requested any formal opinion.

Later, when Joel Brenner, the inspector general, suspected activities that he deemed to be in violation of the laws and regulations binding the NSA, he, along with acting general counsel, Vito Potenza, asked for permission to see the OLC opinion that reportedly justified the actions as legal. Vice President Cheney's counsel, Addington, brusquely refused to make the opinion available, saying the legal reasoning was none of the NSA's counsel's business.

The position taken by the White House was that all the many operations of the executive branch, defined and limited in countless ways by statute, can be found definitively legal or illegal by a single office and a single official chosen by the president. In this case, OLC and Yoo. An alternative view is that each agency is obligated to stay within a reasonable interpretation of the law and cannot be relieved of that obligation by unreasonable interpretations, that is, interpretations outside the penumbra of lawfulness.

The considerations at stake go far beyond questions of knowledge and effectiveness, but such factors are also relevant. The law and regulations that bind the National Security Agency are extraordinarily complicated. Lacking the assistance of the NSA general counsel, Yoo is said to have blundered in his interpretations. There is no indication that General

Hayden asked his lawyers to suggest lawful alternatives for some of what was proposed.

It is clear that General Hayden could not legitimately defend his own actions against charges of lawlessness by relying on an opinion he knew constituted a highly idiosyncratic interpretation of the law. OLC does not have the power to make unorthodox law by interpretation. Not even an order of a president or general permits a soldier to obey unreasonable interpretations of the law. Thus, if it was clear to General Hayden that the activity he was engaged in had been ordered without concern for—indeed, in defiance of—traditional notions of legality for NSA action, then his failure to support his counsel's effort to review the legality and implications of Yoo's opinion was indefensible.

National security concerns did not stand in the way. Hayden's general counsel had every necessary clearance and could be trusted. The only explanations for keeping him uninformed were to prevent his confirming and recording his concerns and making them known.

If the president decides that occasions of emergency require an executive form of civil disobedience, the general counsel of NSA has no responsibility for that. But if the president says that a particular agency's actions are legal, and the general counsel of that agency believes they are rather plainly illegal, the latter has an obligation to raise that difference with the head of the agency and perhaps with members of Congress as well. The same is true if the general counsel is "put on notice" of likely illegality by being denied access to the opinions said to authorize his agency's actions. He and his agency have responsibilities to Congress and to the statutes it has enacted, as well as to the president. This is substantially the path followed by Navy General Counsel Alberto Mora when he believed the interrogation methods authorized by the secretary of defense, in reliance on the advice of his general counsel, were illegal. Calling that view to the attention of the secretary and the department counsel was enough to halt the proposed actions.

The Final Acts: A Clash of Powerful Ideologies

Goldsmith Refuses to Certify the Legality of the Program
A new assistant attorney general for the Office of Legal Counsel, Jack Goldsmith, was named to replace Assistant Attorney General Jay Bybee, who was appointed to a judgeship on the Ninth Circuit Court of Appeals.

John Yoo left to return to teaching. Goldsmith had to decide what to do with a number of opinions by his immediate predecessors that he believed are outside the penumbra of permissible interpretations (and many of which President Obama would immediately renounce on taking office). In making these decisions, Goldsmith had to confront several major obstacles before he could apply his own judgment to determine what falls within the category of acceptable interpretation of the law.

The first question was whether he needed to reconcile his duty to the law with his obligation to protect national security. His answer to Addington was entirely correct. Balancing these concerns was not his responsibility; rather, it was the responsibility of the president, who could reject Goldsmith's legal judgment or assume the law-surpassing emergency power that Jefferson and Hamilton had endorsed and that Lincoln and Roosevelt had exercised. The public understanding of the role of OLC was that it would provide objective advice to the president and that the public could therefore trust the president's law-abidingness when he relied on that advice. For Goldsmith secretly to change that understanding would be to deceive the public needlessly.

By insisting on a law-bound role, Goldsmith was not only supporting the expectations of past and present OLC members, but was also attempting to salvage and preserve for future presidents the office's reputation for law adherence. Once its credibility was lost and OLC became known as simply a zealous advocate of the president's interests, it would be difficult for it to recapture the public's trust or to lend that credence to the president.

But in another respect, like a judge deciding a case, Goldsmith had also to decide what weight to give to precedent. As in the case of courts, precedent—as well as the language of the Constitution, statutes, and treaties—constrains the freedom of the party charged with interpreting the law. This deference encourages public confidence of the sort that comes with consistency; the legal opinions of many lawyers over time are valued over the views of any individual lawyer. This consideration might well have led Goldsmith to stand by an opinion he thought was near the margin of widespread acceptability relative to the views of courts and legal audiences, but he seems to have considered Yoo's opinion to be outside the area of permissible interpretation.

As such, Goldsmith still had to decide whether it was his responsibility to correct a decision of his predecessor, or whether his role was simply to decide new matters. The Bush electronic surveillance system required periodic reviews and periodic reconsideration of its legality. That forced Goldsmith to reconsider its lawfulness periodically. In any event, the activities that Yoo had approved were ongoing in reliance on the OLC's claims of legality; this fact created a continuing responsibility on the part of OLC's new head.

If Goldsmith believed that no significant percentage of courts, other legal audiences, or both, would consider the activity legal, he had a responsibility to withdraw OLC's opinion leaving the administration to act or refrain from acting on its own authority. The decision was more difficult if he believed that the president's actions—though taken on the authority of an earlier OLC opinion, which was outside the penumbra of permissible interpretations—would be legal under a proper theory. In that case, his only reason for overruling an earlier opinion would be to ensure that its language could not be used to justify illegal actions.

The hardest question is posed if Goldsmith believed that particular opinions were within the penumbra of judgments that a significant portion of the legal community would accept, but were incorrect in Goldsmith's view of the law. Goldsmith should then have written an opinion stating not only his own view but also that a significant share of legal opinion went each way on the issue and that the president could properly decide on the merits without raising doubts of his commitment to legality.

The attorney general, even more clearly than the president, can reject the legal advice of OLC and substitute his own. Thus, had Attorney General Ashcroft been healthy—rather than being hospitalized in severe discomfort and sedated—Chief of Staff Card and White House Counsel Gonzales could quite properly have urged him to reverse the decision of Goldsmith and Comey.

In the circumstances, putting pressure on a seriously ill attorney general to reverse legal opinions of his staff reflects a continuing indifference to the law, as does Card's action in then summoning Deputy Attorney General Comey to the White House to chastise him for honestly defending his legal judgment. Card's actions amount to a clear claim that national security and loyalty should dominate over obligations to legality in the decisions of OLC.

The White House Seeks to Rely Instead on the Opinion of White House Counsel

When it was clear that Deputy Attorney General Comey, Assistant Attorney General Goldsmith, and others were unwilling to certify the legality of steps they saw as plainly illegal, despite their possible usefulness to our security, Vice President Cheney turned to White House Counsel Gonzales to sign the certification of legality. The public recognizes that part of the job of the White House counsel may be to write, on request, opinions supporting the interests of the president, whether or not he regards the president's proposed actions as ones that courts would be at all likely to consider authorized. There is thus no more deception in his making the argument or finding as to legality than there is when a private lawyer writes an opinion supporting the highly questionable legality of the actions of a private client. However, such opinions of one's private lawyer do not generally constitute a legal defense against charges of knowingly engaging in criminal conduct.

Judges and lawyers can evaluate the credibility of the source—a lawyer whose loyalty and responsibility is entirely to the president and not to the Congress or the public. They are not misled as they would have been if Goldsmith had set aside his judgment of the scope of acceptable arguments in order to render a favorable opinion for the president.

There is nothing wrong with substituting for OLC or the Department of Justice a lawyer of the president's choice who is almost totally committed to the president's interests. It might be preferable, when intelligence secrets ought not to be compromised, for the president to act as Lincoln did, openly doing what he regarded as necessary for the safety of the country, although acknowledging it was beyond his duly granted authority. But the president may seek a favorable opinion from his White House counsel or from a large law firm or from whomever he wishes, so long as the opinion is widely understood to have no greater force than the opinion of any other lawyer who is hired and paid by his client.

President Bush Backs Down

When Goldsmith, Comey, FBI Director Robert Mueller, Solicitor General Theodore Olson, Attorney General Ashcroft, and others all threatened to resign if the program continued, they were asserting the dominance of their view of both the law itself and the role of lawfulness as they see it over the president's powers in situations of emergency—the mirror image of the insistent claims of the dominance of national security over law made by Addington and Cheney. The view of the law held by the Department of Justice cannot automatically trump the executive's moral claims of the urgent need to save American lives or to assure national security. Lawfulness and emergency requirements such as national security are powerful and equal competitors for the attention of the president in times of dire need.

From this perspective, Deputy Attorney General Comey was wrong to feel compelled to resign on the ground that the president was about to do something DOJ said was not legally supportable.

Goldsmith was also surely right to argue that the president, as chief executive with the constitutional duty to "take care that the laws are faithfully executed," could make a determination that the secret PSP program, as practiced, was lawful. Goldsmith concluded that this determination was binding on the entire executive branch, including Comey, in his exercise of the powers of the attorney general. But if this understanding precluded open challenge, it still did not require personal participation in a course of action that seemed unmistakably illegal. So FBI Director Mueller was morally justified to threaten to resign, as he did, rather than help to carry out an order or authorization he considered clearly illegal, especially when the Department of Justice had so concluded.

The Department of Justice has no capacity, and thus no responsibility, for assuring that the president acts only legally, let alone always in conformity with OLC's views of the law. Its responsibility is only to determine and state honestly what are the mainstream views of the authority of the president in a particular circumstance. It cannot reasonably be asserted that the legal views of the Department of Justice are beyond the questioning of the president, the White House counsel, or anyone the president might choose for a second opinion. It has come to be understood that the legitimate interpretation of the law is vested in courts; it has not been understood as vested in a particular lawyer or set of lawyers that the president has appointed and whose views he is free to later reject, with or without removing them from office.

The political dimension offers a different perspective. The president's aides were plainly correct to see that a mass resignation from the top of the Department of Justice would be understood by the American people as a convincing statement that the president had declared himself free of the bounds of law in a far broader way than any emergency exception would allow. The president was wise to back down, despite Vice President Cheney's urging to the contrary, for with the American people unsure about the clarity of the law and also uncertain about the reality of the emergency claims of the president, they were more likely to be persuaded by the extraordinary willingness of a number of officials of the Department of Justice to resign than by the unsubstantiated claims of the president to need particular powers. If the ideologies of law and national security went to battle on this occasion, the law would have won because of public trust in the Department of Justice's willingness to distinguish between legitimate and exaggerated claims of illegality and because of the deep historical suspicion Americans feel for claims of presidential powers unlimited by law.

Conclusion

Government lawyers' proper roles in dealing with national security law in emergency situations are decipherable but complicated. Government lawyers are *not* responsible for keeping the president's actions consistent with *their* judgment of the law, or even with the president's own conception of the law, so long as there is no suggestion that *they* have agreed that the actions are legal. If the president chooses consciously to disregard the law in the face of dire emergency, that is his prerogative, so long as he is willing to openly face the public consequences. A recorded statement of the lawyers' views on illegality is what we should expect. In other ways, moreover, their duty is not just to the president or their superior. Part of their responsibility is to provide honest certifications of executive lawfulness to the public; part is not to be used in a misleading way where they find an action unlawful; and a final part is to represent Congress's interest in executive obedience to its laws. The ultimate responsibility for reconciling the public's concurrent demands for lawfulness and security remains with the president.

Part II

On Coercion

There are at least three major dimensions to our national goals for counterterrorism. We want to preserve an adequate and high level of security for the American people and allies. We want to preserve as many as possible of the traditions that are deeply valued by the American people and identified with our constitutional tradition. And we want to justify and maintain our position as a leader among free and democratic states—one accepted for the quality of its leadership, not for its economic or military power alone.

The Bush administration, from the earliest days after September 11, 2001, developed a strategy of maximizing our security, as if we were in a great war where our very existence was at stake, leaving little time or energy for the second and third dimensions of our national goals. It quickly decided to detain, free of judicial review, suspected terrorists and to try them under lax rules of evidence before military commissions. It promptly asserted a power that it found inherent in the presidency to ignore statutory and normal constitutional limitations on a president's capacity to search, wiretap, or otherwise monitor communications of Americans within the United States in the name of national security. It sought and obtained from its lawyers interpretations that can fairly be described as challenging almost any legal limits on the methods it might use in interrogation. As a matter of practice, it was far more protective of American citizens and of anyone within the United States than of others; the courts might intervene in these cases but not to protect rights claimed by those outside the United States. But its claims of power were not so limited.

Most dramatically, law was considered an enemy and not a fundamental part of the structure with which we would deal with terrorism.

As we have noted, Secretary of Defense Donald Rumsfeld referred to law as being, like terrorism, one of the weapons of our enemies who lack the capacity to fight real wars. Statutes forbidding detention without congressional approval and torture were set aside as quickly as was the Foreign Intelligence Surveillance Act (FISA). The feeling was that there was no time for such things when we were at war with Al-Qaeda and its supporters and that, in any event, what were being asserted were powers that really belonged to the president, free of interference by Congress or the courts—powers that had been unwisely shared since the 1970s. Reasserting executive independence was considered a great benefit in itself. So was freeing ourselves—the world's only superpower since the fall of the Soviet Union—from the efforts of other nations to limit our freedom of action in a world that our military was thought able to dominate easily.

The Bush administration approached issues like interrogation, detention, and surveillance almost deductively linked. It saw the September 11 attacks on the United States as "war." It reasoned that in war, anything furthering the national security could and should be done—and that no one should expect deference to traditions, the attitudes of allied nations, or anything more than the narrowly construed letter—not the spirit—of the law of war. And the administration reasoned that in war, it is the executive that must make the decisions, for the views of Congress, the courts, the career civil servants, or the public (which would in any event not know and generally shouldn't be told the precise nature of the danger) would be too unreliable, too slow, and perhaps too cautious.

In this framework, there was little reason to pay attention to bringing along the public or Congress. There was even less reason for a superpower to defer to the reactions of allies. Attending to widely held views of legality would ignore the very special dangers of the situation and would entrust our independence to a dangerous international law; certainly, the broader spirit (rather than "letter") of domestic or international law could and should be ignored if terrorism fell into a gap between the laws of war and of peace. In war, the Bush administration officials believed, forward-leaning boldness was an attribute of strength; tentativeness in the face of uncertainties, a weakness. Finally, a warring nation's need for secrecy created opportunities to be free of executive accountability that could and should be exploited by the administration.

If these were not deductions from the firm belief that we were fighting a war, indeed a particularly dangerous one, it must have seemed very much to be the case to those deciding for the Bush administration and especially to those, like the vice president and the secretary of defense, who felt that the president's needed independence had been harmfully shackled by Congress and the courts since the 1970s.

In short, the Bush administration found a justification for considering only national security in deciding upon measures whose harshness affected public and congressional support, the support of other nations, and the legality of government actions. The justification lay in a new understanding about the powers of the president, the extent of the emergency, and the nature of "real" leadership in dangerous times. Nor were choices about harsh coercive measures—initially justified to prevent another imminent attack—calibrated later on, when no attack followed. When scaling back did occur, it was at the instruction of the Supreme Court (ruling on monitoring and review mechanisms for detainees) or a response to public outcry (when the torture at Abu Ghraib became public).

But the Bush administration's justifications could not supersede the law of nature that if one takes actions designed to maximize only one type of valued consequence, without due consideration of other values, the outcome is likely to be costly in terms of the values ignored. Consideration of national security alone, subject only to a very narrow (if at all plausible) reading of the Constitution, statutes, and international obligations, inevitably resulted in a significant loss of public and congressional support, cooperation of allies, and legitimacy. Moreover, actions that much of the bureaucracy, Congress, and the public are sure to reject legally or morally are very hard to shield behind a veil of secrecy. Even the most trusted individuals revolted in cases such as the decision to ignore FISA in authorizing wiretaps.

The Bush administration's strategy proved deeply flawed. It overstretched our military with two wars, only one of which was directly related to the "war on terrorism"—wars in which our immense kinetic advantages were less useful than the ability of our opponents to operate while hidden within a population that we did not want to attack. Cooperation from our allies began to fade. There was little military support in Iraq and a growing unwillingness to cooperate with the effort to capture, detain, and interrogate suspected terrorists as our allies worried about international prohibitions of torture, saw the infamous pictures of Abu Ghraib, and found their own citizens detained in Guantanamo.

Lawyers in the career military and FBI agents balked at interrogation practices deeply opposed to our traditions. A substantial opposition to administration methods developed among the media and our citizens. Appointed officials in the Department of Justice revolted, as we have seen, against White House dictates concerning electronic surveillance. Secrets leaked to an increasingly hostile press. The U.S. Supreme Court entered the fray with a surprising number of decisions, reversing the detention policies and legal arguments of the administration, first for citizens and then for aliens. Under the leadership of Senators John McCain, Lindsey Graham, and John Warner, a long acquiescent Congress imposed at least vague restraints on highly coercive interrogation and regulated the criminal trial procedures of military commissions.

What could have been done instead? Action was needed to combat terrorism and to prevent another attack. However, this could have been accomplished—and can be accomplished in the future—without rejecting law and transparency. Instead, the Bush administration could have tried to accommodate additions to national security protection as far as possible within the limits of law, tradition, and values widely shared in Western nations. In the most exceptional cases in which law imposed impossible constraints, the departure from legal constraints should have been as narrow as possible and with due deference to the rationale behind the original constraints. Our policies need not have been rooted in recently discovered loopholes. Had President Bush done this, he would not have had to claim, without proof of necessity, the full array of powers a president like Lincoln or Roosevelt needed when the very existence of the United States was at stake.

The Bush administration rejected laws—both domestic and international—because it thought the law did not allow the executive enough power to combat terrorism effectively. In this section, we show that this is not true. Through examples of targeted killings, detentions, and interrogations, we show that by starting from a framework that recognizes the concerns of due process, in both domestic law and the law of war, only minor modifications are needed to create an effective yet protective counterterrorism strategy. Such a strategy would have enabled the administration to pursue most of its counterterrorism goals without jeopardizing the other American interests. We illustrate this in the chapters that follow.

The practice of targeted killing, the most coercive tactic employed in the war on terrorism, clearly displays the difference between labeling terrorism a crime and labeling it an act of war. After the attacks of September 11, 2001, President Bush authorized the CIA to target Al-Qaeda leaders anywhere in the world and justified the targeted killings of suspected terrorists as lawful battlefield operations against enemy combatants. President Clinton had already experimented with the same authority. But since the war on terror is not a conventional war bounded by location, duration, and readily identified allegiances, this paradigm is unnecessarily broad in allowing the targeting of any terrorist suspect in any place at any time. Instead, we argue that the executive must assume further limitations to ensure the legitimacy and effectiveness of targeted killing operations, whether under a war paradigm or a law enforcement paradigm.

Guantanamo Bay is emblematic of the Bush administration's rejection of the "process" protections. Guaranteed both by our constitution and, to a lesser extent, by the law of war, these procedures could not be bypassed without inviting interventions by the Supreme Court to reverse the administration's policies. Detention can be made far less error-prone and far fairer, even if it is continued under the wartime paradigm. The Obama administration has attempted this path, even while repeatedly failing to convince courts of the basis of the detention. We believe that a war paradigm, with some important due process guarantees, is indeed the right one for battlefield detainees captured in Afghanistan and Iraq. For others captured in various places around the world and detained at Guantanamo Bay, taking the minor steps necessary to place detention under a criminal law paradigm will preserve much of the security provided by the widely unpopular military detention schemes while adding legitimacy and reliability that has so far been lacking.

The costs of highly coercive interrogation, even torture, do not support the thin (and controversial) evidence of its security advantages over what domestic law and international law plainly allow. If coercion does have security advantages—a much-debated point—they are bought at the price of violating the American people's dedication to fair and humane treatment, impairing relationship with our allies, and making it easier for terrorists to recruit supporters. The president may need to make exceptions to any law in very rare, grave emergencies where many lives are at imminent risk and there is no alternative—a "prerogative" suggested by American leaders, such as Jefferson, Hamilton, and Lincoln. But the more general rules for interviewing purposes should not permit anything for which we would condemn another nation if used on an American citizen. These general guidelines, accompanied by rules of accountability to make transparent what is being done, will serve us far better than radical departures from widely accepted domestic and international prohibitions.

4

Targeted Killing

Introduction

Imagine that the U.S. intelligence services obtain reliable information that a known individual is plotting a terrorist attack against the United States. The individual is outside the United States, in a country where law and order are weak and unreliable. U.S. officials can request that country arrest the individual, but they fear that by the time the individual is located, arrested, and extradited the terror plot would be too advanced, or would already have taken place. It is also doubtful that the host government is either able or willing to perform the arrest. Moreover, even if it did arrest the suspected terrorist, it might decide to release him shortly thereafter, exposing the U.S. to a renewed risk. Should the United States be allowed to kill the suspected terrorist in the foreign territory, or must it at least attempt to capture, detain, and try him?

More than any other counterterrorism tactic, targeted killing operations display the tension between addressing terrorism as a crime and addressing it as a war. The right of a government to use deadly force against a citizen is constrained by both domestic criminal law and international human rights norms that seek to protect the individual's right to life and liberty. In law enforcement, individuals are punished for their individual guilt. Guilt must be proven in a court of law, with the individual facing trial enjoying the protections of due process guarantees. Killing an individual without trial is allowed only in very limited circumstances, such as self-defense (where the person poses an immediate threat) or the immediate necessity of saving more lives. In almost any other case, it would be clearly unlawful, tantamount to extrajudicial execution or murder.

When agents of a state seek to engage in enforcement operations outside their own territory without consent of the foreign government, they are further constrained by international norms of peaceful relations and the respect for territorial boundaries among states. Ordinarily, when a criminal suspect finds refuge in another country, the United States would ask the other country for extradition to gain jurisdiction over him. Even interviewing a person outside of U.S. territory would be unlawful; executing him would be an extremely egregious offense. Violations of these norms run the risk of replacing law with force and spiraling international violence.

In wartime, governments may use deadly force against combatants of an enemy party, in which case the peacetime constraints are relaxed. But in war the enemy combatants belong to another identifiable party and are killed not because they are guilty, but because they are potentially lethal agents of that hostile party. Moreover, soldiers are easily identified by the uniform they wear. Once in the uniform of an enemy state, any soldier, by commitment and allegiance, is a potential threat and thus a legitimate target, regardless of the degree of threat the soldier is actually posing at any particular moment. The relaxing, unarmed soldier, the sleeping soldier, the retreating soldier—all are legitimate military targets and subject to intentional targeting. No advance warning is necessary, no attempt to arrest or capture is required, and no effort to minimize casualties among enemy forces is demanded by law.

The identity and culpability of an individual not wearing a uniform but suspected of involvement in terrorism is far less easily ascertained. While combatants should not benefit from defying the obligation to distinguish themselves from civilians (wearing civilian clothes does not give a soldier legal immunity from direct attack), the lack of uniform does raise concerns about the ability to identify individuals as belonging to a hostile force.[1] Moreover, joining a military follows a distinct procedure that allows for a bright-line rule distinguishing between those in the military and those outside it (although it hides the dangerous responsibility of civilians who take part in hostile activity without being members of the armed forces). Joining a terrorist organization does not necessarily have a similar on/off switch; individuals might join the organization or support it in some ways or for some time, but then go back to their ordinary business without any ritual marking their joining or departing. Identifying individuals as terrorists grows more difficult as organizations, such as Al-Qaeda, become a network of small dispersed cells, or even individuals, making the association with a hostile armed group even more tenuous.

Despite these difficulties, both the United States and Israel (as well as several other countries) have made targeted killing—the deliberate assassination of a known terrorist outside the country's territory (even in a friendly nation's territory), usually (but not exclusively) by an airstrike—an essential part of their counterterrorism strategy. Both have found targeted killing an inevitable means of frustrating the activities of terrorists who are directly involved in plotting and instigating attacks from outside their territory.

Adopting a position on targeted killings involves complex legal, political, and moral judgments with very broad implications. Targeted killing is the most coercive tactic employed in the war on terrorism. Unlike detention or interrogation, it is not designed to capture the terrorist, monitor his or her actions, or extract information; simply put, it is designed to eliminate the terrorist.

A targeted killing entails an entire military operation that is planned and executed against a particular, known person. In war, there is no prohibition on the killing of a known enemy combatant; but for the most part, wars are fought between anonymous soldiers and bullets have no designated names on them. The image of a powerful army launching a highly sophisticated guided missile from a distance, from a predator drone, against a specific individual driving an unarmored vehicle or walking down the street starkly illustrates the difference between counterinsurgency operations and the traditional war paradigm. Moreover, the fact that all targeted killing operations in combating terrorism are directed against particular individuals makes the tactic more reminiscent of a law enforcement paradigm, where power is employed on the basis of individual guilt rather than status (civilian/combatant). Unlike a law enforcement operation, however, there are no due process guarantees: the individual is not forewarned about the operation, is not given a chance to defend his innocence, and there is no assessment of his guilt by any impartial body.

The uneasiness about classifying and evaluating targeted killings further grows as these operations are carried out outside an immediate battlefield, such as in Yemen, Pakistan, or Somalia. Justifying targeted killings in those countries faces the challenges of the constraints of peaceful international relations or else a potentially unlimited expansion of the geographical scope of the armed conflict beyond the immediate theater of war. There are slippery-slope concerns of excessive use of targeted killings against individuals or in territories that are harder to justify. Recent reports about a U.S. "hit list" of Afghan drug lords, even though supposedly taking place in an active combat zone, have sparked criticism that drug lords, even when they finance the Taliban, do not fit neatly within the concept of "combatant," and must instead be treated with law enforcement tools.[2]

Concerns about the use of targeted killings grow as collateral harm is inflicted on innocent bystanders in the course of attacks aimed at terrorists. Collateral damage to civilians, if proportionate to the military gain, is a legitimate, however dire, consequence of war. In domestic law enforcement, the police must hold their fire if they believe that there is a danger to innocent bystanders, except where using lethal force against a suspect is reasonably believed likely to reduce the number of innocent deaths.

To make this tactic acceptable to other nations, targeted killings must be justified and accounted for under a set of norms that, even if it may not correspond perfectly to either peacetime or wartime paradigms, is nonetheless respectful of the values and considerations espoused by both. In this chapter we consider the advantages and disadvantages of choosing either paradigm as our starting point, thereafter subjecting the paradigm to necessary modifications for application to the counterterrorism context. We do so by assessing the American and Israeli experience in employing targeted killings and its legal, moral and strategic implications.

The Practice of Targeted Killing

The United States

Countries have been in the business of targeted assassinations for centuries. The United States has been a more recent participant. The U.S. Senate Select Committee chaired by Senator Frank Church (the Church Committee) reported in 1975 that it had found evidence of no less than eight plots involving CIA efforts to assassinate Fidel Castro, as well as assassination plots against President Ngo Dinh Diem of South Vietnam and General Rene Schneider of Chile. During the Vietnam War, the Phoenix Program planned the assassination of Viet Cong leaders and sympathizers. In 1986, President Ronald Reagan ordered Operation El

Dorado Canyon, which included an air raid on the home residence of Libyan ruler Muammar Qaddafi. Qaddafi remained unscathed, but his daughter was killed.

Assassination plots by both the United States and other countries were not publicly acknowledged, justified, or accounted for. Rather, they were taken to be an element of that part of foreign relations that always remains in the dark, outside official protocol or lawful interaction, unspoken of, but understood to be "part of the international game." Many of the plots never became public knowledge; few, if any, enjoyed enduring public acceptance.

The political fallout of the Church Committee's criticism of the covert assassination program during the Cold War brought President Gerald Ford to promulgate an executive order banning assassinations, a prohibition that was later incorporated into Executive Order 12333 (1981), signed by President Ronald Reagan, and that remains in effect today. The executive order was part of the reason that those responsible for planning military actions prior to 1998 took great care to avoid any appearance of targeting specific individuals.

However, following the 1998 bombings of the American embassies in Kenya and Tanzania, and on the basis of a (secret) favorable legal opinion, President Bill Clinton issued a presidential finding (equivalent to an executive order) authorizing the use of lethal force in self-defense against Al-Qaeda in Afghanistan. Shortly thereafter, seventy-five Tomahawk cruise missiles were launched at a site in Afghanistan where Bin Laden was expected to attend a summit meeting. Following the attacks of September 11, 2001, President Bush reportedly made another finding that broadened the class of potential targets beyond the top leaders of Al-Qaeda, and also beyond the boundaries of Afghanistan. Secretary of Defense Donald Rumsfeld ordered Special Operations units to prepare a plan for "hunter killer teams," with the purpose of killing, not capturing, terrorist suspects. Using the war paradigm for counterterrorism enabled government lawyers to distinguish lethal attacks on terrorists from prohibited assassinations and to justify them as lawful battlefield operations against enemy combatants, much like the uncontroversial targeted killing of Japanese Admiral Isoroku Yamamoto while he was traveling by a military airplane during World War II. According to reports, President Bush also gave the CIA, and later the military, authority to kill U.S. citizens abroad if there was strong evidence that an American was involved in organizing or carrying out acts of terrorism against the United States or U.S. interests.[3]

The first publicly known targeted killing of terrorists outside a theater of active war under the most recent presidential finding was in Yemen in November 2002, when a Predator (unmanned and remotely operated) drone was launched at a car carrying Abu Ali Al-Harethi, suspected of the USS *Cole* bombing, along with four others, one of whom was an American citizen. The attack in Yemen was executed with the approval of the government of Yemen, thereby eliminating some of the international legal difficulties associated with employing force in another country's territory.

Later, the United States engaged in a number of targeted killing operations in Pakistan, not all of which were authorized or approved by the Pakistani government. One of those operations, carried out in January 2006 and directed at Bin Laden's deputy, Ayman al-Zawahiri, left eighteen civilians dead while missing al-Zawahiri altogether and drawing fierce domestic criticism of Pakistani President Pervez Musharraf.

Since 9/11, Predator drones have reportedly been used dozens of times by the United States to fire on targets in Afghanistan, Iraq, Pakistan, Yemen, and elsewhere. The targeted killing operations have successfully killed a number of senior Al-Qaeda members, including chief of military operations Mohammad Atef.

President Obama's administration has not changed the policy on targeted killings; in fact, it ordered a "dramatic increase" in the drone-launched missile strikes against Al-Qaeda and Taliban members in Pakistan. According to commentators, there were more such strikes in the first year of Obama's administration than in the last three years of the Bush administration. CIA operatives have reportedly been involved in targeted killing operations in Yemen and Somalia as well, although in Yemen the operations are carried out by Yemeni forces, with the CIA assisting in planning, munitions supply, and tactical guidance. Obama has also left intact the authority granted by his predecessor to the CIA and the military to kill American citizens abroad, if they are involved in terrorism against the United States.[4]

Israel

Since its creation in 1948, Israel has assassinated various enemy targets, including Egyptian intelligence officers involved in orchestrating infiltrations into Israel in the 1950s, German scientists developing missiles for Nasser's Egypt in the 1960s, Black September members following the Munich Olympics massacre of 1972, and prominent leaders of Palestinian and Lebanese terrorist networks such as the secretary general of Hezbollah in 1992. Israel even planned an assassination operation against Saddam Hussein after the Gulf War.

But it was only during the Second Intifada, which began in September 2000, that targeted killings became a declared and overt policy in the fight against terrorism. Since the first publicly acknowledged targeted killing operation by Israel in November 2000, there have been many dozens of such operations, mostly in Gaza and only rarely in the West Bank. The use of targeted killing operations increased with the level of Palestinian violence and decreased with the prospects of peaceful relations between the parties. Following waves of suicide bombings, there was a surge in targeted killing operations; when there were declarations of ceasefire or when political processes were underway, operations were halted.

The process for approving targeted killing operations in Israel involves an intelligence "incrimination" of the target, which identifies the target as a person actively involved in acts of terrorism; a plan for the time, place, and means of the attack (most commonly, an airstrike); consideration of the danger of collateral damage; and a review of potential political ramifications. The complete plan must receive the approval of a top-level political official. There is no external review process, judicial or other.

The stated Israeli policy is that only members of a terrorist organization who are actively involved in an ongoing and direct manner in launching, planning, preparing, or executing terrorist attacks are lawful targets. In addition, targeted killing operations will not be carried out where there is a reasonable possibility of capturing the terrorist alive.

The legitimacy and usefulness of the practice of targeted killings has been hotly debated within Israel ever since it became publicly known that Israel was employing them. No incident illustrates the tension between the benefits of a legitimate procedure meeting due process standards and the national security demands for exigency better than the targeted killing of Salah Shehadeh. Shehadeh was the head of the military wing of Hamas in the Gaza Strip, and was, according to Israeli intelligence, directly responsible for the killing of scores of Israeli civilians and soldiers and the injury of hundreds of others in dozens of attacks.

Initially, Israeli officials had demanded that the Palestinian Authority arrest Shehadeh. When the Palestinian Authority declined, the Israeli government sought to capture him directly, but had to forego such plans when it realized that Shehade lived in the middle of Gaza City, where no Israeli soldiers had been deployed since 1994, and where any attempt to apprehend Shehadeh would turn into a deadly confrontation. It was then that Israel decided to kill him.

On the night of July 22, 2002, an Israeli F-16 aircraft dropped a single one-ton bomb on Shehadeh's house in a residential neighborhood of Gaza city, one of the most densely populated areas on the globe. As a result, Shehadeh and his aide, as well as Shehadeh's wife, three of his children, and eleven other civilians, most of whom were children, were killed. One hundred fifty people were injured.

Israeli officials claimed that the targeted killing of Shehadeh was designed to prevent him from carrying out future attacks against Israelis. They asserted that, according to intelligence reports, at the time of his killing, Shehadeh was effectively a "ticking bomb," in the midst of planning at least six different attacks on Israelis, including one designed as a "mega-attack," involving a truck loaded with a ton of explosives.

In the aftermath of the attack, there was little disagreement that Shehadeh himself was a justified target. Nonetheless, television images of funerals of slain children drew fierce criticism both within and outside of Israel. Legal proceedings were initiated in Britain against the Israel Defense Force's chief of general staff, the IDF's air force commander, and the commander of the Southern Command.[5] A lawsuit under the Alien Tort Claims Statute and the Torture Victim Protection Act was filed by the Center for Constitutional Rights in the Southern District of New York against the head of the Israel Security Agency at the time, Avi Dichter. The claim was subsequently dismissed by the court.[6]

Within Israel, the cars of air force pilots, normally considered demigods in popular Israeli culture, were sprayed with graffiti insults of "war criminal." A year later, twenty-seven pilots declared that they would refuse to carry out any additional bombing missions in Gaza. Israeli leftwing activists petitioned the High Court of Justice to order a criminal investigation into the attack and also to prevent the air force commander—Major General Dan Halutz—from being promoted to deputy chief of general staff (Halutz later became chief of general staff, but resigned after the 2006 war in Lebanon). A criminal proceeding was initiated in Spain by relatives of the victims of the attack on Shehade against seven Israeli officials for alleged war crimes (and was later dismissed by a Spanish court).

In a traditional war context, killing fourteen civilians along with the highest military commander of the enemy could be considered proportionate collateral damage. For comparison's sake, the special report of the prosecutor of the International Criminal Tribunal for the Former Yugoslavia on the NATO operation in Kosovo determined that ten (and according to some reports, seventeen) civilian casualties were legitimate collateral damage for the attack on the Serbian television station.

But public opinion could not disentangle the proportionality question from the broader political context of the Israeli-Palestinian relationship: the legality and morality of the continued occupation of Gaza and the West Bank (Israel withdrew from Gaza three years later); the perception of failure in conducting the war on terrorism; and the frustration over losing the symbolic struggle over "victimhood" to the Palestinians.

A year after the targeted killing of Shehadeh, ten senior Hamas leaders met in a room on the top floor of a residential building in Gaza. Bruised by the effects of the Shehadeh operation, the Israeli security agencies decided to use a laser-guided bomb only a quarter of the size of the one used to kill Shehadeh. The Hamas leaders left the room seconds before the bomb hit. The top floor was destroyed, but the group escaped with minor scratches. Had a larger bomb been used, the building would have collapsed, together with the Hamas leadership and civilian residents.

Two years later, in a newspaper interview, Avi Dichter, while admitting that the preoperation assessment misjudged the level of collateral damage that would result from the attack on Shehadeh, added that "he couldn't say how many Israelis paid with their lives for the fact that Shehadeh continued to operate long after Israel had the operational capability to harm him, but not the moral will to do it." In describing the subsequent failed attack on the Hamas leadership as "a miss," Dichter lamented, "it was the Hamas' dream team . . . the ceiling collapsed, but the team got away. No one knows how many Israelis were killed as a result of the decision [not to use heavier munitions]."[7]

Choosing the Framework

Justifying Targeted Killings—The War Paradigm

The debate within the United States over the lawfulness of targeted killings has remained largely confined to legal scholarship and public commentary; the courts have never addressed it. The Bush administration, to a large extent, relied on a December 1989 Memorandum of Law (an advisory opinion) issued by the Special Assistant for Law of War Matters to The Judge Advocate General of the Army at the time, W. Hays Parks.[8] The Parks memorandum distinguished the prohibition on illegal assassinations in Executive Order 12333 from lawful targeting of individuals or groups who pose a direct threat to the United States. The prohibition, argued Parks, applied to covert acts of murder for political reasons. Legal advisor to the State Department at the time, Abraham Sofaer, emphasized in his own statements that the prohibition "should not be limited to the planned killing only of political officials, but that it should apply to the illegal killing of any person, even an ordinary citizen, so long as the act has a political purpose."[9] Both Parks and Sofaer, however, asserted that this prohibition did not preclude the targeted killing of enemy combatants in wartime or the killing in self-defense of specific individuals who pose a direct threat to U.S. citizens or national security in peacetime. The latter, both argued, was permissible under the inherent principle of self-defense to which every country was entitled under Article 51 of the United Nations Charter (which allows countries to use force in self-defense after suffering an "armed attack") and customary international law. Neither Parks nor Sofaer expounded on what amounts to *direct* threat.

The Bush administration has favored the paradigm of war, treating terrorists as combatants and justifying the targeted killing of terrorists as equivalent to the lawful killing of members of an enemy force on any battlefield. Specifically, the administration deemed terrorists to be "unlawful combatants," targetable and detainable, but denied the rights accorded to lawful detainees, namely, to be treated as prisoners of war if captured. The Bush administration maintained this position even when the targeted killing took place in Yemen or Pakistan, outside an immediate theater of hostilities such as Afghanistan. Given that the war on terrorism was a "global war," the administration maintained, there could be no geographical boundaries to the theater of war.

However, as we noted in the introduction to this chapter, choosing a war paradigm as governing the targeted killings of suspected terrorists is not devoid of difficulties. The killing on the basis of blame rather than status, the difficulties in ensuring the accurate identification of the target, and the fact that operations take place outside of a defined battlefield— all make the war paradigm at best a proximate, but by no means a perfect, fit. The full legal implications of this choice were considered by the Israeli High Court of Justice (HCJ), in its ruling on the Israeli practice of targeted killing operations in Gaza and the West Bank.

A petition was first submitted to the HCJ by a group of Israeli NGOs in late 2001, as the first Israeli targeted killing operations became public, but it was dismissed on grounds of justiciability. In March 2002, another petition was submitted, and this time, Supreme Court President Aharon Barak ordered the state to respond. By that time, 339 Palestinians had been killed by targeted killing operations during the Second Intifada: 201 intended targets and 129 innocent bystanders. No less than seven briefs, covering hundreds of pages of arguments and documents, were submitted to the court. In his last decision before retiring from the court, President Barak delivered the ruling in December 2006.[10] It is probably the most comprehensive judicial decision ever rendered addressing the legal framework, of the "war on terrorism."

Barak began by accepting that, unlike in the era of the First Intifada, there was now an "international armed conflict" with Palestinian militants, which warranted and justified the use of military means, as governed by customary international law, to combat terrorism. For Barak, accepting the armed conflict paradigm was, albeit implicitly, a precondition to the justification of targeting operations, going far beyond any law enforcement. Furthermore, his choice of an *international* armed conflict paradigm was singular among the opinions of the U.S. Supreme Court and of most commentators, which have favored a *non-international* armed conflict model. This choice was possibly motivated by the fact that international armed conflicts are subject to more regulation under international law than their non-international counterparts, thereby further constraining the government. Barak, in his decision, did not discuss the possibility of working within a law enforcement paradigm or the possibility of relying on Article 51 of the UN Charter to justify the practice. Indeed, it would have been hard to justify a general practice, employed hundreds of times in the same territory, as an "exceptional measure" under a self-defense paradigm.

But Barak's acceptance of the war paradigm as applicable to the fight against terrorism was not unqualified. The remainder of the decision was designed to limit the full application of the laws of war and place further constraints on the legitimacy of targeted killing operations, in comparison with traditional combat.

First, in terms of the classification of terrorists, Barak rejected the government's claim that these were unlawful combatants, and found, instead, that terrorists were "civilians taking direct part in hostilities." This choice of a two-group classification (civilian/combatant) vs. a three-group classification (civilian/ lawful combatant/unlawful combatant) was intended to achieve at least two goals. The first was to make sure the protections of the Geneva Conventions applied to the armed conflict with Palestinian terrorists and to avoid the American administration's conclusion that, as "unlawful combatants," terrorists were entitled to few protections under the laws of war.

Second, by refraining from labeling terrorists as "combatants," the ruling ensured that unlike combatants on the battlefield, who were all legitimate targets regardless of rank, role, or threat, terrorists would not be targeted on the basis of mere membership in a terrorist organization; instead, an individual culpability of the targeted person, by way of direct participation in instigating and executing terrorist acts, would have to be proven. A mere membership test in the case of Hamas or some other Palestinian organizations would have been especially prone to overinclusive application, since alongside their military wings these organizations also have broad political, social, economic, and cultural operations.

The ruling also departed from the traditional armed conflict paradigm in that it conditioned the legitimacy of targeted killings on the absence of a reasonable alternative for capturing the terrorist. On the traditional battlefield, no attempt to capture the enemy or warn the enemy in advance is necessary before shooting to kill. In fact, the court's requirement to try to apprehend the terrorist is far more easily situated within a law enforcement model of regular policing operations and signifies the uneasiness that the court felt about the war paradigm.

The Supreme Court's decision also addressed concerns about collateral damage to innocent civilians in the course of targeted killings operations. At the time the petition was submitted, the ratio of civilians to militants killed by targeted killings operations was 1:3—one civilian for every three militants[11] (the ratio has improved substantially since then, and in 2007, the rate of civilians hurt in targeted killing operations was 2–3 percent).[12] Barak acknowledged the difficulty in determining what number of casualties was "proportionate":

One must proceed case by case, while narrowing the area of disagreement. Take the usual case of a combatant, or a terrorist sniper shooting at soldiers or civilians from his porch. Shooting at him is proportionate even if as a result, an innocent civilian neighbor or passerby is harmed. This is not the case if the building is bombed from the air and scores of its residents and passersby are harmed. . . . The hard cases are those which are in the space between the extreme examples.[13]

Accordingly, the decision placed an emphasis on the procedure by which the targeted killing operation was considered and approved and on the post-factum debriefing of operations, all in an effort to improve the record on collateral harm. Importantly, however, the decision did not demand a zero civilian casualty policy. In that, it remained more loyal to the war paradigm than to a policing paradigm.

Barak added that certain incidents might be subjected to judicial review. The concern about collateral damage also brought the court to stipulate that in certain cases in which there was substantial collateral damage, and depending on the conclusions of an investigation into such incidents, it would be appropriate to compensate innocent civilians who have been harmed.[14]

To conclude, the Israeli Supreme Court sought a middle ground between a more aggressive law enforcement paradigm and a tamer wartime paradigm. It chose the latter as its point of departure, but then, in consideration of the unique nature of the war on terrorism, added limitations and constraints on the government's war powers so as to remain as loyal as possible to the basic principles and values of the Israeli legal system.[15]

Justifying Targeted Killings—The Exceptional Peacetime Operations Paradigm

Could the U.S. administration, given the Parks memorandum, justify targeted killings even without relying on the applicability of military powers to a "war on terrorism"? It would have to find the operation lawful under a reasonable interpretation of the domestic law of homicide; it would have to address major issues of peacetime international law, including human rights laws and the duty to respect the sovereignty of other countries; and, of course, it would have to satisfy the constitutional protections found in the Bill of Rights to the extent these are applicable abroad.

Domestic law enforcement operations permit shooting to kill a suspected criminal only under very limited circumstances. These limitations coincide with international human rights norms on the use of force by governments against citizens. When the suspect imposes no immediate and lethal threat, firing at him to affect an arrest is only constitutional if "the officer has probable cause to believe that the suspect poses a threat of serious physical harm."[16] There are even greater common law constraints on shooting a suspect where there is a concern about collateral harm to others around the suspect; in such cases, law enforcement officials are required to hold their fire and refrain from risking innocent bystanders. Still, under the American Model Penal Code §3.02, the defense of "necessity" or "choice of evils" justifies and thus immunizes conduct "which the actor believes to be necessary to avoid a harm or evil to himself or to another" if the harm to be avoided is greater than that sought to be prevented by the law defining the crime (intentional killing, in this case), and so long as there is no reason to believe the legislature intended to exclude this justification. Under this statement of the American rule, the danger of the harm to be avoided need not be imminent and the rule would justify homicide as well as less serious crimes. Thus, in some jurisdictions the wording (of the law) need hardly be stretched to make legal under domestic law the killing of an active participant in a terrorist scheme to kill many others, if that way of aborting the plan is believed to be necessary. In other jurisdictions the law would have to be changed to allow intentional homicides or consideration of nonimminent harms.

As for international human rights laws, the possibility of using deadly force against individuals who are threatening the security of the state has not been rejected altogether even by international human rights bodies. The Human Rights Committee, in its response to the Israeli report on the practice of targeted killings, notes only that "before resorting to the use of deadly force, all measures to arrest a person suspected of being in the process of committing acts of terror must be exhausted." It adds that such operations must never be carried out for purposes of retribution or revenge, thus implying that they may be legitimate if intended at preemption.

The 2002 Inter-American Commission on Human Rights *Report on Terrorism and Human Rights*[17] similarly leaves room for the use of deadly force against suspected terrorists, even under a general law enforcement model. It notes that "in situations where a state's population is threatened by violence, the state has the right and obligation to protect the population against such threats and in so doing may use lethal force in certain situations."[18] It goes on to assert the natural implication that, in their law enforcement initiatives, states must not use force against individuals who no longer present a threat as described earlier, such as individuals who have been apprehended by authorities, have surrendered, or who are wounded and abstain from hostile acts.[19]

And in its decision in the case of *Isayeva*, the European Court of Human Rights acknowledged the right of a state—Russia—to use deadly force against Chechen rebels, even when there was no indication that the latter were posing an immediate threat to the Russian forces.[20]

But outside the territory of the United States, the government is also limited by the international norms protecting each state's sovereignty in using force to capture or kill suspected criminals. As a general principle of international law, a country is strictly prohibited from engaging in law enforcement operations in the territory of another country, and much more so when the law enforcement operation includes killing a person. Deadly attacks by air strikes or drones directly implicate the international prohibition on the use of force between states. How, then, could the government justify targeted killing operations under international law in any way other than relying on a war/combatants paradigm?

The Parks memorandum addresses the question of lawful targeting and unlawful assassinations in peacetime, and argues the following:

The use of force in peacetime is limited by the previously cited article 2(4) of the Charter of the United Nations. However, article 51 of the Charter recognizes the inherent right of self-defense of nations. Historically, the United States has resorted to the use of military force in peacetime where another nation has failed to discharge its international responsibilities in protecting U.S. citizens from acts of violence originating in or launched from its sovereign territory, or has been culpable in aiding and abetting international criminal activities.[21]

Parks goes on to give the examples of an 1804–1805 Marine expedition into Libya to capture or kill the Barbary pirates; a year-long campaign in 1916 into Mexico to capture or kill the Mexican bandit Pancho Villa following Villa's attack on Columbus, New Mexico; the 1928–1932 U.S. Marines' campaign to capture or kill the Nicaraguan bandit leader Augusto Cesar Sandino; the Army's assistance in 1967 to the Bolivian Army in its campaign to capture or kill Ernesto "Che" Guevara; the forcing down in 1985 of an Egypt Air plane in Sicily, in an attempt to prevent the escape of the *Achille Lauro* hijackers; and the 1986 attacks on terrorist-related targets in Libya.

These historical precedents, claims Parks, support the interpretation of the United Nations Charter as authorizing the use of military force to capture or kill individuals whose peacetime actions constitute a direct threat to U.S. citizens or national security. In a footnote, he adds:

In the employment of military force, the phrase "capture or kill" carries the same meaning or connotation in peacetime as it does in wartime. There is no obligation to capture rather than attack the enemy. In some cases, it may be preferable to utilize ground forces to capture (e.g.) a known terrorist. However, where the risk to U.S. forces is deemed too great . . . it would be legally permissible to employ (e.g.) an air strike against that individual or group rather than attempt his, her, or their capture, and would not constitute assassination.[22]

If so, targeted killings, as they have been used by the United States in Yemen, Pakistan, and elsewhere, may well have been justified without ever relying on a "war on terrorism," but instead by being framed as an exceptional use of force in self-defense alongside peacetime law enforcement. Although Parks does not expound upon this point, from his equation of military action in peacetime with that of wartime, it seems he would accept some degree of collateral damage in a peacetime operation under similar logic of wartime attack.

Choosing a peacetime framework with some allowance for military action is not free from difficulties. One obvious problem is that the "exceptional" use of force has been turned, in the context of the war on terrorism, into a continuous practice. In addition, the degree to which countries should be allowed to use force extraterritorially against non-state elements has been debated extensively by both international law and domestic law scholars. The implications of allowing the use of armed force to capture or kill enemies outside a country's own territory, and outside a theater of traditional armed conflict, may include spiraling violence, the erosion of territorial sovereignty, and weakening of international cooperation.

Once the precedent is laid for a broad interpretation of Article 51 of the UN Charter, as existing alongside or as an exception to normal peacetime limitations, it becomes harder to distinguish what is allowed in peace from what is allowed in war. It is for these reasons that not everyone accepts Parks's legal reasoning, with critics arguing that any military attack on another country's territory, outside an armed conflict with that country, amounts to unlawful aggression. Thus, in the case of armed activities on the territory of the Congo (*DRC v. Uganda*), the International Court of Justice went as far as to rule that Uganda had no right to use force against armed rebels attacking it from the territory of the Democratic Republic of Congo.[23] Recently, the U.N. Special Rapporteur on Extrajudicial, Summary or Arbitrary Executions concluded that reliance on the exceptional self-defense argument in support of targeted killings "would diminish the value of the foundational prohibition contained in Article 51."[24]

Even if justified as an exception to a peacetime paradigm, one obvious precondition for the legality of targeted killing operations outside a theater of war, in consideration of the other countries' sovereignty, must be that the state in whose territory the terrorist resides either consent to the operation by the foreign power (as in the case of the collaboration between the United States and Yemen) or else would be unable or unwilling to take action against the terrorist (as in the case of targeted killings in Gaza). On some rare occasions there may be an overwhelming and immediate necessity to act precluding the possibility of obtaining the other country's consent.

Note that under a law enforcement model, a country cannot target any individual in its own territory unless there is no other way to avert a great danger. If so, the Yemeni authorities could not authorize the United States to engage in a targeted killing operation in its territory or themselves execute one on its own if they could safely capture the terrorist alive.

To sum up, targeted killings of terrorists by both the United States and Israel have been justified under a war paradigm: in the American case, by treating terrorists as (unlawful) combatants; in the Israeli case, by treating terrorists as civilians who are taking direct part in hostilities.

It seems that a persuasive argument can also be made that under some conditions, targeted killings of suspected terrorists can be justified on the basis of a law enforcement paradigm. When conducted in the territory of another country, targeted killing must be based on a self-defense exception to the international law prohibition on the use of force, and in consideration of that other country's sovereignty, should only be executed if that other country either consents to the operation or else is unable or unwilling to interdict the terrorist.

In the conclusion of this chapter, we set forth what the legitimate contours of the use of targeted killing must be. We conclude that they seem to fit both a more constrained war paradigm and a more lax law enforcement paradigm (although the latter suits more sporadic and measured use of the tactic). For present purposes it should be noted that if we take the Israeli Supreme Court's decision as controlling, then the conditions for the legitimacy of targeted killings of terrorists in the armed conflict between Israel and Palestinian militants are not very different from those that would apply under a law enforcement model. Both would allow the targeted killing of some terrorists in Gaza and both would prohibit—or place greater constraints—on the targeting of suspected terrorists outside a conventional theater of war if the alternative of capture was feasible.

Strategic Aspects

Even if legally justifiable and morally permissible, the strategic value of employing targeted killings is far from clear and depends very much on the situation. As with any other counterterrorism tactic, targeted killings carry both strategic benefits and costs.

The Potential Hazards of Targeted Killings

An immediate consequence of eliminating leaders of terrorist organizations will sometimes be what may be called the Hydra effect, the rise of more—and more resolute—leaders to replace them. The decapitating of the organization may also invite retaliation by the other members and followers of the organization. Thus, when Israel assassinated Abbas Mussawi, Hezbollah's leader in Lebanon, in 1992, a more charismatic and successful leader, Hassan Nassrallah, succeeded Mussawi. The armed group then avenged the assassination of its former leader in two separate attacks, blowing up Israeli and Jewish targets in Buenos Aires, killing over a hundred people and injuring hundreds more.

Targeted killing may interfere with important gathering of critical intelligence. The threat of being targeted will drive current leaders into hiding, making the monitoring of their movements and activities by the counterterrorist forces more difficult. Moreover, if these leaders are found and killed, instead of captured, the counterterrorism forces lose the ability to interrogate them seeking potentially valuable information about plans, capabilities, or organizational structure.

The political message flowing from the use of targeted killings may be harmful to the attacking country's interest, as it emphasizes the disparity in power between the parties and reinforces popular support for the terrorists, who are seen as David fighting Goliath. Moreover, by resorting to military force rather than to law enforcement, targeted killings might strengthen the sense of legitimacy of terrorist operations, which are sometimes viewed as the only viable option for the weak to fight against a powerful empire. If collateral damage to civilians accompanies targeted killings, this, too, may bolster support for what seems like the just cause of the terrorists, at the same time as it weakens domestic support for fighting the terrorists.

When targeted killing operations are conducted on foreign territory, they run the risk of heightening international tensions between the targeting government and the government in whose territory the operation is conducted. Israel's relations with Jordan became dangerously strained following the failed attempt in September 1997 in Jordan to assassinate Khaled Mashaal, the leader of Hamas. Indeed, international relations may suffer even where the local government acquiesces in the operation, but the operation fails or harms innocent civilians, bringing the local government under political attack from domestic constituencies (recall the failed attack in Pakistan on al-Zawahiri that left eighteen civilians dead).

Even if there is no collateral damage, targeted killings in another country's territory threaten to draw criticism from local domestic constituencies against the government, which either acquiesced or was too weak to stop the operation in its territory. Such is the case now in both Pakistan and Yemen, where opposition forces criticize the governments for permitting American armed intervention in their countries.

The aggression of targeted killings also runs the risk of spiraling hatred and violence, numbing both sides to the effects of killing, and thus continues the cycle of violence. Each attack invites revenge, each revenge invites further retaliation. Innocent civilians suffer whether they are the intended target of attack or its unintentional collateral consequences. Last, but not least, exceptional measures tend to exceed their logic. As in the case of extraordinary detention or interrogation methods, there is a danger of overusing of targeted killings, both within and outside the war on terrorism. A particular concern in the context arises as the killing of a terrorist often proves a simpler operation than protracted legal battles over detention, trial, extradition, and release. The more complicated detention has become, the more attractive the option of targeted killing seems to be.

The Benefits Nations Seek

At the most basic level, targeted killings, which are generally undertaken with less risk to the attacking force than are arrest operations, may be effective. According to some reports, the killing of leaders of Palestinian armed groups weakened the will and ability of these groups to execute suicide attacks against Israelis. By deterring the leaders of terrorist organizations and creating, in some cases, a structural vacuum, waves of targeted killing operations were followed by a lull in subsequent terrorist attacks, and in some instances, brought the leaders of Palestinian factions to call for a ceasefire. The Obama administration embraced the targeted killing tactic, holding it to be the most effective way to get at Al-Qaeda and Taliban members in the ungoverned and ungovernable tribal areas along the Afghanistan–Pakistan border or in third countries. Despite the adverse effects such operations may have on the attitudes of the local population toward the country employing targeted killings, the demonstration of superiority in force and resolve may also dishearten the supporters of terrorism.

Publicly acknowledged targeted killings are furthermore an effective way of appeasing domestic audiences, who expect the government "to do something" when they are attacked by terrorists. The visibility and open aggresssion of the operation delivers a clearer message of "cracking down on terrorism" than covert or preventive measures that do not yield immediate demonstrable results. The result in Israel has been to make a vast majority of citizens supportive of targeted killings, despite all the latter's, perhaps surprisingly, potential adverse effects. And of all the coercive counterterrorism techniques employed by the United States, targeted killings have so far attracted the least public criticism.

Conclusions

Targeted killing operations display more clearly than any other counterterrorism tactic the tension between labeling terrorism a *crime* and labeling it an *act of war*. If a terror attack is simply a crime, counterterrorism forces would follow the same laws and rules as the Chicago or Miami police department do in fighting crime, where intentional killing could rarely if ever be lawful, other than where necessary in a situation immediately requiring the defense of self or others, or in making an arrest of an obviously dangerous felon. From the perspective of international peacetime relations, targeted killings face even greater legal constraints when targeting a terrorist outside the state's jurisdiction.

If a terrorist plan is an act of war by the organization supporting it, any member of any such terrorist organization may be targeted anytime, and anywhere plausibly considered "a battlefield," without prior warning or attempt to capture.

Known or anticipated collateral damage to the innocent is generally prohibited in law enforcement, but is legitimate within the boundaries of proportionality in fighting wars. In fighting crime, the government's obligation to protect its citizens applies to all citizens: criminals, and innocents. In fighting wars, the government's primary obligation is to its own citizens, with only limited concern for the well-being of its enemies.

Assuming, as we do, that states do have a right to defend themselves against acts of terrorism, targeted killings cannot be always illegal and immoral. But because terrorism is not a traditional war, nor a traditional crime, its nontraditional nature must affect the ethical and strategic considerations that inform targeted killings, the legal justification behind them, and the choice of targets and methods used to carry them out.

As we have shown, targeted killings may be justified even without declaring an all-out "war" on terrorism. A war paradigm is overbroad in the sense that it allows the targeting of any member of a terrorist organization. For the United States, it has had no geographical limits.

When any suspected member of a hostile terrorist organization—regardless of function, role, or degree of contribution to the terrorist effort—may be targeted anywhere around the world without any due process guarantees or monitoring procedures, targeted killings run grave risks of doing both short-term and lasting harm. In contrast, a peacetime paradigm that enumerates specific exceptions for the use of force in self-defense is more legitimate, more narrowly tailored to the situation, and offers potentially greater guarantees for the rule of law. It is, however, harder to justify targeted killing operations under a law enforcement paradigm when the tactic is used as a continuous and systematic practice rather than as an exceptional measure. Justifying targeted killings under a law enforcement paradigm also threatens to erode the international rules that govern peacetime international relations as well as the human rights guarantees that governments owe their own citizens.

Whichever paradigm we choose as our starting point, greater limitations than those offered by the Parks memorandum or that are currently operating in the American targeted killings program should be adopted. The limits set by the Israeli Supreme Court—ironically, within the paradigm of wartime operations—are a good place to start.

First, the tactic should not be used unilaterally by the endangered state if the host country of the terrorists is willing and able to act on its own to arrest or disable in a timely manner the source of the threat. Host country cooperation in capture and extradition must be the first alternative considered.

That is, targeted killings must only be carried out as an extraordinary measure, where the alternative of capture or arrest is unfeasible.

Second, only those who are actively and directly involved in terrorist activities are legitimate targets; not every member of a terrorist organization is or should be.

Third, the fact that terrorists do not wear uniforms should not give them an unfair legal advantage to soldiers in uniform. Therefore, in the sense of immunity from deliberate attack, their lack of uniform does raise legitimate concerns about the ability to ensure the correct identification of the target, in terms of personal identity as well as specific culpability. Any targeted killing operation must include mechanisms in its planning and execution phases that would ensure an accurate identification. Such mechanisms need not involve external judicial review; judges are neither well situated nor in possession of the requisite expertise to authorize or reject an operation on the basis of intelligence reports. Rather, the system should be based on verified and verifiable intelligence data from different and independent sources, careful monitoring, and safety mechanisms that would allow aborting the mission in case of doubt.

The concern about collateral damage requires specific attention. Unlike ordinary battlefield strikes, the fact that the targeting forces have control over the time, means, and methods of strike mandates that a heightened degree of care should be exercised to choose an occasion and means that will minimize collateral harm to uninvolved individuals, especially where the operations are carried out outside an immediate conflict zone. In those cases, we believe that where innocent civilians suffer collateral damage, those injured should generally be compensated.

Finally, the aggression of the targeted killing tactic mandates its measured use only in the most urgent and necessary of cases. The government's interest should be to tame violence, not exacerbate it. Where alternatives exist, they should be pursued, not just as a matter of law but also as a matter of sound policy.

5

Detention outside the Combat Zone

Introduction: The Costs and Benefits of Military Detention

We have argued that, in facing international challenges more dangerous than crime and yet less fearsome than more traditional war, three steps are required to reconcile security, liberty, and legitimacy. First, assess what if any departures from normal practices are actually needed for our safety. Then consider whether the possible changes still respect the fundamental principles, if not the letter, of the law of crime or war. Finally, choose the new rules that minimize the change in substance and scope of existing law, whether of peace or war, and make sure that such change remains as loyal as possible to the underlying principles of either legal system. Dealing with the issue of detention of potentially dangerous terrorists suspects provides an opportunity to illustrate this process.

Our discussion addresses only seizures away from any battlefield of familiar armed conflict between organized units. There are in fact ongoing battles between well-armed U.S. military units and similar units belonging to substate organizations in Afghanistan and Iraq. Detention of hostile combatants in such battles must be carried out by the military, near the field of battle, and without the costs and dangers of civil trials. Even if we were to adopt a criminal justice paradigm for other detentions, recognition of the exigencies of battles between armed units would require distinguishing these situations from all others. Units attacking us in combat or in occupation zones implicate issues very different from those presented by small, secret terrorist units hidden among the general population of peaceful and friendly nations. We recognize that the military needs the authority to detain individuals captured while operating against U.S. or allied military forces in organized and armed units. But some such set of words will make the necessary distinction.

The Decision to Adopt the Much Criticized Tactic of Military Detention

No aspect of U.S. policy against terrorists since September 11, 2001, has been more criticized than the detaining of hundreds of individuals in the detention camp at Guantanamo Bay, Cuba. The reasons for criticizing Guantanamo are obvious. Very few of our Western allies now authorize preventive detention. Israel is an important exception. The United Kingdom once used preventive detention but its experience with internment in Northern Ireland and elsewhere has led it to abandon the practice as both unwise and unjust. It is generally triggered by determinations of threat far less precise than those demanded for criminal guilt. Its burden of proof is lower; its rules of evidence, purposely relaxed. Both changes increase the risk of mistake in the form of false positives. It generally has no determinant ending; it is not even clear what new facts might justify release after one has been detained. Detention by the military of any country has incurred particular suspicion because of fear that it reflects a rejection of democratic institutions.

Moreover, establishing future dangerousness is difficult and mistakes are both inevitable and very costly. When the question of dangerousness arises, we have only a few sources of evidence to turn to. An individual can show himself to be dangerous—whether as a criminal or as an insane person or as a terrorist combatant—in any of four ways. First and most familiarly, his past actions can lead to conviction of a crime and then the imposition of a sentence whose duration is normally based in significant part on the risk of future dangerous behavior. Dangerousness shown by past actions sufficient for criminal convictions has been carefully extended to crimes that the individual has started to undertake (or urged or assisted others to take) but has never completed. The laws criminalizing attempt to commit crimes and those prohibiting material support for terrorism are important examples.

Second, an individual can show himself to be dangerous by the commitments he has made to others—powerful social pressures he has willingly incurred—promising to engage in dangerous activity in the future. In criminal law, that is the subject of conspiracy. These first two ways are the "gold standard" for carefully incapacitating the dangerous.

A third and related way an individual can show himself to be dangerous is by declaring his intention, without incurring the social pressures that accompany *promising*, to do something dangerous. That is a very common concern to agents charged with protecting government officials or private individuals. In criminal law, a mere manifestation or statement of intent to do something dangerous without any significant action or promise to put it into effect is thought to be too unreliable as a basis of a crime. (It can, however, justify commitment if it is caused by a mental disease.) Intent is too fickle and too hard to prove.

The fourth and least reliable way to show one's dangerousness is by choosing to develop a close association with other individuals who are known to be planning dangerous activities. Even when a relatively clear form of this dangerousness by association—membership in an organization—is made the basis of a crime, the Supreme Court has held that the Constitution requires the membership for which one can be imprisoned to carry with it a firm commitment to assist or participate in the illegal activities of the others (*United States v. Scales*). This last way of displaying dangerousness is the least reliable but most relevant to our detention decisions since September 11, 2001. It was adopted by some of the federal judges ruling on habeas petitions as the only option authorized by the law of war.

The legal justification for detention at Guantanamo has relied primarily on a law-of-war variation of the last way of displaying dangerousness. The notion has been that we are "at war" or in "armed conflict" with Al-Qaeda and "associated forces" although they are not state forces; that one who is part of such forces is illegally engaged in combat outside the conditions that create POW protection for state forces; and that such "unlawful" combatants may be detained until the "war" is over, just as lawful combatants may be, to keep them from helping organizations dangerously hostile to the United States and its people.[1]

Why then did the Bush administration turn to military detention, a decision subsequently followed on a much reduced scale by the Obama administration? Two benefits of detention promise to increase our safety from attacks by international terrorist groups. The first is that incapacitation can reduce the danger from individuals who are likely to engage in terror attacks. The reduction in danger depends, importantly, upon whether the individual detained is one of one hundred, or one thousand, or one million people who pose a similar risk. Thus the danger avoided by incapacitating a talented bomb maker or a well-established leader or even someone uniquely willing to sacrifice his life (if this is a rare trait) is much greater than in the case of a foot soldier.

Only some of the security benefits of detention depend upon its duration. The primary benefits of detaining even the most hate-filled foot soldier are focused on aborting a particular mission. In the long run, he or she can readily be replaced. Indeed, if he is again "used," the fact that during the short detention we have been able to take identifying characteristics (such as fingerprints) can enable us to prevent him or her from entering the United States. Of course, the released detainee might still be threatening to targets outside the United States.

One more point was critical. Criminal law offered the only alternative rationale available to justify preventive detention for the purposes of incapacitation and intelligence gathering by interrogation; however, criminal law would not allow the detention of dangerous people except on proof of criminal acts and would encumber interrogation of knowledgeable insiders with rules designed to protect against self-incrimination or to preserve the right to counsel.

The second advantage of detention is that interviewing or interrogation of an individual who has important information about the plans or structure of a terrorist organization can be extremely valuable and may only be possible if he or she is detained. In evaluating its importance, one must consider the alternative, often more trustworthy, ways of learning what the individual knows, including electronic surveillance, physical surveillance, undercover offers, the use of informants or spies, and so forth.

It is in light of these benefits—focused on the detainee with unique leadership or technical skills or a willingness to die—that we must consider and seek to minimize the harm done to traditional values and to international support.

For that, we look to the principles underlying the laws of crime and war. Those endangered values include the criminal law principles requiring: personal conduct justifying incarceration; clear advance statement of the prohibited conduct giving warning to the individual and limiting administrative discretion; findings of past facts, rather than far less certain predictions about future conduct; proof beyond a reasonable doubt, leading to a determinant maximum sentence; and evidentiary rules designed to make decisions reliable. Similarly at risk are the protections provided by the law and context of war to assure against: mistaken detention based on false attribution to a hostile army; unlimited duration of detention; conviction for undefined conduct; and, most important, cruel conditions of detention.

The Bush and Obama Approaches: Use of the Law-of-War Paradigm

The Bush administration adopted a theory of "no law" for detention: it began with the determination that *only* the law of war, as opposed to any constitutional or domestic law, was relevant to the detention of terrorists, meaning that all members of such armed and hostile organizations as Al-Qaeda, the Taliban, or associated forces could be detained on the basis of such membership; and then it proceeded to conclude that there was no law of war literally applicable to the detention of terrorists, as the latter did not meet the conditions of lawful combatancy. It thus left detainees stripped of all legal protections: for ascertaining their identity and involvement in terrorism, for guaranteeing minimal conditions for their internment, for third-party monitoring of their detention, or for setting the conditions for their release. The Bush administration's claim of a legal right to detain indefinitely, without reasonable steps to assure due process, never worked well either as a legal position or as a moral argument. It did not satisfy our enemies, our allies, our own people, or our courts. And it ended up with many false positives, meaning with the wrong people detained.

Nor was there a persuasive argument that military necessity made lawless detention necessary under conditions of battle. Prisoner-of-war type of treatment would have been entirely feasible for those captured in battles between well-armed U.S. military units and similar units belonging to substate organizations in Afghanistan or Iraq. Only slight modifications would have been necessary to adapt the Third Geneva Convention on the Treatment of Prisoners of War to the detention of enemy combatants in Afghanistan and Iraq.

Moreover, while the conflicts in Afghanistan and Iraq, like traditional wars between states, might have required temporary military capture and detention of sizable numbers of individuals fighting on behalf of the Taliban or Al-Qaeda or in Shia' or Sunni militias, the same was not true for the capture or indefinite detention of individuals outside these immediate zones of combat. One such case, which came before the U.S. Supreme Court, was that of Lakhdar Boumediene and five other Algerian natives who were seized in October 2001 by Bosnian police when U.S. intelligence officers suspected their involvement in a plot to attack the U.S. embassy there. The U.S. government classified the men as enemy combatants in the war on terror and detained them at Guantanamo.[2] In these types of cases, the risk of mistakes is far greater. On the battlefield, there can be a presumption that those captured and detained are in fact enemy combatants who are engaged in hostilities against the U.S. soldiers. They are captured not so much as individuals, but as obvious and self-identified agents of an entity fighting the United States. But the Bush doctrine of a "global war on terrorism" claimed the right to detain, without judicial review, and to try before special military commissions people appearing to be civilians seized anywhere in the world, so long as it was somehow concluded they were associated with or supporting in any way Al-Qaeda or its allies. As in the case of battlefield detainees, neither the protections of the laws of war nor those of the laws of peace were considered applicable to their capture, detention, or trial.

This effort to create a no-law zone for those detained as terrorists collapsed when the Supreme Court ruled in the case of *Boumediene* that the habeas corpus provisions of the U.S. Constitution guaranteed the availability of judicial review of military decisions to detain, at least for those suspected terrorists detained within U.S. jurisdiction, including Guantanamo. By that decision, for those who were denied prisoner of war status, the protections of a vigorous judicial review were superimposed on indefinite military detention far from a battlefield. As we have argued, extraordinary measures used to fight terrorism—which do not fit neatly into either a crime or a war paradigm—should be accompanied by protections closely analogous to those provided by either the law of peace or the law of war. We were thus left with a hybrid variation of the law of war with the greater protections that due process would require in dealing with people not easily identifiable as combatants.

The *Boumediene* decision did not decide on the protections due two other categories of detainee: (1) those detained in war zones where judicial oversight might well not be feasible but POW treatment (with or without some adaptation) could have been made available as a matter of policy; and (2) those detained in U.S. custody or at U.S. request outside the United States but not in zones of active combat (e.g., secret CIA prisons in Eastern Europe or Southeast Asia).

In the course of rejecting the adequacy of the evidence for detention in a startlingly high percentage of the first few dozen cases to be reviewed after the Supreme Court's decision, district court judges disagreed on a number of critical issues, one of which related to the second part of the government standard; a number believed that using substantial support as the basis for detention lacked a grounding in the necessary laws of war. They also required something more than passive membership as evidence of dangerousness, whatever "passive membership" might mean in an organization that did not have membership ceremonies or induction cards. Sympathy and moral support were not enough of a basis for detention.

In March 2009, the Obama administration continued much the same standard for detention, based on membership in Al-Qaeda or a related terrorist group, adding only the word "substantially" to the additional authorization to detain those who "substantially supported Taliban or Al-Qaeda forces or associated forces." It based this very similar power on congressionally granted authority rather than on the laws of war.[3] The federal courts reviewing on a habeas corpus procedure the grounds for detention have, as we have noted, often rejected the "substantial support" basis as unauthorized by the laws of war.

The Obama team did try to reduce by 75 percent the number of detainees (as well as to move detainees from the Guantanamo detention center to prisons in the United States). The Bush team had already reduced the number greatly. In early 2010, according to press reports, a working group reporting to Attorney General Holder suggested, on the basis of a case by case review, that of the 200 detainees remaining at Guantanamo, 110 should be deported, 40 should be tried criminally, and 50 should be detained indefinitely. In the meantime, habeas corpus reviews of military detention decisions by federal district courts have begun to establish and insist upon a number of judicially created standards for detention.

There has been little or no discussion of the issue of future seizures off the battlefield for detention. Rules restricting detention and interrogation practices, as well as outrage among our allies, may have made that option a less attractive one for a future that contains increased use of

sophisticated missiles targeted on terrorist leaders as well as local detention by Iraqi and Afghan authorities.

An Alternative: The Use of a Criminal Law Paradigm
An only slightly creative use of the same system that allows us to try
dangerous drug lords and paramilitary leaders extradited from Mexico
or Panama would allow us to return safely to the very important American traditions of (1) probable cause for detention and (2) freedom from
the risk of having any statement that was compelled, or taken in the
absence of a required attorney, used against one at trial—while still
serving the purposes of incapacitating dangerous terrorists and providing
an adequate chance to gather urgent intelligence by interrogation. This
alternative would simultaneously deal with the issue of criminal trials by
military commission—another contested power that the Obama administration tried to maintain.

The criminal law alternative would work in the following way. To be
seized and detained by the United States, anyone, whether a U.S. resident
or an alien and whether in the United States or abroad, would have had
to violate a criminal statute of the U.S. government.[4] Many of the critical
statutes are already extraterritorial in their application to plans and steps
designed to lead to an attack on the United States, U.S. citizens, or prop-
erty of either the United States or its citizens. Other statutes against
terrorism might have to be extended to have this reach. Such extrater-
ritoriality of application of statutory duties to obey the law has already
been asserted on a number of occasions by the United States and is relatively easily justified under international law in terms of what is called
"the protective principle"—a rule of customary international law allowing national assertions of criminal jurisdiction over activities planned to
attack the nation's government security or functions (some terrorist
activities might fall under an even broader basis for extraterritorial
jurisdiction—namely, "universal jurisdiction").

From arrest on, the present rules of criminal procedure would, with
one relatively minor modification, allow us to serve our security goals
while preserving traditional freedoms. The individual arrested in the
United States or, in the absence of cooperation from the state where he
or she is found (which could elect to try the suspect), seized by U.S. forces
abroad, would not be sent to a military installation like Guantanamo but

would "appear," as Rule 5 of the Federal Rules of Criminal Procedure requires, "without unnecessary delay," for arraignment in a federal district court within the United States. The "appearance" could be virtual. Such seizure by U.S. officials in a foreign territory, without the foreign government's consent, might be a violation of international law (as it is today when suspects are seized and taken to Guantanamo Bay), but would not affect the legitimacy of the arrest from a domestic point of view. The time of presentation to the federal court for an initial arraignment on the complaint in the case of seizure abroad would have to be somewhat longer than the normal forty-eight hours for individuals arrested at home; Rule 5 of the Federal Rules of Criminal Procedure already contemplates this. The data from which a secret source or informant working with the United States could be identified need not be revealed in the affidavit presented to the court as justification for the arrest or seizure.

Similarly, the source of information justifying detention pending trial can be kept secret from the defendant under normal rules we now apply in organized crime cases and terrorism cases whenever revealing the source of critical information would endanger that source (see U.S.C. 3142[e] and [f]). The detention hearing, like any later preliminary hearing, is not ex parte and the defense might press in either context for information the government was unwilling to reveal (such as how a reliable informant came to know what he alleges), but this is also a problem already handled in the system.[5] Traditionally, the court itself can, but rarely does, demand to know who or what was the source of the information leading to an arrest or search. The next step, indictment by a grand jury with its strict conditions of secrecy and loose rules of evidence, would not threaten national security. In short, preserving pretrial secrecy about the basis for detention may be crucial in many terrorist cases, but it can be done under familiar criminal law we already apply to protect informants in cases of violent crime.

At trial, the evidence showing that the defendant committed a crime of terrorism must be made public. And normally the trial would take place with a promptness dictated by the federal Speedy Trial Act. There's the rub. In some cases, the evidence that the individual had committed or was planning or preparing to engage in a violation of our federal statutes against terrorism would be based on information that could not be revealed without endangering sources and methods of intelligence gathering or important diplomatic secrets. When those security needs—as well as the classified evidence of the detained suspect's guilt of the crime—were shown to the satisfaction of a district court, the judge would, at the request of the prosecutor, delay trial while the prosecution sought usable substitutes for the sources that must be kept secret. Meeting these challenges may require legislation, although the Speedy Trial Act already allows some delays in the interests of justice.

Only if substitute evidence could not be found after a period reasonable in light of the seriousness of the danger would the judge dismiss the case and release the detainee. As in France, a statute or regulation might set maximum periods of delay of trial of a detained suspect while usable evidence is sought; or, alternatively, the matter might simply be left to the normal system of judicial review for abuse of discretion. It might well prove wise, for several reasons, to provide for liquidated damages for time any suspect was held by the government in the hope—later frustrated—that it could find the usable evidence of guilt that generally is a precondition of indictment.

The Advantages and Disadvantages of Using Criminal Law Rather than the Law of War to Justify Detention

First, consider very carefully the four possible "disadvantages" of using this criminal law structure compared to detention of the suspect as an unlawful enemy combatant. The first disadvantage is that it does not allow seizure or detention without probable cause (albeit sometimes in classified form) that the individual has violated a federal statute. Thus, two groups of people could not be seized and detained at all: (1) those whose dangerousness is manifested in a way that would not constitute a crime under federal statutes; and (2) those whose suspected activities would be a crime but as to whom the suspicion has not risen to the level of probable cause. The former is a very narrow category because of the breadth of the federal prohibitions of terrorism—particularly the prohibition of even agreeing (conspiring) to provide material support (even one's own services or training) to a listed terrorist group. The latter category—those suspected on grounds that do not add up to probable cause—necessarily and inevitably includes a very high percentage of mistaken attributions of dangerousness.

The alternative of relaxing the standard from probable cause would thus necessarily mean that we would detain a very large percentage of false positives (innocent individuals). The choice is real. Do we want anyone—U.S. citizen, resident alien, visiting alien, or foreign citizen and resident—detained if there is not probable cause to believe that he has at least agreed to support a terrorist group and, if so, what is the cost not only in terms of risks to the innocent who are seized but in terms of insecurity of even those not seized who know themselves to be innocent but detainable? There are no exceptions to that requirement for murderers, rapists, spies, or saboteurs; it is the general rule for all dangerous people. We can and should live with locking up an individual only if there is probable cause to believe that he is involved in terrorism.

A second disadvantage of the criminal law system is that an individual seized and detained pending trial would have to be released if the government could never find useable evidence or if he was tried and unanimously acquitted. (If the jury is not unanimous, he can and will be tried again.) Once again, this is a matter of policy choice. Many would say that the United States should not continue to detain a suspect indefinitely, under any scheme of the law of war or of criminal law, unless a unanimous jury found him to have violated any of the extremely broad statutes forbidding assistance to terrorists or terrorism. Certainly, the individual should not be detained as a form of punishment despite such a jury verdict.

As in the case of someone who could not even be brought to trial because of an absence of useable evidence, the individual might still be detained until he could leave the country or be deported after acquittal (provided he is not a U.S. citizen), but no longer. As to continued incapacitation of the suspect as dangerous, if additional criminal statutes are necessary, enacting them is the way to go rather than to continue detention despite an inability to convince any sizable number of jurors that the individual is guilty, beyond a reasonable doubt, even of assisting or agreeing to assist terrorism or terrorist organizations.

The last two disadvantages of abandoning law-of-war analogies and relying, instead, on a criminal law paradigm are these. First, while statements elicited from a suspect without torture are now used as evidence warranting detention, statements obtained by questioning a suspect after arrest (under the Fifth Amendment and *Miranda* doctrine) or after indictment (under the Sixth Amendment) might not be admissible as part of the prosecution case in a criminal trial in federal court unless and until the suspect has been offered the assistance of an attorney during the interrogation and warned of his right to remain silent. Interrogation could still continue without warnings and without the presence of the suspect's attorney, but any resulting statement, although not necessarily all "leads" derived from it, would be barred as evidence. In a federal district court there would and should also be judicial supervision of the duration and manner of interrogation after the individual was formally detained for trial, although the standards used would not be the extremely protective ones designed to guarantee the right not to incriminate oneself or not to be taken advantage of at a stage critical to his later trial so long as there were other assurances against these consequences occurring.

Second, the use of pretrial detention in a federal district court as the means of detaining dangerous people depends upon a decision to try the individual before a federal district court and not before a military commission, making a successful criminal prosecution more difficult. Article Three prosecutions differ from military commissions in three major ways favorable to the defense. First, prosecutions in federal courts depend on a jury system, as opposed to a decision by military officers. Second, civilian prosecutions forbid using confessions at trial if they were compelled from the suspect or the result of denying the suspect counsel. Finally, in federal district courts almost all hearsay (evidence given by X of what he learned from Y about the suspect) is considered unreliable and therefore inadmissible. The primary purpose of having military trials, much like the reason for military detention, is to give the government greater freedom from these three protections in order to provide greater assurance that the individual will be detained or convicted or both.[6]

Because we seek this greater assurance only to make sure that terror suspects are in fact incarcerated, the advantages of departure from those three basic protections is desirable only if the protections themselves provide *unwise* or *unnecessary* encumbrances to conviction. One way of assessing whether this is the case is to examine the extent to which, in similar circumstances, other Western democracies do without these protections or, more broadly, use military commissions to find the facts in particular classes of cases. To the extent to which those three protections can be loosened in only very limited ways even in trials before military commissions, there will not be any major difference in the results of trials. Certainly, a jury of American citizens is as likely to convict as the military commissions at Guantanamo have so far shown themselves to do.

Against these manageable costs, there are many benefits to be weighed. By reverting to criminal processes, we would be able to impose credible punishment for criminal acts. At the same time, we will have eliminated one of the greatest criticisms of, and sources of reluctance to cooperate with, the United States among our Western allies. Moreover, we would be showing ourselves to be principled enough to apply the same rules to Americans suspected of terrorism as to citizens of other friendly and not-so-friendly countries. By placing overall control in the hands of judges we would be displaying our belief in the rule of law in a way that is essential if we hope to promulgate to other nations the notion that commitments made with regard to executive power must be kept. Finally, in rejecting the paradigm of unlawful combatant in war, we avoid defining the issue in a way that threatened a lifetime of detention without trial for anyone, however minor his actions, who gives loyalty to any offshoot of Al-Qaeda. These are great benefits compared to relatively small, somewhat improbable costs.

Conclusion

The individuals seized and detained for our safety may be inside active combat zones or outside of these areas of armed conflict. For the former, the best analogy is to the international laws of war and the rules and protections that pertain to POWs. Those can be applied, by way of analogy, to insurgents using terrorist tactics in the area of hostilities, with only minor adaptations. For the latter group, the ordinary criminal law paradigm offers the best guarantees for ascertaining identity and involvement in terrorism, for providing due process in fact findings, and for assuring humane and secure conditions for internment and release.

Only by showing a dangerous boldness in rejecting our peacetime traditions could we adopt a third, sometimes discussed, alternative. As South Africa, the Soviet Union, and others have done much to the regret of their citizens, the United States could legislate a detention regime with analogies to the systems that allow detention of those who are (a) mentally ill and (b) likely to harm themselves or others. The equivalent of "mental illness" could be purposeful association with an organization planning attacks on the United States. The equivalent of "dangerous to himself or others" could be evidence of the commitment of the individual to carrying out such activities. Except for more protective procedures and standards and an important shift to judicial authority and supervision from military authority and supervision, this would be not unlike the present system for determining combatant status at Guantanamo and for establishing combatant status review boards.

As in other commitments for dangerousness without criminal convictions, there would be, as there was at Guantanamo (and in Israel, which has a much greater infusion of courts in the review process) periodic reviews for continued dangerousness. To get rid of the danger of permanent detention because of lethargy in the review process, there could be presumptive limits on detention based on an initial determination of the dangerousness of the individual.

The most serious problem with abandoning both the law of peace and the law of war in favor of a broad new government power lies in the grave risks of creating a type of regime for the United States that has had a frightening history in totalitarian states and has proved a dangerous failure in most other Western countries. Beyond this, using any such innovative detention regime on an individual seized abroad in a country that rejects detention would constitute an unparalleled assertion of national, extraterritorial power compared to asserting a right to try the individual for violation of our criminal statutes. The gains from this regime would have to be very great to warrant this form of departure from hundreds of years of Western criminal justice traditions. They simply are not. If we can extradite, try, and convict dozens of powerful and violent paramilitary warlords for drug trafficking charges, we can and should do the same with those who have violated our terrorist statutes.

In contrast to this boldness, on careful examination, it is clear that only very minor steps, perhaps best legislated but already within the authority of judges, would be necessary to turn detention of terrorist suspects into a normal part of a criminal justice system that already detains pending trial. There are great advantages to taking this route rather than relying on habeas corpus reviews of military detentions or a new judicial detention scheme. We believe that this, rather than continuing military detention of even the most dangerous suspects, is the strategy that President Obama should follow going forward.

6

Interrogation

Introduction: Where We Are Now and How We Got There

The Collapse of Secrecy about Interrogations

The Bush administration tried to keep secret three sets of facts about our policies on interrogation: (1) the very high level of officials participating in the decisions leading to the use of specific highly coercive techniques of interrogation; (2) the legal opinions of the Office of Legal Counsel (OLC) that authorized such coercive techniques, sometimes in frighteningly bureaucratic detail; and (3) the actual practices of the CIA and Department of Defense as each pursued intelligence through interrogations. The efforts at secrecy failed. Leaks to the press, followed by several good books by reporters, revealed the names and responsibilities of officials involved. The extent of the outrage over Abu Ghraib opened up to scrutiny the first of the OLC opinions, even before the Obama administration took office and released the rest. Reports by outraged career professionals, inspectors general, and defense counsel, as well as interviews by the International Committee of the Red Cross, laid out the actual practices.

Early in his administration, President Obama and his attorney general, Eric Holder, made clear that they would not prosecute anyone who had acted under the authority of the OLC opinions. In August 2009, Holder announced that he had authorized a preliminary investigation into whether crimes by CIA interrogators had occurred that did not fall within that protective umbrella. The decision was broadly controversial although, throughout this period, Vice President Cheney was almost alone among Bush officials in insisting that what was done was necessary and legal.

The Unsuccessful Effort to Institutionalize Cruel Interrogation Authorized by U.S. Officials

This much seems clear from well-documented, published accounts. There was an immense early concern about the possibility of a further, second-stage attack like that of September 11, 2001. Our intelligence agencies did not have the penetration into terrorist organizations that would ensure any likelihood that we would know of such plans. The administration believed that members of the Taliban or Al-Qaeda captured during the course of our invasion of Afghanistan might well know the answer to the extremely important questions about enemy intentions. To obtain information from captives, the administration quickly turned to the CIA, which disparaged the slow, patient methods of the FBI, starting when the first seemingly high-level member of Al-Qaeda, Abu Zubaida, was captured.

Having no expertise in interrogation, the CIA turned to psychologists who had worked for the military on its Survival, Evasion, Resistance, and Escape (SERE) program. Relying on a psychological theory of "learned helplessness," they set about reverse engineering the training we had been giving our military to resist the severe techniques used by the communists decades earlier. Through this process, they unsurprisingly produced many of the same techniques which we had trained against and protested—ironically, as "torture."

In the meantime, individuals in the White House and the OLC worked together to produce interpretations of national and international law that would provide the president nearly unlimited power to order any form of interrogation he wished, despite our adherence to the Geneva Conventions and to the United Nations Convention against Torture and Cruel, Inhuman and Degrading Treatment, and despite two statutes making torture an extremely serious crime. These assurances of legality were required by the CIA interrogators; indeed, they wanted a guarantee against prosecution to be supplemented by relatively specific White House directions to proceed with the type of techniques the CIA had now embraced and briefed, enthusiastically, to the White House. Our highest officials met and agreed. The Bush team also created an accelerated program of secret renditions of suspected terrorists to nations where we must have known the suspects would be tortured for information sought by the United States as well as recipient nations.

The Defense Department quickly imitated the CIA. Dissatisfied, first with the pace of intelligence flowing out of Guantanamo, to which detainees from Afghanistan had been sent, and two years later with the pace of information coming out of detentions in Abu Ghraib prison, Defense Secretary Donald Rumsfeld approved a set of coercive techniques for Guantanamo; they soon spread to Iraq.

The Backlash

Meanwhile, the FBI (and representatives of legal and investigative units of the armed forces) began to challenge the efficacy, the legality, and the wisdom of the interrogation techniques that were spreading. Unauthorized pictures of the crude mistreatment of prisoners at Abu Ghraib caused an outpouring of angry reaction from our citizens and our allies and from the states and populations from which terrorist groups like Al-Qaeda would look for recruits. The resulting demands for an explanation led to the release of the first of a set of OLC legal opinions. Rather than quieting outrage, the novelty of the legal arguments revealed in the first release only seemed to raise further questions and demand further explanation.

At the same time, the efforts of the military to develop criminal cases before military commissions against the detainees were repeatedly disrupted by the discovery of interrogation practices that no one wanted to defend but that may have led to critical information. The most dramatic example was the dismissal in January 2009 of charges in the case of Mohammad al Qahtani by Susan Crawford, the convening authority for military commissions, because of the accumulation of authorized cruelty and degradation to which he was exposed over months of constant interrogation.

At last asserting its own role and responsibility five years after the terrorist attacks, Congress rejected any legal argument that denied the applicability of the international convention prohibiting torture. Of more practical importance, it overruled the administration's contention that our commitment under the same convention not to engage in cruel, inhuman, or degrading treatment—which certainly had happened at Abu Ghraib and in Guantanamo—had no application outside of U.S. borders because of the reservation that was added by the United States when ratifying the convention: that we accepted a prohibition of such conduct only if it were unconstitutional under the 5th, 8th, or 14th Amendments. Mistreatment of aliens outside the United States, the administration had argued, could not be unconstitutional because the pertinent clauses of the Constitution only applied within our boundaries. In December 2005 Congress passed a new statute banning cruel, inhuman, and degrading treatment by U.S. personnel wherever it occurred. A prolonged debate among U.S. attorneys general and members of Congress about whether simulated drowning ("waterboarding") was or was not torture only added to the appearance of moral and legal disarray.

The most persuasive policy argument the Bush administration could put forward to the American people for its interrogation policies relied on the need for an emergency exception. Described as the "ticking bomb" case, the claim was at its strongest: where a number of lives were imminently at risk; where individuals had been discovered who knew the facts that would allow us to eliminate the threat; in which there was no other way besides highly coercive interrogation to get that needed information; and in which such an intervention was likely to succeed. Although we had (and have) not yet confronted such a situation, cruel interrogation was authorized and the authority broadly delegated in a much wider set of categories where several of the ticking bomb conditions did not apply. Still, the hope of saving lives by extracting information, it was argued, justified setting aside our treaty obligations and our criminal statutes, and using secrecy to hide our behavior from our citizens, our Congress, and our courts.

The Obama Repudiation of the Bush Rationale

On taking office in January 2009, President Obama reversed much of this strategy. Unlike his predecessor, he took seriously the potential impact of U.S. action on three priorities: to remain faithful to deeply held American values, to maintain respect for domestic and international law, and to uphold American leadership among allies and other states in a world where we need cooperation and support. These priorities had to be accommodated within any strategy for interrogation.

As the limit on what could be done to obtain information from a suspect, the president specified the set of techniques described in a recently amended, 2006 Army Field Manual[1]—techniques designed to be consistent with the Geneva Conventions. He declared waterboarding to be forbidden torture. He ordered a review under Attorney General Holder of the adequacy of the revised Army Field Manual as an upper boundary on coercion and asked for advice about what should be done in the future with regard to interrogation and renditions to other countries as well. Over severe criticism by conservatives, the new administration released many more of the OLC opinions, revealing the Bush administration's obsession with detail at very high levels, as permissible interrogation came to be meticulously redefined to permit very cruel treatment of detainees.

In August 2009, the attorney general released a report of his conclusions. Nothing more coercive than the techniques in the Army Field Manual would be authorized in the future, although efforts would be made to develop a far richer understanding of how to use noncoercive means of interviewing to elicit valuable information. To accomplish this, and to organize and train for the interrogations that may be needed in the future, a new multiorganizational unit of expert interrogators would be formed, trained, and, when needed, sent to wherever in the world a high-level suspect had been seized and was being held. At the same time, Holder also initiated his investigation of possible criminal violations of the U.S. statutes in prior interrogations, excluding acts that had been officially authorized. Conservatives denounced many of these steps as undermining our security; liberals decried them as inadequate.

A Final Unresolved Issue

What remained unclear is the extent to which U.S.-assisted or U.S.-encouraged interrogation by others may escape the new rules. The Bush administration had made frequent use of renditions to countries known to torture—transfers that were, according to the accounts of the suspects, followed by torture at the hands of the authorities in those countries. Our legal obligations not to "render to" a country that would torture were considered fulfilled, despite the obvious, by obtaining some form of statement that the receiving country would depart from familiar practices and refrain from torture. The assurances were obviously not reliable, and could hardly have been considered reliable by the relevant officials that received them.

The Bush administration followed the standard that the U.S. Senate had defined as the limit of our treaty obligation in an "understanding" attached to its ratification of the Convention against Torture. Renditions were forbidden only if it was more probable than not that someone would be subjected to torture. Other countries such as the United Kingdom forbid a rendition if there is any real risk of either torture or cruel, inhuman, and degrading treatment. When the intelligence agencies of any of our Western allies became involved in our rendition practices, the public discovery of such cooperation led to a fierce outcry from that ally's citizens.

As to such transfers of individuals held by the United States to other nations where they might be treated cruelly, the Obama recommendations were cautious: basically to tighten the system for appraising assurances that an individual transferred, even to a state that often tortures, would not be tortured. Transfer was still authorized when the likelihood of torture by the state to which an individual was transferred was appraised at less than 50 percent; and a history of extensive use of torture would not disqualify a transfer to that state. By contrast, the United Kingdom forbids taking any "real risk" that its officials may be unintentionally aiding either torture or cruel, inhuman, and degrading treatment.

Nothing at all was said by either administration about urging a country where a terror suspect is located to detain him for the purpose of cruel interrogation or just making a friendly, or dependent but brutal, government aware of our interest in what he may know.

The Importance of Defining the Range of Questions More Broadly than Either Administration Did

The preoccupation of both the Bush and Obama administrations with the question of whether U.S. interrogators should be allowed to practice coercive interrogations has missed at least two important questions: The first is the responsibility of the United States for coercive interrogations practiced by other countries in the context of the war on terrorism. The second, even broader than the first, involves alternative means of intelligence gathering other than interrogations.

By missing these two questions, any assessment of the merits and perils of coercive interrogation is dangerously lacking. Here, we turn to these two issues, setting the ground for the subsequent evaluation of interrogations, and, in particular, coercive interrogations.

For What Type of Coercive Interrogations by Other Countries Would the United States Accept Responsibility?

Treaties, statutes, almost universal understandings about morality, and expectations of allies all assume that any constraints on our interrogation practices that we accept should apply not only to the actions of our own officials but also to what the United States does indirectly through private parties or the officials of other governments. In domestic criminal law the critical notion is complicity (being an accomplice to conduct by assisting or encouraging it) and conspiracy (agreeing to bring about the conduct cooperatively). In domestic civil law the critical concept is being an agent or partner. Much the same categories apply to international law whether criminal or civil.

Everywhere in the United States an individual is held criminally responsible for actions he requested, encouraged, or assisted. This makes it obvious that government officials and the government itself cannot encourage or purposely assist forms of interrogation in which it is legally forbidden from engaging itself. Article 3 of the Convention against Torture goes beyond purposeful complicity to cover recklessness as well. It applies whenever one country turns a prisoner over to a second "where there are substantial grounds for believing that he would be in danger of being subjected to torture."

During the Bush years, the United States was widely believed to treat its obligations under the Convention against Torture as satisfied if it received some form of statement that the receiving country would not torture—even if the assurance was from a country sought out in part because it was known to use torture routinely. It is easy, and correct, to reject this as disingenuous and unworthy. President Obama's tightening of the rules for soliciting and assessing assurances should help, but still leaves too much of the problem as it was.

The issue goes beyond renditions. Even if we dealt adequately with transfers of detainees, it would not fully address the problem. A critical question remains: how close may a nation come to requesting or assisting the torture or cruel treatment even of someone we have never held or transferred—of someone captured or held by a friendly or dependent nation? About this, nothing has been said. The problems arise from the wide range of relationships—going well beyond physical transfers of detainees—in which we may bear some responsibility for what is done to terror suspects by independent nations. No effort was made to address these.

At one extreme, one party is responsible for the acts of another party who the first has purposely urged or assisted to engage in that conduct. This is the familiar law of complicity. Thus if, in order to get information, representatives of the United States asked Syria to torture a particular individual whom Syria had detained, the United States would be fully responsible for the actions Syria took. At the other extreme, if Syria were, unprodded, to furnish us with information it had beaten out of a suspect we knew nothing about, we would not be responsible for that violation of the Convention against Torture.

It is in the middle that the practical problem arises. For instance, knowing of the information we seek, a state appreciative of assistance we have furnished in any of a number of spheres may torture a suspect, in whom it has no interest of its own, to please us. So how far can we go in exploiting that desire to please? What if we had simply taken steps to make known our interest in what the individual knew about a particular subject? If that is not enough, what if we had located him and requested his arrest, letting the other country know of our interest in the information he possesses?

If the boundaries of our responsibility are set very narrowly, nothing we do or refrain from doing ourselves will make any difference; others will torture for us. The cost in support from citizens and allies, in the hatred of opponents, and the dangers of encouraging similar measures will all remain much the same.

With What Options, beyond Noncoercive Interrogation, Should We Compare the Benefits and Costs of a Practice of Highly Coercive Interrogation?

The issue facing the Bush and Obama administrations was not whether to authorize cruelty or to forego critical information. It was, more broadly, what we should do when we have reason to believe that a particular suspect, whom we can locate and detain or surveille, has information critical to preventing lethal attacks. Depending on the situation, the alternatives differ in feasibility, benefits, and costs. Information gathering about terrorist threats begins with a tip from an observer or general suspicion from analysis of accumulated knowledge about an organization that may be planning attacks or about a particular plan. The first, and by far the most important, decision our intelligence agencies have to make is whether to then gather information about the organization or plan by covert techniques or to rely on overt techniques that would make members of the organization aware that they were being investigated. The British have relied primarily on covert techniques with notable success.

The covert techniques that can be used to gather information without tipping off the organization include human surveillance, technologically enhanced physical surveillance, various forms of electronic surveillance, secret agents and informants, undercover officers, secret intelligence searches, and reviews of records with or without computerized data mining. These covert techniques have two vast advantages: they produce reliable and accurate information because the suspects do not know that information is being gathered about them; and they produce information in real-time. In contrast, overt techniques such as detention followed by interrogation allow the terrorist group to know, rather promptly, that one of its members has been captured and is being interrogated. Using that information, the group will take steps to retreat to backup plans as substitutes for whatever plan was under way and to make it more difficult for us to disable the other members of the organization.

Comparing the Costs Associated with Different Forms of Interrogation

Assume that we have identified a category of cases where overt efforts to question a suspect believed to know of dangerous plans have more promise in terms of their benefits than covert investigation of the sort we have described. A second question then remains: how do we choose which type of interrogation to pursue? The benefits sought from any option are reliable information or verifiable leads about serious dangers that might be prevented with that information and those leads.

We have seen that, except in the case of the ticking bomb, which we will discuss shortly, there is wide disagreement about the comparative benefits of cruel as opposed to other methods of interrogation. So, even in the cases where our analysis leads to the conclusion that averting an imminent danger requires paying the high price of alerting the group by moving quickly to detention and interrogation of a suspect, the marginal benefits of torture or other forms of highly coercive interrogation are widely disputed. Compared to less coercive forms of interrogation, cruel methods may be more likely to elicit a statement, but frequently one that is false. It was this disadvantage of unreliability that first caused our Supreme Court to forbid the use of coerced confessions. Any accurate information furnished can therefore only be detected by time-consuming verification. The problem is most severe when dealing with a carefully planned operation; for the plan is likely to include a cover story that is hard to unravel in any short period of time.

The information furnished in response to coercion is likely to be more narrowly focused as well as less reliable. A tortured suspect is unlikely to reveal matters about which we did not know to ask; nothing will be volunteered. In sum, as the Army Field Manual of September 2006 states, torture often "is a poor technique that yields unreliable results, may damage subsequent collection efforts, and can induce the source to say what he thinks the HUMINT collector wants to hear" (at section 5-21).

We *should* know more in light of thousands of interrogations since 9/11, some highly coercive and others without coercive means, but the Bush administration made no attempt to use data rather than anecdotes to prove that coercive techniques were effective. A CIA memo, claimed by Vice President Dick Cheney to establish the effectiveness of coercion in particular cases and released at his insistence in August 2009, was supportive of Cheney's claim but hardly proved that extreme coercion was either necessary or sufficient to obtain that information and left most readers unchanged from their prior beliefs.[2]

The greater unreliability and narrowness of torture-induced statements have led a large proportion of highly trained interrogators to prefer any of a number of alternative techniques. The FBI had notable success in investigating the Nairobi and Dar-A-Salaam U.S. embassy bombings in 1998 by developing a mutually supportive relationship between the suspect and the agent. As documented by a report of Inspector General Glenn Fine of the Justice Department, this is plainly the FBI's preferred practice. Hanns Scharff, the very successful Luftwaffe interrogator of World War II allied pilots, embraced a similar technique, as described in *The Interrogator* by Raymond Toliver.[3]

There are a variety of other alternatives to coercion for interrogation. For example, some of our allies have used deception about the privacy of conversations stimulated while an individual is detained; or they have gathered enough information to make the suspect believe that he is simply confirming what is already known, leaving him with little reason to bear the dangers and costs of silence—a technique that, as the memos requested by Cheney showed, was used by the CIA with some success. A number of interrogators consider it to be crucial to create resentment or suspicion of the detainee's former colleagues, believing that loyalty is the major barrier to cooperation. U.S. prosecutors rely primarily on offers of reduced sentences in exchange for information.

All this is only common sense and disputed judgments of experts. There is little or no scholarly knowledge and no known systematic internal review of the comparative advantages of different forms of interrogation (let alone of the advantages of covert methods of intelligence gathering or interrogation in this situation). Without researching these areas, choice among the present set of options will remain uninformed. Moreover, some present options have been exercised in less than optimal ways. As the Obama recommendations of August 2009 reflected, our choices have to include structures for recruitment, training, and support of interviewers—structures that can make one or another option seem far better than it may appear now—and our choices must involve deciding what to do to learn more about the comparative advantages of various options whose costs and prospects may be worth examining.

In offering a coherent way to think about coercive and noncoercive interrogations, it is important to weigh and compare different types of costs associated with each form, including in terms of legitimacy and legality. Some are far more closely associated with cruel interrogation methods than with other forms of interrogation. Others are likely to vary with the situation and not simply with the type of interrogation pursued.

Consider first the different types of costs, some of which favor one or another form of interrogation:

• costs in legitimacy of violations of U.S. and international law;

• reputational losses with regard to compliance with U.S.-signed treaties and conventions;

• increased danger to captured military and other personnel of the United States;

- disruption of cooperation with allies;
- unintended aid to terrorist recruiters seeking to create new terrorists;
- encouragement of undesirable interrogation practices by friendly nations abroad;
- encouragement of disregard for treaties and conventions abroad;
- harmful effects on our interrogators;
- disrespect for, or fear of, the interrogating organization, thereby reducing its prospects for recruitment and other needed cooperation; and
- demoralization of domestic publics.

Any discussion framed in terms of costs and benefits necessarily transforms discussion of the deep moral or social commitments of many people into a psychological or sociological question of "demoralization." This is not likely to be a comfortable transformation for those who believe deeply in the deontological immorality of a particular way of obtaining information. Similarly, with regard to the first category, transforming the emphasis on a government's moral obligation to obey the law into a discussion about the costs of defying statutes or treaties hides very serious questions of moral and political theory. We adopt these two transformations here only to maintain a useful conceptual structure for comparing costs and benefits.

Important variations in the particular situation or specific context can make a major difference in the cost and benefits of using each possible option. There may be very good reason to have general rules that do not make such fine distinctions, but the desirability of the results dictated by the rule will inevitably depend on this second set of variables. In other words, each of the concerns we have just considered will be more or less serious depending upon the following aspects of the situation.

- How high is the probability that the individual has the information we seek?
- Is the individual a terrorist or an innocent bystander or someone somewhere in between?
- How imminent is the feared attack?
- How lethal is the attack likely to be?
- How important is obtaining the information from this suspect as a way of dealing with the danger in light of other information sources and possible prevention measures?

- Are we seeking pieces of information to help complete a broader picture, or do we lack any information and require a complete account?
- How dangerous would it be to leave the individual on the street—

  under surveillance or

  not under surveillance?
- What do we know about the suspect's characteristics that reflect on the likelihood of success of any option for gathering information from him?
- Is the critical information something we can verify quickly if the suspect is attempting to deceive us?
- How, if at all, does the location or nationality of the suspect affect the practical, moral, or legal availability of any option?

It would be a serious mistake to ignore one variable more within our control than the others, one that affects both costs and benefits. The costs and benefits of each option also depend on the knowledge, training, and resources brought to bear in using it. We had no knowledge and little training to make a success of interrogation when the Bush administration turned to the CIA in the early years after September 11, 2001 (including only a handful of Arabic speaking agents). This lack of capacity reduced the possible benefits and greatly increased the possible costs of any choice the Bush administration made.

As emphasized in the August 2009 recommendations of the Department of Justice task force on interrogation, even in the limited category of interrogation, options should include the use of a cadre of experts in the use of well-researched noncoercive interrogation methods. Such experts, organized into teams, could bring to bear informed judgments on ways of questioning and deep knowledge of the suspect's culture and language as well as the subject being explored.

In Pursuit of Legitimacy

Why Rules?
One question is preliminary to discussing the Holder recommendations of August 2009 for interrogation for intelligence purposes. Even if the Bush administration gave far too little attention to the costs of what it allowed and had far too little basis for believing it would realize the

benefits it sought, why is the answer not simply to consider far more carefully the costs and benefits in every individual case—considering all the variations in particular situations that we have just described? Why would we want to burden intelligence officials with *any* comparatively clumsy rules and laws (such as the 2006 Army Field Manual to which President Obama adhered) rather than leaving them free to decide within far broader boundaries how much coercion to use after balancing all the factors discussed here? Why announce publicly more detailed rules when *any* rule we come up with will fail to consider some relevant advantages or drawbacks?

Two reasons explain much of the need for rules for interrogation. Many of us want law in this situation because we are unwilling to trust the judgment of the interrogator who would be applying a balance of costs and benefits. Others would distrust the standards set for the interrogator by a remote executive official.

A list of factors and considerations such as those we have outlined in this chapter can be used to justify decisions wholly unacceptable or frightening to citizens and our allies if the party applying them gives either too little or too much weight to various costs and benefits. We have particular reason to worry about the bias, in exercising any very broad discretion, of someone whose role is to find out what dangerous plans are underway and who is rewarded for succeeding in this.

We may even be prepared to accept the judgment of intelligence officials on the "benefits" side as to which option has the best prospects of obtaining political information that an individual possesses. But we may still believe that they should not be the primary source of judgment on costs or on the balance between the benefits and risks of any particular option. As to the political official setting standards for interrogation, history shows that in times of emergency, there is often overreaction and an exaggerated perception of the threat and the necessary responses. Finally, as Lord Acton warned long ago, we have very good reason to fear the effect of unconstrained, unreviewed power on personality.[4]

A comparison to our Western allies shows that rules for interrogation are feasible. Australia seems to have sought ways to maintain the broadest executive discretion to avoid any constraining rules, to exercise the resulting discretion in the deepest secrecy, and to preclude judicial or legislative oversight, but it is an outlier. In contrast, the United Kingdom, Germany, France, Israel, and Japan have made public their rules, which, in the case of interrogation, do not differ greatly from the rules for investigating crime, and in all these countries, the rules and practices are subject to oversight.

The Discretion that Comes with the Power to Interpret Rules

There is, of course, an irreducible ambiguity inherent in the words used to describe impermissible coercion in international conventions and the national statutes that implement them. But it is greatly reduced for European countries by the availability of judicial review by the European Court of Human Rights. Our Western allies also have civil and criminal sanctions for abuse of the rules and standards. These forms of review are far less available in the United States.

Whatever the rule the U.S. agrees to adhere to, we will inevitably retain greater scope for presidential interpretation than will our allies for whom the courts can review the judgment of the national leader. Still, the president's interpretive discretion is not unlimited. Any interpretation of a treaty that departs very sharply from the understanding of our closest allies will be taken as at least a limited repudiation of the text to which we have expressed commitment. Our interpretation of "torture" or "cruel, inhuman, or degrading" in the Convention against Torture and Common Article 3 of the Geneva Conventions must respect the reasonable expectations of many other nations, for some of whom our own compliance would be a consideration in their own adherence to a treaty. Any interpretation of domestic law that is far from the understanding and expectations of many Americans will also be understood as executive lawlessness.

The Likely Options

President Obama selected from among three major contenders the structure to guide interrogation of terror suspects by U.S. officials. The first was the one that the Bush administration adopted—almost unlimited discretion for the United States and its president to use morally rejected and legally prohibited methods of interrogation whenever he saw fit. This required secretly construing our treaty and statutory obligations in a way that largely left them without meaning or effect.

The second alternative would be to meticulously honor our obligation not to engage in torture, and under our reservation to the prohibition of cruel, inhuman, or degrading treatment, not to engage in any form of interrogation that "shocked the conscience" and thus would violate the due process clause of the 5th Amendment to the Constitution. That is substantially the path, without much further specification and without provisions to assure compliance, which Congress took in response to the Abu Ghraib debacle. Congress made clear at that time that this obligation applied wherever the United States placed or held detainees.

A final alternative was to go beyond any narrow reading of our treaty commitments in order to bring our interrogation practices in alignment with our major allies such as the United Kingdom, France, Germany, Spain, and Japan. That would mean adopting a stricter set of rules that were absolute and not dependent on how great our need was for information. That is broadly what the Army Field Manual required of our soldiers and what the FBI required of its agents.

Benefits and Risks of Abandoning Highly Coercive Interrogation

Preliminary Matters

It is important to begin the process of analyzing our choices by dealing with some preliminary matters. As we have noted, each of the set of present options with regard to deriving information from a suspect who is believes to possess relevant information and can be either detained or monitored could be enriched and improved by both research and training. There is, moreover, little or no public knowledge and no known systematic internal review of the comparative advantages of different forms of interrogation, let alone of the advantages of covert alternatives to interrogation in this situation. Without research in these areas, choice among the present set of options will remain uninformed. Moreover, some options will be exercised in less than optimal ways. As the Obama administration recommendations of August 2009 reflected, our choices have to include structures for recruitment, training, and support of interviewers—structures that can make one or another option seem far better than it may appear now—and our choices must involve deciding what to do to learn more about the comparative advantages of various options whose costs and prospects may then be worth examining.

A second preliminary matter is that in deciding what we should do in the immediate future—our emphasis here—we must consider not only the set of written constitutional, statutory, and treaty provisions to which we did, or will, commit ourselves but also the interpretation we would give those texts. Any interpretation of a treaty that departs very sharply from the understanding of our closest allies will be taken as at least a limited repudiation of the text to which we have expressed commitment. Our interpretation of "torture" or "cruel," "inhuman," or "degrading" in Common Article 3 of the Geneva Conventions and the Convention against Torture must respect the reasonable expectations of many other nations for whom our own compliance would be a consideration in their adhering to a treaty. Any interpretation of domestic law that is far from the understanding of many Americans will also be understood as executive lawlessness.

The third important preliminary matter is to clarify the stages through which we will proceed in discussing what the U.S. position should be with regard to highly coercive interrogation. Too much of the debate has been about what to do in the very rare event of a ticking bomb case— one for which (a) we can identify a guilty suspect, (b) whom we confidently believe has information that is urgently needed to save lives, and in which (c) we have no way (other than highly coercive interrogation) of obtaining that information in time to prevent the threatened catastrophe, and (d) we have adequate reason to believe that cruel methods may work. Defined in that way, where the need is exceptionally compelling and the situation extremely rare, how we will handle a ticking bomb case should not define what we will do in the far more general case of simply wanting information about the resources, plans, and practices of a hostile force from a known suspect who can be surveilled or detained.

The extraordinary case of a real and calamitous emergency must be dealt with, but it can and should be dealt with as a separate emergency category and not allowed to define the normal case where the need for the information is far less imminent, the certainty that the suspect has the information is unclear, or the decision on all of these matters would necessarily—because of the far greater frequency of the issue arising—

have to be delegated to a large number of less accountable individuals. So we reserve the issue of the ticking bomb to later in this chapter.

The Options

We have noted that there are essentially three options as to standards we could apply to interrogation of those suspected of having critically important information that could not be obtained as reliably or at lesser cost by options other than detention and interrogation.

Each of these standards can be interpreted in different ways, depending upon how reliable a partner of our allies we hope to be and how consistent we want our actions to be with long-held public and international expectations about American behavior. Although the hardest choices President Obama faced had to do with the meaning of "cruel, inhuman, and degrading" treatment, we should begin with the more straightforward case of torture itself.

Torture

Only a few, perhaps including former Vice President Cheney, still argue either that torture should be regarded as within the rules for fighting terrorism or that waterboarding is not torture. As to the applicable law, the prohibition of torture in the Convention against Torture, in Common Article 3 of the Geneva Conventions, and in the statutes passed by Congress to enforce each of those conventions—is an absolute prohibition of certain, defined conduct, whatever the situation or exigency. Article 1 of the convention defines prohibited conduct as "any act by which severe pain or suffering . . . is intentionally inflicted on a person." Article 2 of the convention then stipulates "no exceptional circumstances whatsoever, whether a state of war or a threat of war, internal political stability, or any other public emergency may be invoked as a justification of torture."

Adhering to the convention, the Senate stated its understanding of what should constitute severe mental—as opposed to physical—pain or suffering prohibited by Article 1, but it stated no objection to the unqualified obligation to avoid torture that Article 2 demanded. The force of this general prohibition, even if not its precise boundaries, does not seem to be contested except, perhaps, by former Vice President Cheney. In its second periodic report to the Committee against Torture (a body of independent experts that monitors implementation of the convention), the Bush administration stated on May 6, 2005, "The United States is unequivocally opposed to the use and practice of torture. . . . No circumstances . . . may be invoked as justification for or defense to committing torture."

The issue for the United States, instead, has involved two aspects of the interpretation of "torture." The first aspect was whether or not waterboarding constitutes torture. The Bush administration would not label waterboarding *torture*, even though in the eyes of most of our allies and domestic communicators, it should have. Any interpretation of "torture" that departs very sharply from the understanding of our closest allies would be equivalent to our renouncing the treaty as far as they were concerned. The cost of either an explicit or interpretive withdrawal from the prohibition of torture would be immense while the comparative advantages of waterboarding or other extremely cruel behavior are unproven although asserted. An interpretation that concluded that waterboarding was not torture because it was not intended to inflict severe physical suffering—despite the past severe punishment of those using it against Americans—would be outside the limits of plausible interpretation. Thus, the Obama administration denounced waterboarding as torture in 2009; the practice (although not the claim of permissibility) had already been abandoned for years by the Bush administration. It had also been very broadly rejected by the American people. In other words, the costs of continuing to rely on this technique are far too high.

The second interpretive issue with regard to torture was illustrated by the decision announced in January 2009 by Susan Crawford, the convening authority for the Pentagon, that "we tortured [Mohammed al-Qahtani]." The Defense Department seems to have initially proceeded on the notion of inducing a state of "learned helplessness" by purposefully cruel treatment that often did not involve severe pain. Al Qahtani may not have been subjected to severe physical pain, but for fifty-four consecutive days he was interrogated for eighteen to twenty hours a day, humiliated, subjected to relatively extreme temperature changes, and otherwise purposely treated cruelly. Distinguishing sustained cruelty from torture as a way of obtaining information from a suspect involves a distinction too narrow to be persuasive to allies or the American people, as Susan Crawford found. The new administration reached the same conclusion.

Cruel, Inhuman, and Degrading

Since 2006, statutes also now prohibit any violation of our treaty obligation under the Convention against Torture to not engage in cruel, inhuman, and degrading treatment. But our statutory and treaty obligations to not engage in such treatment are subject to a reservation added upon ratification of the convention, to the effect that we would interpret this obligation as congruent with constitutional obligations not to engage in actions that "shock the conscience."[5]

The interpretation of "shocks the conscience" in Supreme Court decisions quite arguably allows the consideration of the benefits—that is, the anticipated payoffs from a cruel treatment in a particular context or situation—as well as its costs. In other words, if the benefits are sufficiently great, even cruel forms of interrogation that would not be lawful otherwise, could be acceptable (see *Chavez v. Martinez*, 538 U.S. 760 [2003]). While the exact boundaries of the limitation remain unclear, under at least one plausible interpretation, our obligation to avoid cruel, inhuman, and degrading treatment leaves very great discretion to interrogators and to those who direct their activity.

The Holder task force report to the Obama administration rejected the extra leeway that the reservation to the convention could provide for cruel methods in demanding circumstances, but without explaining why—simply noting that none of our interrogating agencies now saw the need for more than the Army Field Manual allowed. But there are strong reasons to support this rejection. The highly coercive techniques short of torture approved in the years immediately after 9/11 by the Defense Department, as observed by FBI agents in Guantanamo, included prolonged solitary confinement, hooding, stress positions, prolonged standing, sleep deprivation, temperature variations, and various forms of humiliation—all practices banned by the Israeli Supreme Court from use by Israeli interrogators. At best, these are techniques that operate slowly, in the hope of gradually inducing a state of so-called learned helplessness. They are useless in dealing with any possible ticking bomb situation.

As tactics for gathering other, more strategic intelligence, these methods are, as far as we now know, no more promising than the alternative techniques the FBI endorses. During the early days of battling the IRA, some British officials argued that such coercive methods obtained important information. Frank Steele, a former British intelligence officer, disagreed sharply. In an interview with journalist Peter Taylor, he said, "As for the special interrogation techniques, they were damned stupid as well as morally wrong . . . in practical terms, the additional usable intelligence they produced was, I understand, minimal."[4] Steele's statement applies to strategic information as well. Many interrogators in Western countries believe that other forms of interrogation are more useful to obtain accurate information important for understanding an enemy or its strategies.

On the "cost" side, the fact that we reserved this discretion at the time of ratifying the Convention against Torture would not reduce substantially the costs of engaging in cruel tactics rejected by our allies and recognized as illegal police behavior within the United States. Most basically, a prohibition that reaches only the level of shocking the conscience incorporates, with its notion of surprise and horror to American minds, too permissive a bar to be acceptable to allies and many American citizens. And so a central question for the Obama administration became whether to accept restrictions that went beyond a narrow reading of the "shock the conscience" obligations found in our reservation to the treaty and beyond President Bush's executive order giving a less restrictive interpretation to Common Article 3 of the Geneva Conventions. The benefits were clear. Only by drawing sharper and narrower limits could the United States shed a newly attained notoriety for the use of forms of interrogation that we have condemned in the past, would condemn now, and would not tolerate if applied to American citizens. Only by drawing narrower limits could we make the need for intelligence information fit with the need to be able to subject dangerous people to prosecution (where coerced confessions are forbidden even if they do not "shock the conscience").

The other broad option—accepting greater restraints than "shocking the conscience," accepting only the practices that our citizens and our courts would find acceptable if applied to a U.S. citizen or if used within the United States for gathering important intelligence—a category almost identical to what our major allies would find acceptable if used within their borders and generally captured by the standards of the revised

Army Field Manual. Roughly congruent with those that the FBI has insisted on for a number of years, these measures could go beyond what is permissible if a confession is to be used at trial, so long as the information is not to be used to incriminate the suspect at his trial. They would, however, exclude the harsher methods used earlier by the Department of Defense and the still crueler methods used by the CIA, and would be in line with the interpretations by the European Court of Human Rights of what is prohibited as "cruel, inhuman, and degrading."

President Obama adopted the second option to realize the benefits of returning to standards that are understood and accepted by the American people and consistent with the views of our allies. Only this would largely eliminate the major costs we have borne as a result of the earlier measures. This also eliminated the anomaly of having different limits on interrogation binding on the CIA, the FBI, and the military.

The years immediately after the adoption of such limits on our interrogation activities will provide an opportunity to research and review the records of the years since September 11, 2001, for purposes of learning far more about the comparative advantages of different methods of interrogation. During that time we should develop the world's best capacity for forms of interviewing or interrogation that do not bring with them the grave costs of a U.S. policy embracing purposeful cruelty.

Back to the Case of the Ticking Bomb
Pressed by arguments emphasizing the costs of the early Bush practices, the supporters of cruel practices turned quickly to the example of the ticking bomb placed in a major population center. They pointed out that other interrogation techniques require more time to work than brutal force and that harsh interrogation is less cruel than the mass murder that it may prevent.

The Obama administration did not discuss this issue. Even in this case the benefits of torture are greatly exaggerated. We often have the wrong person. Or we may have the right person, but the information he has may be inadequate to prevent the event. He may deceive us in a costly way to the benefit of his colleagues or delay us long enough for the other conspirators to make alternative plans. Even under the pressure of torture, he may fall back to a cover story that was chosen to be not only false but also difficult to disprove.

Perhaps most important, since 9/11, we have not had a true case of a ticking bomb. To recall, this is a case where (1) we can identify a guilty suspect (2) who we firmly believe has information that is urgently needed to save lives (3) where we have no other (than cruel) covert or overt way of obtaining that information in time and (4) have an adequate basis for believing cruel methods may elicit the life-saving information.

Abandoning the international obligations we have solemnly accepted at the costs described in this chapter seems a very bad trade to preserve the mere possibility of using torture in a situation unlikely to ever arise.

But the question remains: what if the president was confronted with such a case? In chapter 1 we discussed the options available for the president if he believes that a massive disaster confronts us. A ticking weapon of great destructive power would fit into this category. The best option is that suggested by Thomas Jefferson and acted on by Abraham Lincoln: to openly acknowledge that the president will disobey a law that prevents him from taking the steps essential to save many lives in an emergency; and that he will do so transparently, accepting the political, if not legal, risks of violating the rule of law in a situation that is unexpected and is highly unlikely to occur.

The question is not about the president's constitutional powers as commander in chief. It is rather what we want the president to do in the face of unanticipated emergencies, many of which may have nothing at all to do with war. Most nations grant their chief executive extraordinary powers to deal with grave emergencies. Our Constitution does not have emergency powers, but that does not avoid the problem. The emergency may be the flooding of New Orleans, the sudden arrival of a lethal flu, a disastrous earthquake such as those China and Haiti recently experienced, or any of a number of events that the framers of our Constitution and Congress could hardly have anticipated in limiting the powers the president is authorized to execute. In each of these situations, which have nothing to do with armed conflict or the president's powers as commander in chief, the president also has to decide whether to exceed his authority in order to save lives. The choice is inevitable for risks too rare to be the subject of legislated powers and too calamitous to be ignored.

Conclusions

There may be extraordinary emergencies where the president must act despite, and in conflict with, laws designed for more ordinary situations. Along with unexpected natural or medical disasters, one imaginable set of such situations involves a prospective and imminent terrorist-caused disaster that could only be avoided by using highly coercive interrogation forbidden by the Geneva Conventions, domestic U.S. law, and human rights law.

For every other situation, the United States will be far wiser to operate under clear rules, sharply limiting the discretion of its military and intelligence officers, and restricting itself to what our FBI has used to obtain reliable information when it has been seeking intelligence (rather than a confession of guilt) and what the most recent Army Field Manual permits for military interrogations.

The case for making highly coercive methods illegal cannot sensibly be restricted to those interrogations carried out by our agents themselves. The same rules must also apply to renditions for the purpose of interrogation by countries known to torture and to any other effort to utilize other countries or other groups to do what is forbidden to American agents.

The U.S. experience with coercive interrogations demonstrates that departures from domestic and international law, from U.S. tradition in war and peace, and from the practices of our closest allies are extremely costly. Nor is there any indication that the security benefit from these departures was worth the costs. In fact, using interrogation is not generally the best way to obtain reliable information from an individual believed to possess it; covert techniques are often more useful. Within the realm of interrogations, there is no empirical evidence to suggest that highly coercive interrogations yield more or better information than professional noncoercive interrogations. And noncoercive interrogation can be further improved by forming a multi-branch expert unit and drawing on all that is known by our allies and social science.

Ultimately, the most effective solutions to the new challenges of obtaining intelligence on transnational terrorism lie within existing legal boundaries, whether crime- or war-related.

Part III

Beyond Coercion

In his first State of the Union address after the attacks of 9/11, President Bush famously resuscitated the "good vs. evil" World War II paradigm, complemented by the "you're either with us—or against us" challenge to the world. Evil was to be eradicated by force, by declaring a "war on terrorism." And in that war, there could be no compromise over values, no negotiation with the enemy, and no accommodation of competing ideologies.

The administration was careful to make some crude distinctions; upon the invasion of Afghanistan, American leaders reiterated that their feud was not with the Afghan people, whom they were seeking to liberate from the true enemy—the same one threatening the free world.[1] The bargain was simple: in exchange for denying support to Al-Qaeda and the Taliban, the Afghan people would receive liberation, development aid, and democratic self-rule. Conversely, those who would support, harbor, or assist the enemies of the United States would pay dearly. Much the same choice was offered in Iraq.

The bargain was also implied by the enduring concept of "a war on terror." The very label presumes a contained, definable enemy—the terrorist—who can be interrogated, detained, and, if need be, targeted; it also assumed that the terrorist is separable and distinguishable from the innocent population, which can be spared from harm. The evil can thus be separated from the good, and every individual categorized as one or the other and treated accordingly.

But the realities of the war on terrorism soon proved that individuals were part of their community and could not always be easily categorized as good or evil, ubiquitously and around the clock, and that the seemingly crisp distinction between those "with us" and those "against us" was impossible to apply with precision on the ground in Pakistan, Yemen, or even Britain.

It is easiest to see the problem if we begin not with terrorism as a case apart but contextualized, as when insurgents employ the tactics of terrorism against us. In Iraq and Afghanistan terrorist tactics are used by insurgents embedded in a local population, reliant on its backing, and encouraged by its moral support. Fighting without uniform or clear insignia, insurgents are often indistinguishable from uninvolved civilians around them. No "surgical strike" is neat enough to excise insurgents from among a group of civilians, who might well be family, neighbors, or community members. Insurgents are part of an already war-torn country now experiencing yet another war. Civilians are forced to take sides and face the consequences.

Throughout the two campaigns—in Iraq and Afghanistan—the lines separating the two groups, insurgents using terror tactics and civilians have been—and continue to be—in constant flux. Civilians outraged by the occupation of their country by what seemed like yet another expansionist foreign empire, and resentful of the violence inflicted by their "liberators," joined or support insurgents; and even where there is no ideological or nationalist motive, war lords and drug lords promise employment and income to people seeking a future in an uncertain world. In consequence, many "innocent" civilians have become less innocent as these wars continued without end.

The blurring of the lines between the "enemy" and the "ally" or "innocent" at once bore, from the very start, two opposing implications. The first was that we were not only fighting against an enemy, but also fighting for, and over, something positive, namely the "hearts and minds" of the local population. In order to win over the hearts and minds, the occupation forces in Afghanistan—and later, in Iraq, too—could not focus only on killing and capturing the bad guys, but, as General David Petraeus had urged in revising the military's Counterinsurgency Manual, had to employ even greater resources to ensure that the promise of a better future for the civilian population would be credible and fulfilled.

Oftentimes, the two missions of the war were, and are, in direct conflict and winning a military victory in a battle against insurgents often entails damage to and injury of the local population. On the other hand, the missions are often interdependent: the coalition forces could not effectively kill and capture the enemy without, to some extent, intentionally incorporating the civilian population into the war effort. The need for human intelligence, tracking insurgents hiding in villages and discouraging successful recruitment of civilians by insurgents, create dependence on civilians in order to fight insurgents. Every action taken—whether aggressive or accommodating—would invariably have mixed effects, some contrary to the ones intended.

As civilians in large numbers become the inadvertent victims of the war on the havens of terrorism, the United States loses ground in its war over the hearts and minds of the local population, a war that, to a large degree, is about collective self-identity. By unintentionally inflicting harms on the uninvolved, the United States feeds collective support for terrorists and insurgents. Instead of making the local population its ally, the aggressive campaign inevitably turns large portions of the population into foes.

The difficulty of separating terrorists from their surrounding communities and the importance of treating the innocent differently from the guilty arises equally when dealing with terror outside the context of insurgency.

As chapters 7 and 8 demonstrate, drawing a marked contrast between combatants and civilians, "bad guys" and "good guys," or "those with us" and "those against us" is a reductive simplification that amounts to more than just a rhetorical reduction. Labeling through sharp dichotomies makes it harder to tailor nuanced responses to a complex and fluctuating problem or to monitor the effects, intentional or unintentional, of our actions on different groups.

When thinking about a comprehensive counterterrorism strategy, the government must seek to change what motivates the actions of terrorists. Doing so requires some mix of coercive and noncoercive means that do not necessarily correspond to a good/evil distinction or "with us/against us" formula. The mixed response must consider the collective aspects of terrorism: the inevitable tension between frustrating the terrorists' goals and keeping the rest of the population out of harm's way. It must assess the effects of coercive measures aimed at terrorists on those uninvolved, as well as the ways in which those uninvolved can be harnessed to frustrate the capabilities of the terrorists.

Offering a detailed picture of such a comprehensive strategy goes beyond what we set out to do in this book. Instead, we focus on two aspects of the government's counterterrorism strategy that highlight the limits of coercive strategies and register heightened sensibilities for the collective nature of the war on terror. The first is negotiating with terrorists; the second is reducing moral support for terrorism within Muslim communities, as they were primarily affected by the aftermath of 9/11 and became the primary source of recruitment for terrorist attacks on the West.

Regarding negotiating with terrorists, we believe that even though the government should be wary of bargaining, refusal to bargain should not be an absolute position. Moreover, the government should distinguish between hostage or other crisis negotiations, intended to end a particular, often repeatable, terrorist threat, and broader negotiations that are intended to transform the relationship between the government and the terrorist group altogether. Whatever presumption the government should hold against negotiation in the first instance of crisis negotiations, the opposite presumption—one in favor of negotiation—is often appropriate in considering broader negotiations.

In discussing the need for an effective campaign for hearts and minds, one that seeks to reduce the moral support for terrorism among large populations, we look to other countries' efforts to reduce support for terrorism, as well as to our own previous experience with public diplomacy during the Cold War. We then test some of the most common assumptions about what drives support for Muslim terrorism against the recent polling data dedicated to this question. These data shed new light on the promises and limits of engaging the world's Muslim population. Rather than economic conditions, levels of education, or even religious commitment, the data reveal that what generates moral support for terrorism are perceptions of the United States and the West that do not conform to our own perceptions of ourselves or indeed to our intentions and that can be avoided. There are, however, substantial constraints that limit our freedom of action, namely our commitments to our own core values, to our allies, and to furthering various strategic interests. It is along this path and around these obstacles that a campaign to reduce moral support for terrorism must proceed.

7

Negotiating with Terrorists

Introduction

Numerous democratic countries around the world, including the United States, have a stated policy of never negotiating with terrorists. However, it is perhaps a policy almost as often honored in the breach as in the observance. Britain negotiated with the Irish Republican Army (IRA), Israel has negotiated with the Palestine Liberation Organization (PLO) and other Palestinian factions, Colombia has negotiated with various domestic rebel groups, and Spain has negotiated with the Basque ETA (Euskadi Ta Askatasuna [Homeland and Freedom]). Even the United States under President Reagan provided TOC missiles to Iran to win the release of hostages held by Hezbollah. In each of these cases, a (despite a stated policy of "no negotiating with terrorists") state negotiated with a group it had deemed to be a "terrorist organization." In some cases, negotiations addressed limited incidents involving hijackers, skyjackers, and kidnappers, in attempts to save citizens in immediate danger. In other instances, negotiations were much wider in scope, intended to transform the relationship between the government and the terrorist group altogether.

Despite these exceptions and distinctions, it remains the accepted wisdom that governments should not negotiate with terrorists in any situation. The Bush administration held fast to this position in ringing phrases, especially when addressing Al-Qaeda. In one instance, Vice President Dick Cheney remarked: "This enemy holds no territory, defends no population, is unconstrained by rules of warfare, and respects no law of morality." The consequence, he argued, is that "such an enemy cannot be deterred, contained, appeased, or negotiated with. It can only be destroyed, and that's the business at hand."[2] And former House Majority Leader Tom Delay, in a speech before the Israeli Knesset, said: "It's a battle between good and evil, between the Truth of liberty and The Lie of terror. This war is the moral extension of World War II and the Cold War, and like the Nazis, fascists, and Communists before them, the terrorists are going to lose." His conclusion about negotiation was the same. "History, as always, will judge harshly those who would accommodate evil's aggression."[3]

The Bush administration expanded this stance beyond terrorists to include rogue regimes around the world. Several media sources reported Cheney as having said, in a White House meeting on North Korea in December 2003, "I have been charged by the president with making sure that none of the tyrannies in the world are negotiated with. We don't negotiate with evil; we defeat it." As is widely known, the United States has frequently departed from this stance. We have engaged with North Korea in negotiations, and the Obama administration has extended its hand to Iran in an effort to negotiate our extreme differences over Iran's atomic program.

In this chapter we ask the following question: to what extent is it useful for a state to have a no-negotiation policy with terrorists and, indirectly, with the rogue regimes that may be backing them? In our analysis we suggest how to identify the relevant factors for consideration of this question, and compare how adhering to or else rejecting a no-negotiation policy may fit in with the broader goals of fighting terrorism.

Scope of the Question

The term *terrorist* famously lacks any definitional consensus. No less malleable, when thinking about negotiating with terrorists, is the term *negotiation*. Every tactical or strategic move between parties in conflict, including military strikes, may be interpreted as tacit bargaining, signaling, or in fact negotiating. For example, President Johnson sometimes used bombing strikes in North Vietnam for this purpose. Politicians often try to distinguish the term *negotiation* from related terms, such as *talks*, *dialogue*, or *contact*, in order to give themselves more room for maneuver while still maintaining nominal consistency with a no-negotiation policy.

For the purposes of this discussion we choose a much more constricted scope for the term *negotiation*, as defined by negotiation expert Robert Mnookin: "a joint decision making process involving interactive communication in which parties that lack identical interests attempt to reach agreement."[4]

We also assume that, in attempting to reach agreement, the parties are willing to make some concessions or tradeoffs, however nominal. This excludes from our discussion ultimatums of the kind issued by President Bush to the Taliban in the aftermath of 9/11. We believe that a good-faith negotiation must include some readiness to meet the other party's interests, whether the other party consists of terrorists or not, and whether any concessions are made directly by the government or by an interested third party.

Moreover, we exclude from our discussion cases in which the use of negotiation is merely a tactical ploy, intended to buy time for operational alternatives or else to draw terrorists out of their hiding places and capture them. In 1996–1997, for example, the Peruvian military used the ongoing negotiations between the government and the Tupac Amaru group that had taken over the Japanese Embassy in Lima as a cover for preparing its successful assault and release of hostages from the embassy. Using a promise to negotiate in this way is likely to be effective only initially and may destroy a state's ability to negotiate credibly in the future. If anything, such tactics on a government's part can only help to sustain a credible commitment *not* to negotiate with terrorists in the future.

The contexts in which negotiations occur vary widely, but we wish especially to distinguish between two scenarios, placed at opposite ends of a continuum: tactical negotiations in the context of a crisis or imminent threat intentionally created by an opposing party (e.g., a hostage crisis) and peace negotiations intended to end, or restrict the scope of, an ongoing conflict. In crisis negotiations, a state must quickly respond to a threatening act. Its immediate goal is to confine negotiations to the one act and resolve the crisis. In the case of peace negotiations, or transformative negotiations, the negotiations are intended to define a new relationship between the state and the terrorist organization, hopefully one that would exclude all terrorist activities against the state (at the price of granting the terrorists at least some of their demands). As we proceed to show, the different characteristics associated with these two scenarios affect the cost-benefit analysis of pursuing negotiations.

Within these categories there is, of course, great variation. Some terrorists seize hostages for the sole purpose of extracting concessions. Others use the attack to dramatize a particular issue or ideology, and capture the attention of a valued audience. The terrorists may be political actors with political demands, ranging from the release of sympathetic prisoners to the state's withdrawal from certain territories. The question of whether or not to negotiate may arise in the context of consistent demands and repeated pressure by a sizeable group or in the context of a sole individual holding hostages or engaging in a terrorist act that he will have difficulty repeating. The groups, in turn, may be state actors, or actors closely affiliated with a state, or else nonstate actors whose geographical location spans different states and territories.

All these differences necessarily affect a government's response. Governments may find themselves better able to justify negotiating with domestic terrorist groups than foreign groups, simply because they are the state's own constituents. At the same time, however, the political, symbolic, and practical challenge to a government's legitimacy and power from an armed group within its population is often greater than that which a challenge from the outside can generate, making domestic negotiations harder. The domestic context may make it easier for the government to use coercive measures to end attacks, since other nations would consider the issue fundamentally an internal domestic matter; but on the other hand, it may also make the use of coercive measures more susceptible to domestic legal constraints.

The government's response may also depend on the whether the terrorists are acting on behalf of a foreign state or a foreign nonstate actor. In the case of a nonstate actor operating from within a foreign state (e.g., Al-Qaeda attacks on the United States or Hezbollah attacks on Israel), it may be less clear with whom it would be productive to negotiate: the group, the government of the foreign state, or a third power that supports the group. Also, any threat of a military response is likely to be complicated by possible effects on the relations between the victim state and the country where the terrorists are located or of which they are citizens. Deterrence and retaliation are generally more complicated and less effective where there is no state involved and where the armed group need only be concerned about its own interests.

Despite these differences, many of the considerations of whether—as opposed to how—to negotiate with terrorists are similar across the board. There is a general revulsion at the methods employed by terrorists and a corresponding reluctance to "deal"; similarly there is difficulty in weighing the short-term threat from terrorism against the potential for greater long-term harm that may arise from rewarding terrorism. Therefore, although the particulars will vary from case to case, it is possible to glean some generic insights from the myriad of cases.

We will begin by laying out some of the common arguments against negotiating with terrorists and then examine some of the arguments in favor of negotiations. Next, we will establish a framework for thinking about how to weigh the costs and benefits that may accrue from the choice to negotiate. We will then briefly set out some additional considerations regarding how such exchanges should be conducted in the event that a government decides to negotiate. We round off the chapter by analyzing how these considerations fit within the larger context of the war on terrorism.

The Costs of Negotiating with Terrorists

Those who support a policy of never negotiating with terrorists tend to make one of five arguments. The first, most common objection to negotiating with terrorists is that it sets a bad precedent and encourages future attacks. In his essay "Negotiations with Terrorists," Richard Hayes cites a series of studies conducted by Defense Systems, Inc. that traced government counterterrorism policies in France, Brazil, Colombia, and Israel from 1968 to 1982 and measured them against the number of terrorist attacks during the same time period.[5] The study found that the number of terrorist incidents in France rose significantly after 1973, when the French made substantial concessions to resolve the crisis at the Saudi embassy in Paris and rose again as the French continued to make concessions for the next few years. However, in three major events in 1976, the French adopted a firm approach; with that, the number of terrorist attacks directed against France leveled off. As the French government continued to take tough stances against terrorists over different attacks, the number of attacks decreased.[6]

Another example provided by Grant Wardlaw concerns negotiations with members of "The Revolutionary Movement 8th of October" in Brazil. In September 1969, the U.S. ambassador to Brazil was kidnapped by the group and then released in exchange for the release of fifteen terrorist prisoners. In June 1970, the Peoples' Revolutionary Vanguard group kidnapped the West German ambassador to Brazil and forty prisoners were set free in exchange for his release. In December of that same year, the same group kidnapped the Swiss ambassador and demanded the exchange of seventy prisoners.[7] Eventually the Brazilian government cracked down on the practice, but it is clear that initial successes had fueled later efforts.

A second argument against negotiating with terrorists is that the very act of negotiation legitimizes and affords recognition to terrorist organizations. The purpose of calling a group a "terrorist organization" is in large part to delegitimize that group and its tactics, which are always criminal under the domestic law of the state.[8] The formal designation of a group as a terrorist organization is generally a contentious process, often taken because it "stigmatizes and isolates designated terrorist organizations internationally."[9] Having attempted to delegitimize and isolate a particular organization, it is self-defeating for the state to then agree to negotiations.[10] A corollary to this argument is that, in agreeing to negotiate with terrorists, a government is implicitly granting legitimacy to the terrorists' demands as well as to their means.

There is, moreover, a risk that, in negotiating with one terrorist group, a government signals to other would-be terrorist groups that violence is a relatively easy way to gain the government's ear and so encourages the further use of violence. When a terrorist act goes unpunished, a condition that is often a terrorist demand in the negotiations, terrorism becomes an even more attractive way to pursue a political agenda. This was one of James Zackrison's main criticisms of Colombia's policy toward domestic insurgent groups that had committed terrorist acts. According to Zackrison, the government would repeatedly enter into peaceful negotiations with insurgent groups and grant a general amnesty for all involved. This, of course, provided no incentive for the groups to stop kidnapping diplomats, or indeed, to refrain from forming new insurgent movements later.[11] This form of costless exit meant that the risks and costs of forming an insurgent group were drastically lowered.

A third argument against negotiating is that terrorists (by nature of their occupation) are simply not trustworthy and therefore make bad negotiating partners. An example from the late 1700s illustrates this point. The Barbary pirates would kidnap the crews of European and American vessels and demand ransom. The U.S. Congress set aside $80,000 for payments to the Barbary states (the North African states of Tripoli, Tunis, Morocco, and Algiers) in return for halting the kidnapping. This figure ballooned into more than $2 million in the course of ten years, but the Barbary pirates continued to seize American hostages.[12] Finally, in 1795, the United States concluded a peace treaty with Algiers, one of the state sponsors of Barbary pirates, by agreeing to pay Algiers nearly $1 million in cash, annual tributes, and naval arms.[13] Not only did this encourage other Barbary states to increase their demands, but Algiers itself also continued to take hostages.[14] It was only when the United States established the Marine Corps, and dispatched U.S. Marines "from the halls of Montezuma to the shores of Tripoli," that the threat of piracy subsided.

A more recent—and similarly unsuccessful—example of this approach occurred in 1985, when the United States sold arms to Iran, expecting that Iran would order Hezbollah to release its American hostages. Instead, Hezbollah took replacement hostages, probably with Iran's encouragement.[15]

Even if it were otherwise acceptable to negotiate, dealing with non-state terrorists poses further challenges that would make reaching an agreement extremely difficult for a state, especially when the deal exceeds the scope of any one particular incident. One such difficulty derives from the fact that terrorist groups often lack formal accountability to any constituency; and so, even if a deal is reached with a particular leader, the effort will be futile if that leader cannot make others in his organization abide by it. The Al-Qaeda network is a case in point. As Peter Neumann notes, the Al-Qaeda leadership serves mostly to provide ideological inspiration and moral sanction to a range of associated factions rather than actually to organize the operations of the network.[16] This means that the chances for a negotiated solution with Al-Qaeda are slim because, although Osama bin Laden and Ayman al-Zawahiri have offered ceasefires to the United States and Europe, it is not clear that local Al-Qaeda members would follow them.[17] Moreover, a group like Al-Qaeda "has global aspirations and no firm territorial base, and there is no clearly defined territory in which its aims could be satisfied through constitutional means."[18] These attributes suggest there would be very few limitations on what Al-Qaeda or similar groups could potentially demand, making conventional compromises nearly impossible. Dean Pruitt echoes these concerns by emphasizing the unlikeliness that Al-Qaeda could enter the mainstream. After all, Pruitt asks, what government could Al-Qaeda join?[19] Extranational, and to an extent antinational Al-Qaeda makes it impossible to conceive the terms of any agreement it might sign.

A fourth, strategic consideration against negotiating with terrorists has to do with the removal or weakening of more coercive means to address the terrorist threat. The government's ability to harness domestic support as well as international assistance to battle the terrorist threat could be diminished if negotiations were under way. Even if negotiations were to fail, domestic and international constituencies might be inclined to believe that further negotiations must be attempted before—or in lieu of—the use of force. Despite the obvious differences, an example of this concern may be found in Winston Churchill's refusal to negotiate with Adolf Hitler in May of 1940. Churchill feared that, having opened the door to negotiations, he would not be able to convince his constituency of the necessity to fight should negotiations fail. Debates on appeasement in Churchill's War Cabinet were kept secret, partly out of fear that discussion of doubt and appeasement would weaken the national morale needed to fight the Germans. Churchill also feared that by entering negotiations he would be "dragged down the slippery slope" and that the whole approach was "intended to get us so deeply involved in negotiations that we should be unable to turn back."[20]

Finally, and Churchill's case is no exception to this, the refusal of governments to negotiate is often driven by a strong moral aversion to "dealing with the devil." As Guy Oliver Faure cautions, "[o]ne should not deal with the devil without the risk of losing one's soul."[21] Even aside from the potential effects on one's reputation and the possibility of future attacks, there is a general reluctance to deal with people whose means and methods fill us with deep repugnance. This type of sentiment resonates in U.S. government officials' statements, cited earlier in this chapter, admonishing the idea of negotiating with Al-Qaeda or the Taliban. It should be noted that governments often couch their choices in moral terms, even when their decisions are strategically driven. Even Winston Churchill, who is widely believed to have been a moralist leader, suggested that appeasement was wrong, not so much because it was immoral but because it was futile: "An appeaser," he famously said, "is one who feeds a crocodile—hoping it will eat him last."[22]

If there are absolute nonconsequential moral costs to dealing with the evil, such costs reflect a more fundamental perceived problem with negotiation: the lack of common values or moral perceptions or tradable advantages that must form the basis on which to begin negotiations. If two parties differ so fundamentally not only in their values but even in the very meaning they attach to certain words and concepts—if the parties' starting assumptions are diametrically opposed—then there might not be any grounds on which to begin, let alone sustain, engagement. There is no zone of possible agreement because the very debate suggests the surrender of one's most deeply held values. This was reflected in President Bush's statement that "no nation can negotiate with terrorists. For there is no way to make peace with those whose only goal is death."[23]

The Cost of Not Negotiating with Terrorists

Just as there are risks and costs of negotiating, there are risks and costs in *not* negotiating.

First, there is an obvious immediate harm if the terrorists' threat is carried out. This prospect is most apparent in the case of a hostage crisis in which any would-be negotiator has two conflicting challenges: to get the hostages freed and to discourage the terrorists, by the response, from taking hostages in the future.[24] A government will not want to risk future attacks by negotiating but it also has a real interest in the safety of those now held hostage. The latter concern is likely to be increased by great pressure from domestic constituencies and the families of hostages. By negotiating, a government may be able to secure the release of some of the hostages, "reduce the dimensions of the problem it confronts and save a number of innocent lives, whether or not an all-encompassing agreement to end the crisis is ever attained."[25]

A second argument in favor of negotiating concerns the opportunity to gather information about the terrorists. For example, negotiating in a hostage crisis may be a way to gather useful information from the hostage takers about their objectives, methods, and supporters.[26] The most dramatic example of this was the identification, after many frustrating years of failure, of Ted Kaczynski as the Unabomber. His identity came to light only after the *New York Times* and *Washington Post*, relying on his claim that he would stop his acts of terrorism if they would publish a "manifesto" he had written and without opposition by the U.S. government, agreed to print the piece. The ideas and writing style of the manifesto indirectly revealed Kaczynski's identity and led to his subsequent arrest.

Such information gleaned from negotiations may be useful not only in the immediate standoff but also in formulating a broader strategy for combating terrorists, which is particularly needed if the threat emanates from a general campaign of terrorism. In discussing Britain's experience with the IRA, Louise Richardson argues that it is necessary to talk to terrorists in order to "get an appreciation of their grievances and a sense of the priorities they attach to different objectives."[27] The information to be gleaned may vary significantly depending on context, but to the extent that useful information is gained, negotiations may prove well worthwhile.

A third argument for negotiating, so long as the terrorists' demands are not fully met, is the potential to strengthen the position of moderates in the terrorist group and possibly to drive a wedge between different factions of the organization.[28] The opportunity for partial success in a high-risk and multiple-objective negotiation can easily divide an organization. The "Real IRA" splintered from the IRA following the 1998 Good Friday Agreement in Northern Ireland. President Obama has suggested negotiating with moderate members of the Taliban in Afghanistan, a strategy that President Karzai has utilized in the past. Many support such a strategy as a means of gaining the support of moderate Taliban members while isolating the more extreme elements.[29] In the case of state-sponsored terrorism, negotiations may also help to drive a wedge between the state parties and the nonstate organizations.

A fourth potential cost of not negotiating is the risk that the terrorists, facing a lack of success with their current means and with no other channel by which to voice their grievances or unite their followers, may respond by escalating their actions. As Bertram Spector states: "Much of the terrorist violence promotes an atmosphere in which negotiation is inoperable, so a government doctrine of 'no-negotiation with terrorists' plays to the strength of the terrorists. If not negotiation, then what? Interaction can become a deadly tit-for-tat, escalating the conflict with no apparent way out other than capitulation or retreat by one side."[30] A blanket refusal to negotiate may weaken the terrorist organization as an *organization*, but could at the same time drive its factions or individual members to the most extreme measures in order to be heard.[31]

Fifth, an approach that seeks to avoid rewarding terrorists by negotiating with them assumes that it is negotiation or immediate concessions that the terrorists seek.[32] In fact, with a long-range goal that depends on mobilizing supporters, the terrorists' immediate objective may be to prevent talks and to invite a harsh response from the government.[33] A government that has offered to negotiate and been rebuffed by the terrorist group may thus be able to garner more support and ensure that criticism is directed at those who are perceived as perpetuating the violence.

A sixth cost of not negotiating concerns the potential for political fallout if hostages are killed. A government that does nothing in the face of endangered citizens, panicked family members, and the horror show of terrorists threatening to execute hostages on every media channel will appear ineffectual or uncaring. The political fallout from storming the site of hostages in lieu of negotiating with them may be as bad as that caused by inaction. This tension was evident during the 2002 Dubrovka Theater hostage crisis in Moscow, discussed in more detail later in this chapter. President Vladimir Putin came to power in Russia with a strong mandate to deal forcefully with the Chechens. Yet the decision to storm the Dubrovka Theater in Moscow was strongly criticized for causing the death of 126 of the hostages.[34]

Last, but perhaps most important, there is a possibility that negotiation could work, not only to resolve an immediate crisis but also, more crucially, to transform the relationship between the government and the group. This may be a very slow process and a government must take steps to protect itself in the meantime. Nonetheless, what seem to be fixed positions in the beginning may evolve into new interests and different priorities as the exchanges progress.[35] What is interesting about this process is that it is not the mere passage of time that results in different priorities, although this may play a role too, but that the act of engaging in dialogue may itself bring about change. A dialogue reframed the varied relationships between Israel and the PLO, the South African government and the African National Congress (ANC), and the United Kingdom and the IRA. Indeed, without some kind of dialogue and engagement it is unclear how any compromise that depended on understanding each other's interests and concerns could ever be reached. Naturally, this kind of dialogue is most relevant when the government is responding to a prolonged campaign of terrorism by a particular group rather than to an opportunistic attack, such as one carried out by kidnappers in Haiti or Colombia, or by Somali pirates.

Some scholars draw a distinction between "absolutist" and "traditional" terrorists. Absolutist terrorists are said to be characterized by an unwillingness to enter into political discourse and by making demands that are "immediate, unconditional, and universal."[36] They are more likely to engage in extreme means such as suicide attacks and their distinguishing feature is their "radical, impossible demands."[37]

But the difficulty of knowing ex ante whether and to what extent terrorists might be willing to negotiate reveals a fundamental problem with attempts to classify groups of terrorists along such lines. One of the functions of negotiation is to gather information about the other parties: their interests, motivations, strength, and support. Without such information, it may be difficult to assess terrorists' demands with accuracy. Moreover, decisions as to which terrorists belong in which category are highly subjective and subject to manipulation.

Emily Pronin and colleagues showed in experimental settings that individuals' perceptions of terrorists' rationality could be influenced by external factors such as newspaper articles depicting terrorists either as rational and objective or irrational and biased.[38] Those who read articles depicting terrorists as irrational and biased were more likely to recommend military action to deal with the problem than those who read articles depicting the terrorists as rational and objective.[39]

In addition, parties' demands may change over time. Indeed, one of the goals of negotiation is to take radical demands and dull their edge, to make them less extreme through engagement. The political engagements with the PLO, the ANC, and (indirectly) the IRA prove that terrorist organizations may indeed transform themselves into political partners. This calls into question the usefulness of classifying terrorists or their goals by the demands they announce at the outset.

Since any strategic decision is necessarily weighed against the alternatives, the context in which the negotiation takes place is important when we come to decide how best to respond. We return to this point later in this chapter.

The Framework

So far we have identified the possible costs and benefits that are associated with the decision to negotiate with terrorists. But without some overarching framework to instruct us on how to weigh these costs and benefits, a government's reaction is more likely to consist of arbitrary, ad hoc, and knee-jerk reactions. Still, if our hope is to discourage the taking of hostages or of using terrorism as a bargaining tactic more generally, we may have to decide, in advance, what our reaction would be to specific terrorist acts in the future. Having a general policy in place is intended to overcome the short-term incentives to resolve a particular crisis and ensure that longer-term considerations are given appropriate weight. It is also intended to resolve domestic disputes that might arise in the face of any given terrorist act about how to react to it. And finally, it is intended to affect the decision-making process for the terrorists. To be able to do that, once a policy is in place, and particularly if it is public, the government must ensure the credibility of its commitment by keeping up on its threats or promises.

In what follows, we outline the benefits of adhering to a predetermined policy of not negotiating over case-by-case decisions. Still, we acknowledge that the case for maintaining a policy (or a very strong presumption) of not negotiating is less clear than it at first appears. As we shall see, exceptions may be necessary, even while conceding that such exceptions necessarily impair the deterring message that the government seeks to convey to the terrorists.

A Fixed Policy Approach

Calculating the cost-benefit trade-off of a decision to negotiate or to not negotiate in any particular instance is extremely difficult, due to the uncertainty of what the result of any particular decision will be. The goal is to protect one's citizens. But how many lives will conferring legitimacy on an organization cost in the long run? What is the human toll of a bad precedent? How does one quantify values such as the transformative value of establishing a dialogue? Also, because so many variables affect the execution of a terrorist act and the formulation of a foreign policy, it is extremely difficult to calculate the impact of any one decision in isolation.

Calculation is further complicated by the fact that the future impact of a decision does not rely on the decision maker's calculations alone. Decisions are made in the context of strategic interaction so that the results of the decision depend largely on the reaction and strategy of the other side as well as on external events.[40] Even to the extent a government can anticipate a particular response, the magnitude of that response and its effects will depend on too many factors to incorporate accurately into one's current calculus. A further difficulty lies in the inability to accurately assess the potential for long-term harm. A decision to negotiate with a terrorists may not confer much legitimacy *now*, but perhaps it will be the first in a series of acts that snowballs into a devastating situation. In the case of a hostage crisis, the potential short-term costs are very clear but the amount of future harm that would result from any given policy is virtually impossible to calculate. Intervening variables of various sorts—political, economic, strategic, or others—are likely to escape the most careful prediction, further complicating matters.

Besides the extreme difficulties of prediction, other factors may distort decision making. Short-term costs and benefits are more visible and calculable. This fact may have important political implications and may affect the discount value political actors attach to future costs or benefits. A national leader facing a hostage crisis may find that she is forced to alleviate the short-term harm in order to save the day and soothe her constituents, thereby leaving the amorphous but more serious threat of graver harm for future leaders to deal with. Alternatively, it may be politically impossible for a leader to be seen cooperating with the enemy, even if she thinks that ultimately her country will be better off if she does. This phenomenon is evident on both sides of the conflict. When the leader of a terrorist organization agrees to negotiate, it often causes a backlash and splintering off of some hardliners in the group (e.g., the "Real IRA").[41]

No course of action is costless. As in any other negotiation setting, a decision maker needs to compare the choice to negotiate against her government's best alternative to a negotiated agreement. Depending on the situation, alternatives include actions such as imposing sanctions, sending in a rescue mission, deploying military force, or accepting the status quo. Alternatives, of course, are themselves laden with uncertainty, are susceptible to change and constraints, and may further be complicated by the opposing party's being a nonstate actor (thereby possibly constraining military strikes outside the country's own borders). In addition, exercising a coercive alternative course of action may help to resolve a current immediate crisis, but at the cost of worsening future prospects. Invading Afghanistan in response to Taliban support for Al-Qaeda, rather than negotiating with the Taliban to end that support, may be a case in point.

All these problems—uncertainty, the outcomes of strategic interactions, intervening variables, and available alternatives—are less material when it comes to assessing the risks and benefits of having a *policy* of not negotiating; in fact, long-term implications may be harder to predict or assess than short-term ones. But a fundamental difference between ad hoc decisions and a policy is that decisions are made once an attack has taken place; the purpose of a policy, conversely, is to dissuade terrorists from future attacks. To the extent that a terrorist hostage taking or bombing campaign is motivated by the hope of concessions by the state, that hope—and therefore, further attacks—can be reduced if the terrorists believe that an announced policy precludes the government from making concessions. If, on the other hand, each occasion of possible negotiation is considered separately, with the outcome that the government sometimes negotiates, the terrorists will see a renewed and valuable prospect of gains from repeating the threat.

Committing to a no-negotiation policy in response to terrorist acts requires predicting (a) whether we can truly adhere to our commitment when tested by reality and thus whether this commitment will be considered credible by our citizens and our enemies; (b) whether our commitment will deny, and be seen by the terrorists to deny, the benefits they seek from their threats; and (c) whether the outcome is that terrorists will decease their actions, rather than escalate them, if both (a) and (b) are fulfilled.

Enhancing the credibility of the commitment in the face of short-term incentives to defect might require tying the government's hands in some ways, for instance, through passing a law prohibiting negotiating with terrorists. Given the prevalence of reneging on no-negotiation policies, it is not surprising that we know of no such law. The closest attempt at such a strategy was Law 40 in Colombia, enacted in 1993, which made it a crime to pay a ransom for the safe return of anyone kidnapped. Specific provisions made it illegal for individuals to pay ransom and also provided for the punishment of financial institutions that offered money or insurance for such ransom. (By way of comparison, the American policy with regard to cases in which American citizens are kidnapped abroad is to advise family members on ransom payment, and not to prohibit or stop them from paying.) Assessing the effectiveness of this legal scheme is problematic: while the policy was in place, there was a nearly 20 percent decrease in the number of kidnappings reported.[42] However, this drop may have been due to a decrease in reporting by family members rather than an actual decrease in the number of kidnappings.[43]

Notwithstanding the question of effectiveness, these provisions were subsequently struck down by the Colombian Constitutional Court in November 1993. The court reasoned that the situation placed the kidnapped individual and his family and friends in a "state of necessity" that justified taking action in order to release the victim. The court ruled that a state cannot block an attempt to save the life of the kidnapping victim and "nobody can deny that to employ one's own goods to protect one's life and freedom is a humanitarian action."[44]

Experience, however, shows that even when the government believes that all three conditions will be met if it makes a no-negotiation commitment, it nevertheless often succumbs to short-term incentives to renege on the commitment and negotiate. Despite clear pronouncements about not negotiating, we and our most adamant allies have found ways to make concessions, in the hope that we will nevertheless maintain the benefits of having committed ourselves to a practice of not making concessions.

In the next section, we evaluate the case for departing from a no-negotiation policy in particular instances. Here, however, the question presents itself: If it is nearly impossible to remain faithful to a no-negotiation commitment, why make one? One plausible explanation for the prevalence of commitments so often honored in the breach is a reflection of the strength of the norm against terrorism: governments wish to emphasize the condemnation of terrorism, even if they at times have to capitulate to it. An imperfect comparison may be found in our earlier discussion of the absolute prohibition against torture and the allowance of some narrow breaches in the face of urgent threat. Another possible explanation is the government's catering to domestic constituencies who prefer a tough stance on terrorism; the departure in any particular case must then be excused or justified on the basis of the exigencies of the moment, but the tough ideology remains a presumptive commitment.

On the whole, we believe that maintaining an official policy of not negotiating in response to crisis events is the appropriate strategy for governments facing a repeated threat of terrorism, even if they find they occasionally need to depart from that commitment.

A Case-by-Case Approach
Why is it that all governments facing terrorism have sometimes negotiated with the terrorists?

Terrorists can affect our willingness to uphold a commitment to not negotiate. A domestic audience would be willing, perhaps, to absorb the harm of a current terrorist attack if it believes that a firm stance by the government would prevent future attacks. But this willingness knows limits; if the threat of immediate harm is very grave, the citizens would pressure the government to avert the danger, even if this aversion must entail conceding to the terrorists' demands. A similar dynamic may take place when the concessions demanded by the terrorists seem very small. The greater the imminent threat and the smaller the terrorists' demands, the more the pressure to negotiate increases. When Ted Kaczynski—the Unabomber—offered to cease his deadly attacks on university and airline employees in exchange for the *New York Times* or the *Washington Post* publishing his manifesto, the newspapers willingly accepted the deal and the FBI did not object. Terrorists can thus undermine the credibility of the no-negotiation commitment by making the commitment appear untenable, either by increasing the size of their threat or by reducing the size of the concession they seek in exchange for withdrawing their threat.

Another reason to break the no-negotiation commitment is the lack of available effective alternative courses of action. The larger the negative gap between the alternative options and the immediate danger, the more likely negotiations are. This is why Israel has remained relatively faithful to its policy of not negotiating with terrorists *inside* Israel, but has been more willing to negotiate with hostage takers *outside* Israel, where its ability to resolve the crisis by other means is more limited.

A final reason to negotiate may be that the message of not negotiating adversely affects not only the terrorists but also other relevant audiences within the state: Israeli society is currently debating whether to release a large number of Palestinian militants in exchange for Israeli POW, Gilad Shalit. In response to opponents' cautioning against the potential incentives for future kidnapping of Israeli soldiers by Hamas, supporters of the deal point tothe need to instill in soldiers the faith that their government would do everything in its power to bring them safely back home.

How Should One Negotiate with Terrorists?

If a government does decide to negotiate with a terrorist organization, there are several ways in which it can attempt to minimize the costs of doing so. These devices are used regularly, sometimes successfully and sometimes not. They carry all the familiar risks that accompany secrecy or deception about government policies.

Backchannel and Secret Talks

One way in which parties seek to minimize the costs associated with negotiation is by conducting the discussions as secretly as possible. The classic example of backchannel talks is the Declaration of Principles signed by Israel and the PLO in 1993 after secret talks in Norway. It was the first agreement between Israel and the PLO and surprised many who were not even aware of the existence of talks until very near the declaration-signing ceremony.

Backchannel or covert negotiations are popular because they are viewed as conferring the benefits of negotiations at a much lower cost. The secrecy severs the public ties between the country and the terrorist group, thereby mitigating the concern about conferring legitimacy on the latter. It enables the parties to maintain more control over the process, to exclude potential spoilers, and to engage in a more creative and flexible exploration of possible agreements than negotiating in the public eye would allow.[45]

If negotiation ultimately fails, the clandestine channel offers the parties "plausible deniability" that minimizes the costs of the negotiation process itself and the risk to reputation or political strategy. It may also be easier to renegotiate a secretly reached agreement because neither party has publicly bound itself. If, however, negotiations culminate in a mutually beneficial agreement, the assumption must be that the benefits of such an agreement are sufficiently great to outweigh the costs of having negotiated secretly.

And yet, backchannel talks are not a panacea for all conflicts. The very secrecy that permits the initiation of negotiations may prove problematic in the implementation stage if excluded parties refuse to abide by an agreement reached without their input.[46] Backchannel talks may also suit some on either side of the table by serving as a stalling tactic, keeping parties trapped in a process of negotiation and renegotiation.[47] Obviously, secrecy does not minimize those moral or utilitarian costs that pertain to the actual engagement with terrorists.

Negotiate through a Third Party

Another way to approach negotiations with terrorist organizations is to conduct them through a third party. Third parties may play many roles in negotiations but the practice to which we refer here is the use of third parties as message conveyors and brokers. Such an approach creates an even stronger opportunity for deniability than backchannel talks for a government hesitant to be seen negotiating with a group it has villainized. It also minimizes the risk of granting terrorist organizations legitimacy because the government has, to all appearances, stayed true to its policy of not negotiating—in public impression if not in fact.

Using an intermediary is not without problems. Adding a middleman increases the risk of communication errors and does not eliminate the risk that terrorists will nonetheless be rewarded for their use of violence. Also, middlemen are rarely devoid of self-serving interests, which may not correspond to those of the parties.

Focus on the Details

When negotiations involve broad political and ideological claims they often seem extremely unlikely to succeed. Many of the conflicts between states and nonstate armed groups have been going on for years and are tied to deeply held values. The narratives at this level are ones of autonomy, culture, identity, self-determination, and religious or political persecution—all values that, when in conflict, are not amenable to simple solutions. If the parties resist a broader political dialogue, and yet believe that an agreement to resolve an immediate crisis would be mutually beneficial, they may try to defuse the clash of values by focusing on pragmatic steps to resolve a more immediate, less central, issue. Focusing on isolatable issues rather than narrative not only makes an agreement more likely, but is also less threatening and more palatable to ideologically committed stakeholders.

Most macrogrievances and demands are unlikely to be met by governments, especially when the appearance is that the government is responding to a threat. Nonetheless, there may be specific manifestations of these grievances that can be addressed. By narrowing the focus and detaching a specific issue from the broader narrative, parties may find some common ground for negotiation. This may be especially useful in addressing the expressive goals of terrorists seeking to draw attention to their cause.

The Dubrovka Theater crisis provides a good example. The Chechens who held hostages in the Dubrovka Theater initially agreed to release foreign hostages who came from countries that were not fighting with Chechnya. However, when the Russian negotiators tried to apply the rationale of releasing innocents to push for the release of women and children, the Chechens refused, arguing that Russian soldiers did not recognize this distinction with respect to Chechen women and children.[48] As Dolnik and Pilch point out, there were several expressive elements to the Chechens' demands throughout this crisis: the stated desire for peace, an end to Russian mop-up operations, and an acknowledgment of human rights violations.[49] The Russian government could have focused on any of these issues as ones on which Chechen and Russian interests were aligned. They could have attempted to negotiate specific, pragmatic measures with respect to these narrow questions without implicating the wider issues of regional independence and cultural autonomy, such as a mutual commitment to spare women and children from the conflict. Whether this was possible in the context of the Dubrovka hostage crisis is debatable. Nonetheless, the case illustrates the types of issues that can arise in the midst of an ongoing conflict that may be more amenable to negotiation than the roots of the conflict.

Such solutions are unlikely to be long-term solutions because they do not and cannot address the underlying causes of conflicts. However, in learning to engage and compromise on smaller issues, parties may develop a means of operating that allows them to start tackling bigger issues. Even if negotiations on narrower issues never progress into discussions on the larger issues, they may help defuse tense situations. This, nonetheless, was the rationale behind the 1996 "understanding" between Israel and Lebanon mentioned in chapter 2. The understanding allowed the armed conflict in south Lebanon to continue but attempted to spare civilians from its destructive effects. The three-and-a-half-year regime under the understanding did not end the conflict, nor did it contribute to a peaceful solution later on; however, it did reduce the number of civilian casualties in both Israel and Lebanon—no insignificant achievement.

Separate the Quid from the Quo

Another way in which states attempt to make concessions without appearing to be doing so is separating the quids from the quos.[50] When the quid can be kept secret, separating it from the quo is even more appealing. The removal of missiles from Turkey to resolve the 1961 Cuban missile crisis was successfully kept secret from the public eye, causing a false perception that the Soviets retreated in the face of the steadfastly principled stance taken by the United States.

This strategy has been employed by Israel with the release of prisoners held in Israel in exchange for the return of Israeli hostages or the remains of soldiers held by the Hezbollah armed group. The bodies of soldiers were returned on a certain day, and prisoners were released some time later. Even though the Israeli public understands that there is a quid pro quo here, the government assumes, whether rightly or wrongly, that this type of deal is more palatable than a simultaneous exchange.

Hunt Them Down Afterward

Finally, a government could grant all of the terrorists' immediate demands, including some substantive ones, allow them to escape, and then hunt them down or somehow deny them the benefits of what they were supposedly promised. In earlier work, Philip Heymann noted that such a tactic need not necessarily be limited to "punishing" the terrorists themselves. Instead, it could involve increasing aid to an ally whom the terrorists regard as hostile to them, thereby rendering the final outcome of the terrorists' acts the strengthening of their enemy.[51] The downside of such a strategy is that, to the extent we believe future attackers learn from previous experiences, it runs the risk of driving higher future terrorists' demands for both concessions and guarantees.

Negotiating with Rogue States

While our focus here has been on negotiating with terrorists, the decision of whether or not to negotiate with rogue states is also debated. Without fully addressing this debate, negotiating with states is likely to be more straightforward than negotiating with terrorists, for several reasons. First, there is less concern about bestowing legitimacy on a state, which already has official standing in the international sphere, than with a nonstate actor whose sole recognition may stem from validation by third parties. Second, it is usually easier to tell with whom one should negotiate. Although there may be rival factions within a state, figuring out who has the authority to speak for the state is likely to be simpler than figuring out which nonstate actor among several similarly situated actors has the authority to speak for all. Third, there are clearer international guidelines regarding how to respond to state action, and there are international institutions and mechanisms already in place that may facilitate various economic, political, and military responses. When reacting to nonstate actors, especially those who are not domestically based, there are obviously greater constraints on the possible actions against them, especially those of a military nature. As we explained in chapter 4, governments are more constrained in their use of force against nonstate actors in foreign territories than they are when responding with military force against an aggressor state.

Negotiating to Transform the Relationship

Much of the foregoing has focused on negotiations intended to resolve crises. As we have noted, we believe that in these types of negotiations, there should be a strong presumption against negotiations.

This presumption, however, does not extend to broader negotiations with terrorist organizations that are intended to resolve the conflict altogether or transform the relationship into a more manageable one. Here we agree with Paul Wilkinson, who notes that "there is a crucial difference between concessions made to terrorists when they are conducting a bombing campaign or holding hostages at gunpoint and concessions made in the context of a peace process designed to bring a permanent end to violence."[52]

Transformative negotiations provide a disincentive for the terrorist organization to continue its campaign of violence that would win them a seat at the table as well. It would be hard for other groups to replicate a prolonged campaign of violence. And the foreseeable benefits of more peaceful relations are much higher than in the case of a single event such as hostage-taking.

In peace negotiations, the relevant parties are presumably all prepared to make concessions in order to achieve a state of affairs preferable to continued conflict. Furthermore, there are generally more issues on the table when the broader relationship is discussed and therefore more dimensions along which to negotiate and bargain. This may help obscure the extent to which concessions are made by the government. Despite any concessions being made in response to a terrorist campaign, the potential benefits of resolving the conflict altogether will almost always outweigh the risks of inviting other aggrieved parties to launch terrorist campaigns to further their own goals. At the very least, we believe that in contrast to the presumption against negotiating with terrorists over crisis situations, there should be a presumption in favor of negotiating about the terms of an enduring peace, or at least, a significant reduction in terrorism.

In October 2008, General Petraeus endorsed a policy of talking with less extreme Taliban members.[53] Although officials emphasized this would not include Taliban leadership, the approach nonetheless marked a reversal from previous policy. The recent willingness to engage in negotiations was part of a general overhaul of American strategy in Afghanistan in response to an increase in violence and a general realization that the problem was not solvable by the military alone.[54] In fact, experts agree that many of the current terrorist threats cannot, in the long term, be solved by military action alone.[55]

Conclusion

Whether and in what situations to negotiate with terrorists necessarily requires a complicated and uncertain cost-benefit analysis; the question cannot be answered by any deontological command never to negotiate with terrorists. There are in fact possible benefits and potential costs of both negotiating and refusing to negotiate. Some benefits and some costs are short-term; some, long-term. Some are relatively certain; others, particularly the long-term, more speculative. The most straightforward case for negotiation is when the likely benefits from negotiating are very great and quite certain and the likely costs are low and speculative.

When the threat is one that can easily and cheaply be recreated by terrorists, there is a strong case to be made for refusing to negotiate. With no shortage of targets, the magnitude and likelihood of the threat are sufficiently grave, even when compared with the great risks of attempting to resolve the crisis by coercive means. Historical data reaffirms the concern that crisis negotiations have often bred more terrorist attacks. This has been the logic behind the 1976 Israeli raid on Entebbe to rescue Israeli and Jewish hostages kidnapped on an Air France flight, or the United States' refusal to negotiate the release of the hijacked cruise ship *Achille Lauro*. And it is for these reasons that we recommend that governments announce and maintain a policy against negotiating with terrorists in such cases, signaling to the terrorists the futility of attacks as means of extracting concessions.

A stated policy, however, offers only a strong presumption against negotiations, not an absolute stance. This must be evident from the frequency of exceptions made even by those explicitly committed to a no-negotiation policy such as the United States and Israel. If the number of hostages at risk is extremely large or the danger to lives is otherwise magnified, the benefit of negotiation grows; the same is true if there is a real risk that refusing to negotiate even in an ordinary case may lead the terrorist to greatly increase his threat in the future. Similarly, if the concession demanded—the short-term cost—is trivial and the long-term cost of negotiation is speculative (e.g., where the threat cannot be easily repeated by these or other terrorists), negotiation to save the lives of those immediately in danger is warranted. The availability of means to reduce the costs of negotiations (such as negotiating secretly or through intermediaries) further impacts the cost-benefit analysis, as do feasible and effective alternatives to resolving the crisis.

Our stance with regard to a presumptive commitment not to negotiate does not extend to broader negotiations with terrorist organizations that are intended to resolve the conflict altogether or transform the relationship into a more manageable one. In these cases, our presumption is reversed, in favor of negotiations. The long-term cost-benefit ratio shifts radically when transformative negotiations are at stake: negotiation is less likely to encourage others from embarking on future systematic campaigns of terrorism; mounting an enduring campaign of terrorism is simply not easily repeatable. The long-term payoffs of ending the campaign, although necessarily speculative, are likely to be greater than the immediate benefits of obtaining the release of particular hostages or ending a single crisis. And the endurance of the campaign up to that point proves that effective alternatives to negotiations have not yet been found.

8

The Case for Sustained Efforts to Reduce Moral Support for Terrorism

Introduction

Over the past nine years, the United States has broadened its strategy for combating Al-Qaeda and other groups targeting civilians from the United States or its allies. During the early years after September 11, 2001, periodic strategy statements from the president, the Department of Defense, and the Joint Chiefs of Staff focused on targeting a somewhat organized group of terrorists making war on the United States. Having no desire to bargain with them, the government's strategy was to incapacitate them by detention or killing. According to its architects, that strategy required new forms of intelligence gathering, including new types of electronic surveillance and highly coercive interrogation; new forms of seizure and detention; and military action against havens such as Afghanistan and, our leaders may have thought, Iraq. To a lesser extent, the plan involved keeping terrorists away from their targets and, to a still lesser extent, keeping them from the resources needed for their weapons of destruction. We couldn't do these things solely by ourselves, so cooperation among allied intelligence and military agencies was critical.

In more recent years, the strategy, or at least the government's way of pursuing it, has grown more sophisticated and nuanced along several dimensions. Killing and detaining terrorists did not adequately cover the range of steps we could take to weaken those determined to harm us. Beyond incapacitating, our objectives now include denying terrorists whatever they need for well-organized attacks. Better border control as well as control over global money transfers are important examples. The Department of Defense has shifted its own policies accordingly, seeking measures of success beyond body and prisoner counts.

However, time has also shown that the model of terrorist motivation, organization, and planning, which informed even the more sophisticated versions of our efforts to weaken terrorist organizations is inadequate. It no longer seems that our danger is concentrated in a single, however loosely, organized group with whom we are engaged in struggle. Most experts now believe that in addition to the hierarchical, relatively small and still very dangerous organization of Al-Qaeda there are bands of followers, outside the formal structure of Al-Qaeda, who are motivated by feelings and beliefs widely shared among millions—perhaps tens of millions—of Muslims worldwide. The independence of the attacks in Madrid (2004), London (2005), and Mumbai (2008) from Al-Qaeda control or direction is a vivid demonstration. Other examples are the 2006 foiled airline terror plot in London, the November 2009 shooting at Fort Hood, and the failed bombing attempt of a Northwest airliner on route to Detroit a month later, on Christmas Day.

The fact is, we cannot greatly increase our safety without greatly decreasing the enthusiasm among large numbers of Muslims for attacking our allies and us. For an idea of the scope of the problem we face, consider a Gallup poll that found that 7 percent of Muslims worldwide believe that the 9/11 attacks were "completely" justified. That fraction, though small, translates into about ninety-one million people on the face of the planet. This suggests a very serious risk, even if only 10 percent of this group constitutes potential recruits for activities ranging from encouraging terrorism through supporting it materially to joining terrorist groups. The point has not been lost on the Obama administration. President Obama addressed these issues in early June 2009 when, speaking in Cairo, he called for "a new beginning between the United States and Muslims around the world; one based upon mutual interest and mutual respect,"[1] starting with the elimination of the negative stereotypes that each side has developed of the other.

The Limits of Coercion

A recent Rand study on how terrorist groups end, for example, recommends that we focus on making policing approaches to counterterrorism more effective, and resort to military action only for special cases of large, densely concentrated terrorist organizations.[2] Ultimately, however, neither a policing nor a military strategy can succeed using coercion alone. As President Obama's trip to Cairo suggested, ending the threat of Islamic terrorism will require still bolder changes in our strategy.

Terrorist movements, if fueled by hatred and fear, have the capacity to more than replace their losses. And their growth potential cannot be eliminated by deterrence or incapacitation with the means realistically available to us. Since 2001 our military leaders have come to recognize the inherent limits to a strategy reliant wholly on power and coercion. As Secretary of Defense Rumsfeld famously noted in a question to his senior aides in October 2003, the actions of our enemies in response to our efforts could increase the pool of terrorists by more than our coercive efforts can reduce it. This is true at least within the limits that we are prepared to accept, as a nation, on our ruthlessness toward suspects, and on our use of group sanctions.

Terrorists can hide among the general population, but it would be both wrong and counterproductive to attack or punish the innocent along with the guilty. Any severe sanction not accompanied by proof of individual guilt creates a sense of injustice that encourages our enemies and discourages our friends. Notions of collective guilt achieve the same results. Yet there are limits to our hopes to identify and separate terrorists for detention or killing.

Even if we were to invade and occupy, we would need Soviet-like terrorizing methods to pick out the active radicals in a largely unfriendly population. Western nations are at a great disadvantage in gathering the intelligence necessary to identify those with hostile intent who are outside our borders, our languages, and our cultures. Ruthlessness in the use of group sanctions would, in all probability, prove too unpalatable at home to be maintained for a sustained period; shortening our staying power by diminishing support on the home front would drastically reduce the deterrence we seek. The effort to gain the cooperation of Muslim states has not proved promising either. When major governments on which we rely heavily, like Pakistan and Saudi Arabia, cannot unleash their security forces without the danger of domestic rebellion, they are likely to be of questionable help in confronting terrorists.

Changing Beliefs about Justifications for Terrorism

The limits of coercion mean that an overall strategy for countering terrorism must complement policing and military force with noncoercive approaches that make military and police action more effective and less necessary to begin with, and that do what strictly coercive approaches cannot. A promising candidate for such an approach is reducing the moral support for terrorism among key groups—that is, reducing those expressions of approval and encouragement that create the social environment for violence against civilians from the United States and its allies—even where those approving of terrorist actions never allow their approval to become active cooperation or material support.

Both highly suggestive statistical evidence and highly plausible causal relationships support this emphasis on the importance of relatively passive supports for terrorism. An article in the September 18, 2009, issue of the journal *Science* by Krueger and Maleckova describes the result of relating (1) the attitudes in nineteen Middle Eastern and North African (MENA) countries toward leaders of nine (largely Western) states to (2) the number of terrorist attacks on each Western state by residents of those nineteen countries.[3] A 20 percent increase in the disapproval rate of a country's leaders was associated with more than an 80 percent increase in the number of terrorist attacks. The authors offer two explanations: that the correlation reflects the impact of greater material and moral encouragement for active terrorists; or that the difference in attitudes affects the number willing to become active terrorists themselves. Thus, a campaign to reduce moral support for terrorism would make it harder for terrorist groups to recruit, gain financing, and carry out operations. What the authors do not consider is that it could also make it easier for the United States and its allies to launch military and police operations to target terrorist groups and to gain the cooperation of local governments to combat terrorism.

It seems highly likely, if not certain, that the moral support and aid of critical reference groups—including family, friends, and neighbors— makes a big difference in the ability of politically minded terrorist leaders to recruit the people they need to carry out or assist in attacks that are very dangerous—if not suicidal—to their perpetrators as well as to their targets. Anecdotal evidence of this is very strong; so are the obvious inferences from known recruiting practices. A person who feels humiliated can far more easily be tempted to terrorism if a show of courage would make him or her heroic to family, friends, and neighbors. With a little less guesswork, one can simply note that seeking the respect of those closest to us is an immensely powerful, universal motivation. Lowering moral support for terrorism could thus limit the supply of terrorists.

On the enforcement side, denying havens where terrorist groups can safely plan, recruit, train, equip, and communicate obviously hinders terrorist activity. Osama Bin Laden was able to plan and organize a series of attacks safely in Afghanistan and may now be able to do the same safely in the tribal areas of Pakistan. But denying such havens for anti-Western terrorists can ultimately be accomplished—at tolerable moral, military, and financial costs—only by local governments. And a local government, no matter how undemocratic, cannot safely ignore the wishes of very large portions of its population. Thus, lowering popular support for terrorists' efforts to kill Western civilians is necessary for the United States in order to gain effective cooperation from governments where terrorists operate.

Historically, there is much evidence that terrorist movements have ended and terrorist groups dissolved when they lost the backing of a sizeable sympathetic population. That was true in Italy with the Red Brigades, in Northern Ireland with the IRA, in Germany with the Red Army Faction, and elsewhere. A Rand study on the end of terrorist groups, released in July 2008, confirmed the importance of this factor. When widespread support has been eroded, the terrorists' breeding grounds, the community in which they have found the rewards of approval and leadership, disappears. Losing this lifeline also creates a drastically higher risk of penetration by the national security forces, lower access to needed forms of help, including the minimal one of silence, and the burdens of finding new methods of recruitment and operation to replace familiar methods now made cumbersome or risky.

What We Know about Those Who Support Terrorism

A public diplomacy campaign to reduce moral support for terrorism inevitably begins with our own hypotheses about what is generating public support for Islamic terrorism. An effective public diplomacy campaign is one that specifically sets out to target and weaken those attitudes and beliefs that bring about the hostility of large numbers of the Muslim world toward the United States.

Although there are many proffered explanations for Muslim hostility toward the West, the literature gives us ten principle reasons or hypotheses about Muslim beliefs. We will describe those ten and determine whether their assumptions about what Muslims believe about the United States are supported or unsupported by the most recent polls. Even that is not probing deeply enough; hostility toward the United States and its allies may be necessary but is not sufficient for providing a fruitful ground for terrorism. We must focus separately on those beliefs that are most closely associated with actual moral encouragement and assistance for terrorism, not just vague or diffuse hostility toward the United States.

The Ten Possible Sources of Hostility

One: Our Values   In the months following 9/11, many claimed that the perpetrators of the attacks and those who supported them hated Americans for our freedoms and our way of life. Indeed, on September 20, 2001, in his address to a joint session of Congress, speaking to the entire nation, President Bush called the 9/11 attackers "enemies of freedom."[4] There was a sense that Islamic extremists hated America for its core values: democracy, personal freedoms, including the freedom of religion and expression, the central role that liberty and autonomy of action play in our society, and our different (and in the eyes of supporters of terrorism, immoral) culture that comfortably tolerates practices that would be forbidden in strict Islamic societies.

The polls are inconclusive on this point. As of 2008, in at least three Muslim countries polled—Egypt, Indonesia, and Pakistan—the majorities have unfavorable views of American culture.[5] A 2007 Pew Research Center survey, conducted in eight predominantly Muslim countries, found that fewer than 30 percent of respondents rated America favorably, and majorities in most predominantly Muslim countries polled believe that "people in Western countries" are selfish, arrogant, violent, greedy, and immoral.[6] The results as to favorability were much the same in Pew's 2010 poll (Pew Research Center, Global Attitudes Project, June 2010). This is reinforced by a recent Gallup poll, which found that what

Muslims least admire about the West is what they perceive as moral decay and a breakdown of traditional values.[7] Unsurprisingly then, majorities in Egypt, Indonesia, Pakistan, and Morocco support the Al-Qaeda goal of "keep[ing] Western values out of Islamic countries."[8] Nonetheless, attitudes toward our technological drive and our political system are very different. What Muslims around the world say they admire most about the West is its technology and democracy, including political freedoms such as freedom of speech.[9]

The idea that Muslims dislike the United States for our values is an unduly broad, if not an entirely unsupported, statement. While the polls indicate that Muslim majorities have an unfavorable view of American culture and morality,[10] this animosity is not connected to the American political system of democracy or the freedoms and political liberties that Americans enjoy. To the contrary, the "politically radicalized" (see note 9 of this chapter) members of the Muslim world are more concerned with promoting democratic ideals than are their moderate counterparts, perhaps in part because they can and will win elections.[11]

Two: U.S. Military Imperialism Majorities in all six predominantly Muslim nations surveyed by Pew in 2010 are worried about a military threat from the United States.[12] A classified MI5 internal research document, leaked to the media in 2008, concluded that the "the most pressing current threat is from Islamist extremist groups who justify the use of violence 'in defense of Islam.'"[13] A World Public Opinion poll strongly supports the assumption that perceived U.S. military imperialism and aggression are a significant source of Muslim hostility. The recent poll showed that large majorities in Egypt, Indonesia, Pakistan, and Morocco support Al-Qaeda's goal of pushing the United States "to remove its bases and its military forces from all Islamic countries."[14] Furthermore, there is widespread disapproval of our military presence even when the government (such as Saudi Arabia) has requested the assistance of U.S. forces.[15] Indeed, thirteen of fifteen respondents to a 2006 Pew survey believed that the American military presence in Iraq was "an equal or greater danger to stability in the Middle East than the regime of Iranian president Mahmoud Ahmadinejad."[16]

According to Pew's June 2010 poll results, fewer than 20 percent of the people in Pakistan, Egypt, and Turkey "believe the U.S. considers their interest" or "favor the U.S.-led efforts to flight terrorism."

Three: Our Contempt for and Disrespect of Islam   The polls sustain the idea that there is a strong belief throughout the Muslim world that the United States is disrespectful toward Islam and, as will be discussed, that the United States is attempting to undermine Islamic unity and spread Christianity.

A recent World Public Opinion poll found that, on average, 77 percent of respondents in the Muslim countries polled said the United States was disrespectful toward the Islamic world, and substantial numbers believe that the United States *purposely* tries to humiliate the Islamic world.[17] Furthermore, only 12 percent of the politically radicalized associate "respecting Islamic values" with Western nations, while "disrespect for Islam" contributes greatly to their resentment of the West.[18]

Four: Our Religious Imperialism   Related to the idea that the West is disrespectful of Islam lies the hypothesis that the Muslim world thinks that the United States is trying to spread Christianity into Muslim areas. This hypothesis is at least somewhat borne out by the polls. Large majorities in six predominantly Muslim countries believe that our goal is to "to spread Christianity in the Middle East."[19]

Five: U.S. Cultural Imperialism   The polls also demonstrate that a substantial number of Muslims believe that the United States is attempting to impose its beliefs and policies on the Islamic world.[20] Western "cultural saturation" is one of the top reasons for resentment against the United States, particularly among the politically radicalized Muslim population.[21]

Six: Our Position in the Arab-Israeli Conflict   The polls endorse the supposition that the United States' role in the Arab-Israeli conflict is a major source of Muslim hostility. Majorities in Egypt, Morocco, the Palestinian territories, Jordan, Turkey, and a modest majority in Pakistan all believe that the United States favors the expansion of Israel's national territory.[22] This belief leads, in all likelihood, to the broad support that majorities in Egypt, Indonesia, Pakistan, and Morocco report for Al-Qaeda's goal of "push[ing] the United States to stop favoring Israel in its conflict with the Palestinians." This set of beliefs seems to be a significant source of Muslim hostility.[23]

Seven: Our Abuse of Power   The polls demonstrate that, in at least four predominantly Muslim countries, majorities believe that the United States has extraordinary power over world events.[24] Moreover, significant numbers believe that their own government adjusts its policies at least some or much of the time out of fear of the United States.[25] Furthermore, substantial majorities see the United States as hypocritically failing to abide by international law while pressuring other countries to do so.[26] Given the pervasive belief that the United States seeks "to weaken and divide the Islamic world," the polls support the assumption that a sizeable number of Muslims believe the United States is illegitimately wielding its power.[27]

Eight: U.S. Economic Imperialism   The polls show that fear of economic imperialism is present and intense in the Muslim world. Huge majorities of those polled in predominately Muslim countries believe that the United States wants to "maintain control over the oil resources of the Middle East."[28] Indeed, majorities in Muslim nations and some Western European nations view the entire war on terrorism as just "an effort to control Mideast oil or dominate the world."[29]

Nine: Our Support for Unpopular Governments in Predominately Muslim Countries   American support for the unpopular and repressive regimes in Saudi Arabia, Egypt, Jordan, and Pakistan may or may not be an important reason for Muslim hostility and serve to reinforce the belief that such governments are illegitimate. On the one hand, in a recent poll, pluralities or majorities in those particular countries responded that they regard their government as legitimate. Still, substantial numbers oppose U.S. military aid to countries like Jordan and Saudi Arabia.[30] Approximately 40 to 50 percent of those polled in each country agreed with the Al-Qaeda goal of getting the United States to stop supporting Egypt, Saudi Arabia, and Jordan.[31]

Ten: Disagreements about Critical Facts, Such as Who Carried Out the 9/11 Attacks   The polls demonstrate that there is significant disagreement between the United States and the Muslim world as to who was responsible for the events of 9/11. The conviction that Al-Qaeda carried out the 9/11 attacks has been a driving force of U.S. and Western foreign policy for the past eight years. However, large majorities in the Muslim world do not believe that Al-Qaeda perpetrated 9/11,[32] and majorities in numerous predominantly Muslim countries believe that Arabs did not carry out the attacks at all.[33] Perhaps most startlingly significant number of respondents believe that the United States itself carried out the 9/11 attacks.[34]

Targeting the Most Dangerous Beliefs

Although long-term U.S. public diplomacy should strive to address all or at least most of those beliefs that spawn deep hostility within the Muslim world, our biggest and most immediate concern must be those beliefs that are most closely associated with actual moral support for terrorism, not just hostility toward the United States. Here the most relevant data identify the convictions and attitudes that distinguish from the general (often hostile) population those who believe in the desirability of terrorist attacks.

In *Who Speaks for Islam?: What a Billion Muslims Really Think*, a book based on a seven-year-long Gallup poll study, the authors found that the two beliefs most closely associated with the 7 percent of respondents who believed that 9/11 was completely justified[35] are (1) that the West is denying respect to and is responsible for the humiliation of Islam,[36] and (2) that Islam's territory and its culture are under aggressive attack from the West and must be defended.[37] A fear of Western political control and domination, in all its forms, and a sense of lacking self-determination feed into the politically radicalized group's sense of powerlessness.[38] Moreover, the politically radicalized individuals are significantly more likely to believe that Western societies do not "show any concern for better coexistence with the Arab-Muslim world."[39] Familiar social and economic measures of well-being do *not* distinguish between the groups on these points. Nor does religious piety.

In some ways, this is good news. It appears that distaste for Western culture and values do not lie at the heart of Muslim anger; distaste for real or perceived disrespect for Islam and attempts at cultural and political domination do.[40] Therefore, to reduce moral support for terrorism, we need not (nor should we) attempt to change ourselves, but we will have to decide what behaviors that convey threat or disrespect we are willing to change in order to address those two most dangerous beliefs.

Taking overt steps that demonstrate a respect for Islam may also be an easier task than confronting the desire of the politically radicalized/marginalized for "concrete changes in certain aspects of foreign policy."[41]

Although we may not be able to, and should not, change all of the factors that incite Muslim hostility, designing a public diplomacy campaign with an accurate picture of the views of the Muslim world is a start. There is a second step. Besides weakening views of the United States that can lead to public support for terrorism, we must also seek to build up preexisting objections to terrorism and its target of innocent civilians. Human sympathy for other people and cultural and religious objections to killing civilians are at least two factors that inhibit support for terrorism. The polls show that they are about as prevalent in the Muslim population as in any other.

The Prospects for a Successful Strategy to Reduce Moral Support for Terrorism

The Doubts

Before we begin to suggest how we ought to go about reducing moral support for terrorism among crucial reference groups, there is the lingering question of whether it is realistic to hope to do so—whether any effort on our part stands a true chance of success. Trying to reduce terrorism by a campaign to reduce popular support for it depends, implicitly, on two assumptions, either of which could be wrong.

First, the United States may lack the capacity to change the relevant root beliefs held by large numbers in Muslim countries by any material degree, as they may not be subject to argument and evidence. They may be deeply grounded in the sociology of group membership or the psychology based in the individual's—or a community's—history. Much literature in social psychology gives reason to doubt that changing beliefs is an effective way to change behavior, positing that causation runs the other direction. President Obama's announced exchange programs and working partnerships are consistent with such social theories. Even if the convictions underlying hostility are generally subject to change by arguments, the targeted audiences may have a distrust-based immunity to *our* efforts to change them. Or else, the price of reduced moral support may be one we are unprepared to pay, such as the termination or radical modification of valued relationships with allies like Israel or Egypt.

The second, more subtle, assumption in doubt is that, in light of the vast numbers involved, a successful campaign could lower support enough to matter. A stunningly successful campaign might cut down to half or even a quarter the number of people now radical enough to be firmly convinced that September 11 was completely justified. But the people it would least affect would in all likelihood be the most angry and suspicious to begin with. Even a wildly successful program—eliminating the moral support for terrorism of almost 90 percent of those now enthusiastic about the 9/11 attacks—would leave more than nine million very radical people with a deep hatred for the United States and the West. Not all would be prime recruits for active terrorism, but even if 10 percent were, we would still be facing almost a million of the hardest-core prospects for terrorism. The extreme danger from those might be much the same as the danger we now face.

Factors Supporting the Possibility of Success

The Reasons for Hope   As to the second concern—that any number we reach may be too small to matter—note that we may not need to accomplish the Herculean task of cutting the population of active or potential terrorists to a number that cannot pose a threat. A condition of successful terror operations might be the existence of a community in which a very high percentage of people encourage and protect his or her group. A loss of the allegiance of that high percentage would both aid local government policing operations against terrorists and make it easier for the United States to secure cooperation from local governments. And the potential gains from success make even a very uncertain undertaking worth trying.

To address the other troublesome possibility—that we may not be able to change greatly the beliefs of any sizeable part of the audience we address—note that we may not need to "greatly" change beliefs. Even if we gain only enough credibility to raise new doubts about the presently accepted justifications for killing civilians, that may be enough if many among the 7 percent are already skeptical of these same justifications. Additional doubts may be enough to deny moral backing for an activity (terrorism) that is very costly to the population in terms of their reputation abroad, safety from retaliatory steps, and for an investment in local economies.

The evidence, historical and contemporary, suggests that affinity with and encouragement for terrorism can be reduced. According to the Pew Global Attitudes Project, during the period 2002–2007 the proportion of people believing that terrorism against civilians was justified in defense of Islam fell from 74 percent to 34 percent in Lebanon, from 33 percent to 9 percent in Pakistan, and from 43 percent to 20 percent in Jordan. The changes are real, although they may be largely motivated by dismay at terrorist attacks within these countries themselves. Furthermore, the most recent polls reveal that there is a growing perception, in at least some countries, that attacks on civilians are simply an ineffective way to "change the situation," "as a tactic in a conflict."[42] Hence, opinions about terrorism are not as rigid as we are prone to suppose.

Nor are Muslim radicals exempt from this trend. More recently, many former Al-Qaeda mentors, affiliates, and supporters—people who often still share much of Al-Qaeda's radical interpretation of Islam—have begun to denounce the group.

Around the sixth anniversary of 9/11, Sheikh Salman al Oudeh, a father of the awakening of fundamentalist Islam that swept Saudi Arabia during the 1980s, delivered a harsh rebuke: "My brother Osama, how much blood has been spilt? How many innocent people, children, elderly, and women have been killed . . . in the name of Al Qaeda? Will you be happy to meet God Almighty carrying the burden of these hundreds of thousands or millions [of victims] on your back?" Sayyid Imam al Sharif, Ayman al-Zawahiri's ideological mentor, tendered a similar condemnation. In most cases, such denunciations encompass all attacks on civilians, not just those that kill Muslims.[43]

These shifts make this a promising time to launch a new campaign to reduce moral support for terrorism in the Muslim world; the momentum is against Al-Qaeda. Western governments cannot claim credit for this. Declining support for terrorism in the Muslim world likely reflects terrorists' missteps, more than successful U.S. efforts. Public opinion has shifted against terrorism most dramatically in countries that have experienced terrorist attacks themselves; Al-Qaeda's disregard for Muslim lives in Jordan, Iraq, Indonesia, and even London has cost the group much goodwill. Still, there are at least three reasons to think that a U.S.

campaign to reduce moral support for terrorism can make an additional, useful difference.

The Historical Analogies   Experiences outside the Muslim world suggest that governmental and private actions can reduce moral support for terrorism—and that such actions can facilitate counterterrorism. Consider terrorism in Greece and Ireland. For decades the Greek government was unable to crack down on leftwing terrorists groups like November 17. Such groups commanded wide popular sympathy, and the memory of military dictatorship meant that many Greeks worried more about broader counterterrorism powers for the government than about the dangers of terrorist groups. But public and government attitudes began to change after the murder of a British defense attaché in June 2000, a publicity campaign led by his widow, and growing concerns that the country's reputation as soft on terrorism would undermine the 2004 Olympic Games. International pressure combined with dwindling domestic sympathy for terrorism translated into far more aggressive and effective counterterrorism campaigns.

For decades, too, the Irish American community helped perpetuate IRA-sponsored terrorism in the British Isles, providing money, weapons, and political support in the U.S. political arena. The widespread perception among Irish Americans that the British were backing a discriminatory Protestant government made it hard for either the U.S. or British government to fight the IRA and its American supporters. The Irish cause was viewed as basically legitimate. Over time, however, U.S. public support for the IRA began to decline. Thanks in part to a vigorous British campaign, Irish Americans became more aware of IRA excesses. Just as reports and images of British overreactions harmed the government's cause, so too did opposite campaigns undermine the IRA's popular image. Meanwhile, the British government gained credibility as an honest broker that desired an equitable solution to the conflict, rather than being seen as merely a Protestant partisan.

Summary   Both history and recent events suggest we may be capable of eliminating widespread moral support for terrorism—support based on justifications for killing civilians that have convinced the credulous for years but ultimately failed to maintain their grasp. If many in the 7 percent most supportive of 9/11 are already growing skeptical of these fragile justifications, our task may be feasible. The United States has unnecessarily created a fertile ground for terrorism until now. The invasion of Iraq, furor over detentions at Abu Ghraib and Guantanamo, apparent hypocrisy in our promotion of democracy and the rule of law, and inflammatory rhetoric from U.S. leaders have created ample fodder for terrorist persuasion. Nor has the United States had a plausible plan to engage popular support; it has had no well-considered plan at all. So, at a minimum, the United States is working from a favorable baseline as it tries to achieve what has been too long ignored.

Moreover, the recent denunciations of Al-Qaeda from extremist opinion leaders show that moral support for terrorism can dissipate without solving the most intractable underlying grievances. Salman al Oudeh and Imam al Sharif remain committed to rigid interpretations of Islam. They believe that jihad in defense of Islam is a valid justification for violence. And they support attacks against occupying forces in Iraq and the Palestinian territories. Even so, they have come out against attacks on U.S. civilians and others. Therefore, the United States can focus narrowly on the beliefs and attitudes that it seeks to change—on the specific beliefs that justify lethal attacks on civilians.

The Need for a New Platform and a New Strategy for Relations between Two Often Hostile Cultures

A New Organization and Its Responsibility

If we are right about the importance of even tacit moral support for terrorism, if the polls accurately reveal its causes, and if there is a real possibility of successfully and meaningfully reducing that support, then we should set to that task at once. Surprisingly, the remedy starts with an organizational change. Republican presidential candidate Senator John McCain stated in June 2007:

Across the political spectrum, Americans agree that the war on terror is not just a military struggle, but a battle of ideas. From left to right, Americans agree that our efforts to communicate our message are ineffectual, especially compared to the anti-American information operations of much of the Arab media, Al-Qaeda, and radical Islamists.

Yet if we are all in such firm agreement about the gravity of the problem, why do we have so few ideas about how to solve it? Although there are many facets in the struggle of ideas against violent Islamic extremism, there is one critical step we can take right now to improve our position. If elected president, I would establish a single, independent agency responsible for all of America's public diplomacy. And that agency would report directly to the President.[44]

We would not include all of America's public diplomacy in a new agency; but we believe that only a new organization, whose sole mission is to better the relationship between the West and the people of Islam, can be trusted with the task of finding ways to reduce hostility between our two cultures. That was the history of our Cold War efforts for decades until 1999 when the United States Information Agency (USIA) was integrated into the State Department—a move that Senator McCain described as "unilateral disarmament in the struggle of ideas."

Like the old USIA, the new agency should report to the president through the National Security Council apparatus. It should be unencumbered, however, by the demands of routine diplomatic and national security needs, which should remain for the exclusive control of the Department of State, the Department of Defense, and our other foreign policy agencies. This new agency should speak to a broad swath of the Islamic world, not just to the citizens of any single nation. It should have a voice in governmental decisions separate from the voices of the secretary of state or defense, with a far longer time horizon in mind. Its responsibilities will go well beyond forming relations with other states; its charge will be to create dialogue between cultures. That was the pattern throughout the Cold War during which USIA managed the Voice of America and the Fulbright-Hays Act.

The concerns of the new organization would include the Islamic diaspora in the United States and Western Europe as well as nations with Islamic populations in North Africa, the Middle East, and South Asia.

Learning from the Past

The last time the United States faced a public diplomacy challenge of the present magnitude was the Cold War. As a result, some have proposed that the Cold War be used as a model for combating moral support for terrorism.[45] Although there are clear and crucial differences between the Cold War and the War on Terrorism,[46] there may be some useful lessons we can extract from Cold War public diplomacy in our attempt to design an effective campaign.

Cold War public diplomacy sought "to create qualitatively and visibly positive changes toward the end of fostering understanding and support for U.S. foreign policy initiatives."[47] It consisted primarily of two approaches: efforts at disseminating information and the creation of programs fostering engagement with the people of the Soviet Union and its allies.[48]

The international radio stations Voice of America (VOA)[49] and Radio Free Europe/Radio Liberty (RFE/RL)[50] were at the forefront of the information war conducted by the United States during those years.[51] Although these radio stations were able to successfully avert Soviet blocking technology and reach their target audiences, to this day it remains unclear if successful dissemination of information actually translated into positive changes in attitude among the Soviet population.[52]

Informational public diplomacy faced the initial challenge of deciding what approach American efforts at communication should take. Should radio stations and print magazines be charged with presenting unbiased, yet positive, information about American life and news, or should they engage in aggressive propaganda that some might label manipulation?[53] John Robert Kelley claims that while radio stations such as VOA had a self-stated mission to present the objective truth,[54] both approaches to information campaigns survived and were utilized during the Cold War.[55]

The people-to-people engagement side of Cold War public diplomacy consisted of efforts to "foster 'mutual understanding . . . through international educational and training programs.'"[56] To this end, the United States implemented cultural exchange programs, traveling exhibits,[57] and student exchange programs such as the Fulbright Scholarship.[58] While the frequency of such exchanges and the longevity of the cultural exchange program may suggest success, the absence of reliable statistical data regarding attitudinal changes of participants renders a conclusive assessment of success impossible.[59]

Because of the lack of reliable data we will probably never know the extent of the impact that America's public diplomacy efforts had on the Cold War. Still, we can extract some lessons from that era that may be useful in formulating a post-9/11 public diplomacy campaign. First, the informational side of Cold War public diplomacy was at its best "when prizing credibility and transparency over subliminal persuasion and manipulation,"[60] a fact demonstrated, in part, by VOA's success.[61] In the early days of the Cold War, when the United States used a crude form of propaganda that dramatically slanted the American image, target audiences were at best "unimpressed and at worst offended."[62] Once VOA started reporting American news, both good and bad, it built up credibility and legitimacy with the already skeptical Soviet audience.[63] This is an important lesson of Cold War diplomacy that should shape our approach to the very suspicious audiences for post-9/11 public diplomacy.[64]

Second, the Cold War taught us that adopting such an approach is easiest when there are clear institutional responsibilities and a precisely defined mission shared by the key architects of public diplomacy.[65] During the Cold War, disputes about the proper approach to public diplomacy and the lack of a unified vision among the various agencies and organizations engaged in public diplomacy created friction that compromised effectiveness.[66] Bureaucratic confusion and the lack of transparent institutional duties, problems exacerbated by the State Department and Broadcasting Board of Governors' absorption of USIA,[67] must not be allowed to stifle progress toward an effective public diplomacy strategy.[68]

Finally, throughout the Cold War, when the president and executive branch took an interest in, and made a firm commitment to, public diplomacy, our strategic communication efforts greater success won.[69] The Obama administration must make public diplomacy a priority for it to have a chance at success. This is true not only for the obvious reasons of funding and resources, but also because the executive, as the governmental actor in charge of foreign relations, must be the one defining the public diplomacy approach, instructing those agencies that deal in public diplomacy, and ensuring coherence among the programs of multiple agencies.[70]

We should keep these three broad lessons from the Cold War in mind as we design a post-9/11 public diplomacy campaign.

The Limits of Efforts to Deny Moral Support to Terrorists

The new organization and the American public must understand and openly articulate the parts of our policy and of our national commitments that are not subject to modification in the hope of reducing whatever moral support a terrorist group enjoys. We should not and will not change our basic values to improve relations with those who question our values. We cannot denounce free speech because it offends listeners' or spectators' feelings, as in the case of the publication of cartoons of the prophet Mohammed in the Danish newspaper *Jyllands-Posten* in September 2005. We should not abandon some allies for the support of others who hate them or we will find we are not trusted as an ally. Our commitment to India and Israel cannot be sacrificed although each is highly unpopular with tens of millions of Muslims. We cannot leave ourselves undefended in the hope that enough goodwill can be generated quickly enough to make defense unnecessary. We will have to fight where important interests are threatened as in Pakistan, and we will have to guard our borders assiduously even when this gives offense.

But what is to be done within those broad boundaries involves a multitude of choices among a wide variety of possibilities—choices that will have to be made with advice from the new institution, and with strong support from the president.

Identifying the Most Important Audiences for Our Efforts
Whose Beliefs Matter the Most to Us?   The Gallup poll estimates that about 60 percent of the world's Muslim population views the United States unfavorably. That might not be a source of concern; we don't need to be loved. But the 7 percent whom Gallup concludes believe that the 9/11 attacks were completely justified should concern us deeply. Analyzing what distinguishes that 7 percent is a good starting point for identifying those beliefs that lead some to support terrorism. As noted, these people are far more likely than their neighbors to feel that Islam is under attack from the West and that the United States is responsible for humiliating Muslims. Those beliefs explain as well as justify terrorism, in the mind of the believer.

The beliefs characterizing the 7 percent providing open moral approval of terrorism against us are often driven by and dependent on the mistaken belief that the United States intends to occupy and dominate the world of Islam. We may be able to change this belief if we demonstrate our contrary intent, though not by words alone. The evidence must, in short, undermine their convictions about our intentions—convictions that in the minds of the angry 7 percent justify violence against civilians.

Knowing the common beliefs and attitudes of the 7 percent is just the beginning of identifying our audience. Within that population, it would make sense to target those most likely to respond favorably to evidence that our intentions are not hostile or aggressive, including those residing within haven states. Another subgroup whom it would be wise to target would be those likely to be most dangerous as terrorists: scientists, military officers, and other groups that have the special skills or access that terrorists need. Finally, within the 7 percent we should target those who may have disproportionate influence over other Muslims, particularly over those most likely to be recruited as terrorists (such as the young, the educated, and the unemployed). Religious, cultural, and popular political leaders will be especially important in forming a visible leadership against terrorism.

What Beliefs Should We Address?   Mistrust and dislike of the United States runs deep in the Muslim world. Whether it is linked to U.S. support for Israel, U.S. wars in Afghanistan and Iraq, our alliances with repressive regimes in Egypt, Saudi Arabia, and elsewhere, or a culture many Muslims reject, such feelings are likely to remain for time to come. As President Obama made clear, we should not and will not change our culture, our traditions, or our loyalties to be better liked. If reducing moral support for terrorism depended on changing opinions of the United States from today's quite negative levels to positive admiration and delight at our leadership, the project might well be futile. Fortunately, evidence of the recent shift in opinion away from support for terrorism shows that such support can decline even while the United States remains disliked.

Within this context, we should be testing the assumption that there is a strong aversion among Muslims to supporting or justifying violence against civilians. Only 1 percent, as measured by the Gallup Poll, accepts the legitimacy of terrorism in principle, although 7 percent found the attack on the World Trade Center justified. The discrepancy in the numbers is explained, in part, by distinguishing terrorism as a general phenomenon from terrorism aimed at the United States. Religious beliefs offer a partial explanation. One Qur'anic verse, for example, decrees that, "Whosoever kills a human being for other than manslaughter or corruption in the earth, it shall be as if he has killed all mankind, and whosoever saves the life of one, it shall be as if he had saved the life of all mankind" (5:32). On a more basic level, there is a strong human desire to be seen as part of the moral, civilized world. Average Muslim men and women do not want to be regarded as barbarians any more than an average American does. Terrorism, except as tied to fear of the West, thus enjoys far less than 7 percent support in the Muslim world. Finally, there are also the more practical consequences of being seen as favoring terrorism: lost revenues from investment, tourism, and foreign aid; international isolation; national embarrassment.

Muslim opposition to terrorism—whether rooted in religion, human nature, or pragmatism—can be and, for the 7 percent has been, overcome by the conviction that the United States is attacking or humiliating Islam. In the face of fear, otherwise implausible justifications for attacks on civilians become compelling. We should thus focus, first, on providing evidence that we are not hostile to, or disrespectful of, Islam; and, second, that we are not imperialistically aggressive in cultural or military terms. Take such justifications as the assertions (1) that the workers in the World Trade Center on 9/11 were not civilians because they paid taxes and voted for the U.S. government, or (2) that all Israelis serve in the military and so there are no Israeli civilians. In the charged atmosphere surrounding the U.S. invasions of Afghanistan and Iraq in 2001 and 2003 or among the occupied in the Palestinian territories, such arguments seemed to suffice. But if beliefs about hostility and humiliation subside, these weak arguments may no longer hold.

Our first concern should thus be with the beliefs and attitudes that for too many justify crossing the line between suspicion and dislike of foreign nations and nationals and believing that attacks on civilians of a certain nationality or religion are worthy and desirable. Within that category, we must concentrate on actions that are consistent with our national interests and values and yet can rebut those justifications of violence against the West.

The Critical Role of Polling   The more general point is that intelligent polling can play several helpful roles in a campaign to reduce moral support for terrorism. It can tell us what beliefs and attitudes to target—a crucial set of facts if these are important sources of motivation for terrorists. It can enable us to measure our success in reducing the number of individuals holding extreme dangerous beliefs and attitudes by continuing to monitor polling figures. Changes in figures would go some way toward detecting whether our actions (and which actions) are reducing or increasing the critical number of people so radical that they believe 9/11 was completely justified. We could learn to measure how we are affecting the most dangerous attitudes of those to whom terrorist groups must look for recruits and support.

We can make polling far more useful than it is now. The frequency of surveys can be increased. More refined data sets based on age, economic status, or region would allow our efforts to change beliefs and attitudes to be targeted to more specific groups. We can elicit more useful information about beliefs and attitudes than we receive now—such as *why* an individual believes the West is a source of danger or humiliation.

Limiting Our Objectives   We should not seek to reshape Islam. That point might seem obvious, but U.S. policymaking circles abound with proposals for encouraging strains of Islam that are more moderate, less political, and more liberal-minded. Some analysts urge the United States to promote the more tolerant Indonesian strains of Islam in the Middle East, in order to counter the spread of violent Islamism from Pakistan, Saudi Arabia, and elsewhere in the Middle East or Southern Asia. Others argue that Islam needs a reformation to become compatible with the modern world. Deputy Secretary of Defense Paul Wolfowitz expressed a similar sentiment before the invasion of Iraq. This proposal goes far beyond what the United States could possibly hope to accomplish. It also mistakes the lessons of the European reformation backward.[71]

A campaign should seek to build bridges at a sustainable pace. A still-suspicious Islamic populace would interpret a sudden surge of interest in the welfare of Islam as manipulation. We must also proceed at a pace that creates a realistic level of American expectations about responses. Only this will permit the necessary level of support to be sustained. The bridges themselves will have to be actions because the legacy of mistrust for the United States in the Middle East means that merely talking about good intentions is unlikely to change attitudes. Arguments alone will not work because the messenger is no longer credible. On the extremely likely assumption that the arguments of American leaders or officials will be received with as much skepticism as we express toward the televised arguments of Osama Bin Laden, we will have to rely very substantially on actions that provide, or apparently provide, evidence that is inconsistent with present attitudes and beliefs that "justify" attacks on civilians in the United States and the West. President Obama has promised such actions.

These actions must be convincing from the perspective of Muslims—not just from that of Americans. While Americans might believe that the massive U.S. aid to Egypt is evidence of friendship, few Egyptians see matters in that light. To them, the aid is a bribe to keep the peace with Israel and maintain support for a repressive Egyptian government. Future evidence should demonstrate respect at least as much as generosity. We must look for opportunities to engage in cooperative undertakings with Muslim partners and to honor Muslim achievements. Obama's emphasis on partnerships built around shared pursuit of shared values sets the right tone.

Because Muslim hostility is often rooted in suspicion of our intentions and because even the very nature of our actions, much less our motivations, is likely to be misunderstood, we should seek to build trust in our explanations of what we are doing and why. Admiral Mike Mullen, the chairman of the Joint Chiefs of Staff, emphasized credibility as the heart of strategic communication in an article in the fall of 2009.[70] His language is powerful:

> That's the essence of good communication: having the right intent up front and letting our actions speak for themselves. . . . But more important than any particular tool, we must know the context within which our actions will be received and understood. We hurt ourselves and the message we try to send when it appears we are doing something merely for the credit. . . . We hurt ourselves more when our words don't align with our actions. Our enemies regularly monitor the news to discern coalition and American intent as weighed against the efforts of our forces. . . . Each time we fail to live up to our values or don't follow up on a promise, we look more and more like the arrogant Americans the enemies claim we are. . . . When they find a "say-do" gap—such as Abu Ghraib—they drive a truck right through it. . . . To put it simply, we need to worry a lot less about *how* to communicate our actions and much more about *what* our actions communicate.

In short, our capacity to explain is very limited so long as we are distrusted; dealing with that disabling condition requires actions and credibility, not words alone. Obviously there are actions that we will want to take to protect ourselves, although they may be understood as showing hostility or indifference to the populations they affect; and then we will have to try to explain that they were not motivated by hostility or permitted by indifference.

Dealing with Cultural Differences

Over a very long period of time deep cultural differences between most of the West and most of the Muslim world will remain. We will make enemies among political leaders if we are openly critical of governments that are undemocratic and that threaten dissenters, engage in human rights violations, and generate major disparities of opportunity based on gender. We will make other enemies if we hypocritically ignore those conflicts between our beliefs and our friendships. Much of the Muslim world will remain deeply critical of the apparently unstructured materialism and tolerance of deviant behavior that we have come to take for granted and regard as part of our valued freedoms. We will preserve alliances with nations much of Islam regards as enemies; they will continue support for states we regard as dangerous and cruel. We will continue to take steps to identify, incapacitate, and deter terrorists—steps that much of the Muslim world may regard as unnecessary and prejudiced. In the final analysis, both sides will suffer unless there is a substantial effort to be tolerant of even what we otherwise find objectionable. This will be a price well worth paying for a safer world.

Something less passive than tolerance is also required. Neither side can be indifferent to efforts to instill hatred of the others' people or culture. Without violating our constitutional protection of free speech, we have substantially reduced calumny on the basis of religion, race, gender, and sexual preference by the social force of public opinion. We must do the same with regard to Muslims and Islam at home and abroad. In turn, there should be no room for funding schools that teach hatred of the West. On these issues, we should begin to explore a partnership consistent with our fundamental values.

Conclusion

The costs to both the West and Islam of the level of suspicion, hostility, and distrust with which we have lived in recent years is too great to be comfortably ignored by the reassuring thought, on both sides, that we are the victims and wholly justified in our beliefs, words, and actions. The prospect of substantially reducing the danger of terrorism and the massive costs we now pay to prevent it depends upon creating the beliefs and attitudes that underlie confidence and tolerance. The fruit of success in this effort is well worth the price of trying. There are clear limits to what we can do or should be willing to do but there is still much within those limits. The effort will require wisdom but we have carefully brought down walls of separation before.

Conclusion: After the Next Attack

The likely prospect of another terrorist attack within our borders, whatever its size and dangers, presents final problems for us to address. Throughout this book we have argued for balance and reason as methods of government in a world in which terrorist attacks come in all guises and sizes, can never be completely prevented, and will continue to be a real threat for decades to come. By "balance" we mean that we must reconcile our concerns for our security with our concerns for a bundle of other values: our civil liberties, the human rights of others, historically accepted limits on executive power, and our leadership among democratic nations.

Besides assessing the costs of any technique or strategy in terms of *all* our values, we must also carefully consider the possibility that tactics or strategies may be counterproductive, in the sense that by hardening resentments and heightening fears, they may prove as likely to increase our danger as to reduce it. We have seen law, whether of peacetime or of war, playing a critical role in accommodating our concerns for security with our concerns for our other vital interests—not as the Bush administration often did, as an encumbrance imposed by weaker enemies on our power or a tactic of so-called lawfare.

The next attack will again raise this most fundamental issue: whether increasing immediate physical security should be the touchstone and purpose of everything we do, or whether the U.S. will continue to insist on a place for the less tangible concerns for which we have demanded an equal weight. Any attack to come will spread fear that our leaders have not provided adequate protection and have left us exposed to harm, even if no reasonable protection could have safeguarded against attack. More specifically, it will refuel arguments about whether we could have been far more fully protected by returning to the strategy of the Bush administration, looking only at national security and, within limits, at dollar costs.

The argument will be made that a single-minded pursuit of national security protected us from September 12, 2001, onward, and that we can and should return to that presumed safety in three ways: by greatly diminishing the weight we give any concern other than security in its narrowest sense; by freeing the president from the interference of Congress and the courts; and by setting aside the effort to use respect for the principles and values embodied in law, both domestic and international, as the wisest method for measuring and reconciling competing concerns.

Throughout this book, we have urged a different equilibrium, one that would remain as relevant in times of crisis as in times of peace. Reaching this equilibrium requires a process that recognizes a broad enough array of concerns, develops a wide enough range of options, predicts very carefully (and without presumptive recourse to force) how each option affects each of our major concerns, tries to gather evidence over time to help us make more accurate predictions, and builds legitimacy at home and abroad for our tactics and strategies. In part II of the book, we have tried to outline how that process might be applied, and to show how remaining as faithful as possible to existing legal paradigms, whether of peace or of war, can produce a sound reconciliation of our principal concerns without reducing our safety. A strategy aimed simply at minimizing the most immediate risks from terrorism leaves Americans despised by allies, facing ever-increasing enemies, doubtful of our leadership, and without the protections and benefits of law. But many will contend after another terrorist attack that there cannot be adequate security without following that path.

In crafting rules for the relatively novel reality of life under the shadow of transnational terrorism, we have particularly emphasized loyalty to the readily available principles of domestic and international law. The United States and its allies have come to express as law the balance among the set of a democracy's most deeply valued concerns that we have mentioned. The balance reflected in the law has an acceptance at home and abroad that confers the many benefits of legitimacy. As a result, for more than a century the United States has increased in security, power, and respect—rather than weakened by lawfare.

Laws may have to be modified or adapted in light of the special context of terrorism. Sometimes, we will want to increase our security by expanding powers provided by the law of peace. At other times, we will have to adjust the laws of war to fit the new type of combatants and the nature of the modern battlefield; or else to limit the powers of wartime law to accommodate fairness, respect for national sovereignty, and human dignity. The need to make such changes will sometimes require departure from the letter of the law but not from accepted legal principles—the array of concerns behind these rules. Can this view survive another attack?

Responding Rationally to the Next Attack

Another attack on the United States is bound to spark a renewed debate about the wisdom of the balance among concerns and the recourse to law in a world of ever-present danger. The challenge is particularly grave because a new attack would be likely to reveal new dangers, causing us to reassess the current order of our concerns. What it should *not* do is to make us indifferent to every concern except short-term physical security.

If there is another terrorist attack within the United States, as most people believe will be the case, if it is more than trivial, and if it is related to jihadist beliefs or organizations, we will have to adjust the balance we have struck in light of the increased risk the new attack may demonstrate. The type and amount of increased risk will depend upon the characteristics of the attack. If it reveals a previously unknown capacity to do us harm, that new capacity must enter into our calculations, whether it takes the form of unsuspected, technical skills or new and undetected access to facilities and people we had thought were protected.

Indeed, even if it did not reveal any unexpected capacity, the occurrence of an attack after years without one would change our assessment of the likelihood of future attacks.

In readjusting our assessment of risk in light of new attacks, we must make the following calculation: if, but only if, the resulting increase in risks to our safety tilts the balance among our foremost concerns, should we also be willing to comprehensively change our strategies, our laws, and our sense of acceptable counterterrorism techniques? Our decision must take into account the long run, not just the first surge of panic in the wake of violence. It will also signal toward enemies and allies. An exaggerated sense of our danger may be just what the terrorists sought and others may seek.

The fact that we must, at a given point, give greater weight to a security risk that we are balancing against the preservation of American traditions, liberties, values, and leadership in the world does not mean that the scale necessarily tilts far enough to justify practices of counterterrorism (e.g., torture) that we have previously rejected. Great Britain, Spain, and France have accepted risks that appear great to us without more than limited sacrifices of the other values we share. Even Israel, which has faced a much greater incidence of terrorism, has been more respectful of legal constraints. In making our recommendations regarding interrogation and rendition for interrogation, for example, the arguments for the rules and practices we propose should continue to hold despite a significant increase in the domestic danger.

In only one situation would the risks be likely to increase immensely, fundamentally revising present calculations of the balance of concerns. If we have reason to believe (with or without a new type of attack) that a terrorist group has obtained the capacity to do vastly more damage by the use of nuclear, chemical, or biological weapons, the balance among our concerns will have to shift radically, changing decisions about tactics and strategy. Unlike the time of the Cold War, we would not be able to rely on deterrence against a terrorist group hidden among a hostile but peaceful population; we would not be able to count on 100 percent prevention at our borders; nor would we necessarily be able to identify and incapacitate a critical mass of the group associated with the danger.

The process we have been describing would remain much the same, even if its ingredients were to change dramatically. We would still need to be careful not to take any step that would increase our risk by making more terrorists than it disabled. And some steps that might reduce the risk of future attack would, even in that disastrous situation, be too costly in terms of other concerns. Even if, in a doomsday scenario, a hundred thousand people were killed in an American city, new steps to protect our security would still need to respect old concerns. We should not quickly abandon democracy, free speech, or freedom from arbitrary arrest. We should still hesitate to invade traditional allies in order to use our own forces to disable a terrorist group that we feared might be hiding in the territory of that ally. We should not intern tens of thousands on the basis of religion or ethnicity. As dramatically as our world of danger changes, we must decide never to turn our back on our defining values.

Responding to the Psychological Effects of the Next Attack

The great political mystery of terrorism has been, for decades before September 11, 2001, its remarkable capacity to generate irrational fear and terror, totally disproportionate to the actual danger it poses. That is why terrorism has proved useful to its perpetrators. The most serious problem any new attack will create may be neither the damage it does nor the risk if we fail to adjust our counterterrorism measures appropriately. Instead, it may be the damage it brings, in the long term, to our ethical and legal systems, as well as to our political culture.

The strategy of terrorism rests largely on its effectiveness in spreading exaggerated fear. The most predictable reaction to an act of terror may be *panic*—a word the *Oxford English Dictionary* defines as an "excessive or unreasoning feeling of alarm or fear leading to extravagant or foolish behavior, such as that which may suddenly spread through a crowd of people." The word derives from a reference to the Greek god Pan who "was the source of mysterious sounds that caused contagious, groundless, fear." The shock of unexpected attacks on blameless civilians in peacetime has been observed for decades. It is capable of producing extreme and widespread concern in situations where the risk is small compared to other, familiar dangers. Any wave of excessive, misdirected fear that follows the next attack can lead to a panic gravely damaging the United States economically, politically, and morally; for it will be within a panic-prone context that the debate over values and principles will take.

Panic is controllable by sensible measures, as the pilots of airplanes that have developed difficulties in flight know well and as social scientists affirm. For our purposes, the starting point is to identify the causes of the exaggerated fears bred by terrorism, for those causes are what we must deal with to avoid the harms that can flow from the incessant demands of an urgent sense of uncontrolled danger. The fears particular to a terror attack involve all of the following:

• a sudden awareness of an apparently grave risk;

• a sense of another party's dangerous, continuing, lethal hostility;

• an invisible source mixed within a friendly population;

• targeting of the uninvolved;

• an absence of adequate trust in the capacity of our leaders to provide security; and

• frightening divisions within the population between those who identify themselves simply as targets and those who are grouped by ethnicity or language with the terrorists.

In response, it is wise to begin early to address those causes of irrational, contagious fear. Some of the characteristics that may create panic are beyond our control. A new terrorist attack *will* convey the continuing, lethal hostility flowing from an invisible source and directed at a random group of the innocent and uninvolved. The other characteristics, however, are within the government's capacity to affect.

We can make sure that terrorism, however shocking, does not return as a complete surprise. In times of calm we can update the public's awareness of the risks of terrorism. Terrorism cannot be 100 percent controlled, and the public must know that. We can have—and let it be known that we have—contingency plans for dealing with the next attack. These will be necessary to create a sense of control after the event. We can explain why we are not taking some steps now and under what, if any, circumstances we would consider taking them. Plans can be devised at a time of calm for a time of confusion. This kind of preparation may be likened to the clear, well-considered measures a trained airplane crew takes to manage the passengers' fear in case of trouble on board a plane. Furthermore, we can take steps, such as the military and intelligence agencies take, *after* a sudden loss, to examine what could have prevented it. That is what the 9/11 Commission did.

Last, and most important, consider the central role of the pilot's voice in managing the emotional state on board a plane in difficulty. Panic is recognized to be a contagious, group phenomenon. Besides displaying competence in assessing risk and conveying the confidence of having decided on actions before we face the psychological pressures of panic and the demands of political response, our leaders—like that airline crew—are going to have to make clear what they expect of the American people before and after a terrorist event. And, like that pilot, our president must speak to our deepest concerns while enlisting our resolve.

The Bush administration expected little from the public and acted accordingly. In contrast, Winston Churchill expected much of the British in 1940 through 1945; Franklin Roosevelt similarly expected much of Americans throughout the Depression and deep into World War II. In the event of any new attack, President Obama and his successors must similarly convey to the American people that they expect no less from us than calm resolve, courage, and continuing commitment to the values and relationships we cherish.

Our preparations for the psychological effects of a next attack could offer a crucial bonus: To the extent that such advance measures suggest we have anticipated and in fact largely defused the psychological bomb the terrorists intend will follow the next real bomb or attack, we will have dulled the siting of the expressive power of terrorism.

We must keep in mind that to a large degree, history judges people on the basis of the consequences of their decisions. Decisions about what to do in the face of grave threats, heretofore unparalleled, to the nation, are laden with great uncertainty and risk. Our expectation from our leaders is that they be ready to make bold and responsible decisions, even in the face of such anxieties. Our leaders must recognize that the longer-lasting payoffs of their decisions will not be determined by their response to any one particular crisis, as grave as it may be, but by their ability to preserve the health of the nation—in its broadest sense—in the time to come.

Notes

Introduction

1. Robert Bolt, *A Man For All Seasons* (Oxford: William Heynemann Ltd., 1960), 38–39.

1 The Complicated Relationship between Counterterrorism and Legality

1. In *Korematsu v. United States*, 323 U.S. 214 (1944), the Supreme Court upheld the constitutionality of Executive Order 9066, which had served as authorization for the internment of Japanese Americans during World War II.

2. Clement Fatovic, "Constitutionalism and Presidential Prerogative," *American Journal of Political Science* 48, no. 3 (July 2004): 429, 433–435. Other advocates of the Hamiltonian position—namely, for intraconstitutional prerogative—have included Judge Nelson in the Prize Cases, Justices Davis and Chase in *Ex Parte Milligan*, and Justice Frankfurter in *Korematsu*. Advocates of the Jeffersonian position—namely, for extraconstitutional prerogative—have included Arthur Schlesinger, Jr., and Justice Jackson in *Korematsu*. Larry Arnhart, "'The God-Like Prince': John Locke, Executive Prerogative, and the American Presidency," *Presidential Studies Quarterly* 9, no. 2 (1979): 121, 122.

3. The same is true of efforts to find implicit congressional exceptions to statutory limitations of executive power. Familiar interpretative rules may make less frequent the stark choice we have posited. Often an unanticipated emergency will constitute a justification that would have been assumed by the drafters to permit actions they are otherwise forbidding. Still, it must remain possible for the legislature to make clear that it does not want an interpretive exception made or a justification implied beyond what it has described itself—that there is little or no ambiguity about what it wants done or not done in that circumstance. To deny the legislature this power would be to cut away much of the rule of law.

4. *Bob Jones University v. United States*, 461 U.S. 574 (1983).

5. HCJ 5100/94, *Public Committee Against Torture in Israel v. The State of Israel*, [1999] IsrSC 53(4) 817, reprinted in 38 I.L.M. 1471, 1488 (1999), http://elyon1.court.gov.il/files_eng/94/000/051/a09/94051000.a09.pdf.

6. *Gäfgen v. Germany*, Appl. No. 22978/05 (GC judgment of June 30, 2008), http://cmiskp.echr.coe.int./tkp197/search.asp?skin=hudoc-en.

2 International Law, the President, and the War on Terrorism

1. UCMJ, section 821.

2. Congress can, however, pass statutes that override international treaties and the president then has the authority to execute the statutes and violate the international law.

3. U.S. Constitution at Article II, Section 2.

4. Courts have held that only those treaties that can be characterized as "self-executing" are judicially enforceable in the absence of implementing legislation. What constitutes a self-executing treaty is not clearly defined and is therefore a question that courts, with the advice of the executive, must resolve; on a general level, treaties that create concrete rights or define concrete prohibitions and represent intent by all the signatory parties to be executed automatically are self-executing. Treaties that involve a promise to legislate about a certain topic or that use more general, aspirational language are non-self-executing. See *Medellin v. Texas*, 552 U.S. 491; 128 S. Ct. 1346 (2008).

5. Robert J. Delahunty and John Yoo, "Executive Power v. International Law," *Harvard Journal of Law and Public Policy* 30 (Fall 2006): 73, 75; Delahunty and Yoo argue that elevating "customary international law to the status of law binding on the President would transfer lawmaking authority to a vague, indeterminate process that is not subject to popular sovereignty" (at 113).

6. See note 3.

7. Eric A. Posner and Cass R. Sunstein, "Chevronizing Foreign Relations Law," *Yale Law Journal* 116 (April 2007): 1170, 1201.

8. For example, Posner and Sunstein argue that the executive's interpretation that the Detainee Act (later struck down by the Supreme Court) complied with international law was not unreasonable and should thus have controlled. Others have been willing to go even further and argue that international law is no more than one policy consideration that the president must weigh in deciding how to act when issues of national security are implicated.

9. Derek Jinks and Neal Kumar Katyal, "Disregarding Foreign Relations Law," *Yale Law Journal* 116 (April 2007): 1230, 1234.

10. For fact check, see http://www.icrc.org/Web/eng/siteeng0.nsf/htmlall/annual-report-2008-finance/$File/icrc_ar_08_finance.pdf (p. 431).

11. Sarah Sewall, introduction to *The U.S. Army/Marine Corps Counterinsurgency Field Manual* (Chicago: University of Chicago Press, 2007), at xxv.

12. Ibid., at 1-150.

13. Charles J. Dunlap, "Law and Military Interventions: Preserving Humanitarian Values in Twenty-first-century Conflicts," presentation for Humanitarian Challenges in Military Intervention Conference, Carr Center for Human Rights Policy, Kennedy School of Government, Harvard University, November 29, 2001.

14. Ibid.

15. David E. Kellogg, "International Law and Terrorism," *Military Law Review* 50 (September–October 2005): 50.

16. [The] Hon. Dennis Jacobs, moderator, panel 1, "International Law and the State of the Constitution," Columbia Law School Federalist Society Student Symposium, February 24, 2006, http://expost.blogspot.com/2006/02/what-is -international-rule-of-law.html.

3   The Role of Government Lawyers in Counterterrorism

1. The fact that citizens care about such compliance may be the explanation for a remarkable congruence in a CNN/USA Today/Gallup poll conducted in January 2006, in which the public was asked to comment on the government's wiretapping program. The poll showed a perfect correlation between the numbers of those who believed the program to be illegal under the existing FISA (49 percent) and those who believed the program to be wrong (50 percent). Respondents who believed the wiretapping program was probably legal (47 percent) corresponded to the number of people who replied to the question whether the program was also right (47 percent).

2. Joseph Carroll, "Slim Majority of Americans Say Bush Wiretapping Was Wrong," January 25, 2006, http://www.gallup.com/poll/21058/Slim-Majority -Americans-Say-Bush-Wiretapping-Wrong.aspx.

4   Targeted Killing

1. One such famous case was when the Israeli Mossad assassinated an innocent Moroccan waiter in Lillehammer, Norway, in July 1973, mistaking him for a member of the Black September faction responsible for the Munich massacre.

2. For a report on the U.S. "hit list," see Craig Whitlock, "Afghans Oppose U.S. Hit List of Drug Traffickers," *The Washington Post*, October 24, 2009.

3. Dana Priest, "U.S. Military Teams, Intelligence Deeply Involved in Aiding Yemen on Strikes," *The Washington Post*, January 27, 2010, A01.

4. Ibid.

5. The latter, who in September 2005 following his discharge from the military flew to London, had to stay aboard the plane and return to Israel after being tipped off that he might be arrested.

6. *Matar v. Dichter*, 500 F. Supp. 2d 284 (S.D.N.Y. 2007). The United States Court of Appeals for the Second Circuit reaffirmed the dismissal: *Matar v. Dichter*, 563 F.3d 9 (2d Cir. 2009).

7. Amos Harel, "Dichter: The Targeted Killing of Hamas Leaders Have Brought about Calm," *Ha'aretz*, June 1, 2005 (in Hebrew).

8. W. Hays Parks, "Memorandum on Executive Order 12333 and Assassination," Department of the Army Pamphlet 27–50–204, from *Army Law* 4 (December 1989), http://hqinet001.hqmc.usmc.mil/ig/Div_Intell_Oversight/Supporting%20Documents/EO%2012333.pdf.

9. Abraham D. Sofaer, "The Sixth Annual Waldemar A. Solf Lecture in International Law: Terrorism, the Law, and the National Defense," *Military Law Review* 126 (Fall 1989), at 119. For further analysis of the Sofaer doctrine, see Kenneth Anderson, "Targeted Killing in U.S. Counterterrorism Strategy and Law," Working Paper, May 11, 2009, http://papers.ssrn.com/sol3/papers.cfm?abstract_id=1415070.

10. *Public Committee Against Torture in Israel v. The Government of Israel*, HCJ 769/02 (2005) (Isr.), translation available at http://elyon1.court.gov.il/files_eng/02/690/007/a34/02007690.a34.htm (hereinafter, "targeted killing case").

11. Note that numbers of militants killed include both the intended targets and their armed group associates who were with them at the time of the attack and were harmed as a result.

12. Amos Harel, "Pinpointed IAF Attacks in Gaza More Precise, Hurt Fewer Civilians," *Ha'aretz*, December 30, 2007, http://www.haaretz.co.il/hasen/spages/939702.html.

13. *Public Committee Against Torture in* Israel, note 10, para. 46.

14. *Public Committee Against Torture in Israel*, note 10, para. 40.

15. That the 2008 armed conflict between Israel and Hamas in Gaza looked far more like a conventional war may help explain why, only three years after Barak's decision, Israeli forces struck numerous Hamas members who would not have necessarily met the strict tests he had imposed.

16. *Tennessee v. Garner*, 471 U.S. 1 (1985).

17. Inter-American Commission on Human Rights, *Report on Terrorism and Human Rights*, OEA/Ser.L/V/II.116, Doc. 5 rev. 1 corr., October 22, 2002, http://www.cidh.oas.org/Terrorism/Eng/exe.htm.

18. Ibid., para 87.

19. Ibid., para 91.

20. *Isayeva v. Russia*, Appl. No. 57950/00, European Court of Human Rights (2005), para. 181; see also *Isayeva v. Russia*, Appl. No. 6846/02, European Court of Human Rights (2007).

21. Parks, note 8, at 7.

22. Parks, note 8, at 8n14.

23. *DRC v. Uganda*, ICJ 116 (Dec. 19, 2005).

24. Report of Philip Alston, Special Rapporteur on Extrajudicial, Summary or Arbitrary Executions, Study on Targeted Killings, A/HRC/14/24/Add.6, May 28, 2010, 13, http://www2.ohchr.org/english/bodies/hrcouncil/docs/14session/A.HRC.14.24.Add6.pdf.

5 Detention outside the Combat Zone

1. The Military Commission Act of 2006 defines an unlawful enemy combatant as a non-POW who has purposely provided material support to hostilities against the United States, and then adds "including a person who is part of the Taliban, Al-Qaeda, or associated forces."

2. The Guantanamo detainees came from a total of thirty-two countries. As to the location of their capture, according to a *National Journal* article of February 3, 2006, of the 132 files released by the U.S. Defense Department at that time (out of about five hundred total Guantanamo detainees) only 57 of those detained by the Defense Department were accused of being on a battlefield in post-9/11 Afghanistan. Only 35 percent were arrested in Afghanistan. The CIA seized, detained in secret locations, and then brought to Guantanamo still others.

3. The asserted justifications of detention suggest that anyone detained as a member or affiliated with Al-Qaeda could be held until the "war" against these groups and their affiliates was over. Those individuals might thus be detained as long as any of these groups continue to target us. In both the U.S. and Israeli cases, the unusual durability of the terrorist undertaking led, however, to a process that included periodic reviews for continuing dangerousness, something that would not take place for POWs in a traditional war.

4. Of course, the separate problem of invading the sovereignty of another state to seize a suspect (as in the case of Israel's abduction of Nazi war criminal Adolf Eichmann from Argentina to a trial in Israel) remains under all alternatives. Seizure by U.S. agents abroad would still violate customary international law whether as a prelude to trial or to detention at Guantanamo. That step should depend on the unwillingness of the state where a terrorist planning an attack on the United States is found to arrest and try him locally.

5. An attorney would be appointed at the first arraignment to advise the detainee, but, unless cleared, the attorney would not have access to classified material or be available at interviews, the results of which are never to be used in court.

6. The most important area for potential change is the condition under which hearsay would be admissible as evidence. Without the checks of cross-examination or of an oath, a single unreliable informant could falsely implicate very large numbers of people. That was the history of the British reliance on informants to prosecute IRA suspects. Ultimately, we have to decide: how sure must we be that a source of evidence is honest and reliable; and what mechanisms, other than confrontation at trial, can provide that degree of assurance?

6 Interrogation

1. See http://www.army.mil/institution/armypublicaffairs/pdf/fm2-22-3.pdf.

2. Central Intelligence Agency, Directorate of Intelligence, "Detainee Reporting Pivotal for the War Against Al-Qa'ida," June 3, 2005, http://www.washingtonpost.com/wp-srv/nation/documents/Detainee_Reporting.pdf.

3. Raymond F. Toliver, *The Interrogator: The Story of Hans Scharff, Luftwaffe's Master Interrogator* (Fallbrook, CA: Aero Publishers, 1978).

4. See, e.g., Philip Gourevitch and Errol Morris, "Exposure: Annals of War," *The New Yorker*, March 24, 2008.

5. This is the only relevant standard in the three constitutional amendments by which Congress defined and limited our obligation to avoid CID in the reservations and understandings it attached in ratifying the Convention against Torture.

6. Quoted by Tom Parker, "Combating Terrorism," CQ Congressional Testimony, September 19, 2006.

7   Negotiating with Terrorists

1. From President Bush's speech of September 20, 2001: "In Afghanistan we see Al Qaeda's vision for the world. Afghanistan's people have been brutalized, many are starving and many have fled. . . . The United States respects the people of Afghanistan—after all, we are currently its largest source of humanitarian aid—but we condemn the Taliban regime."

2. John D. Banusiewicz, "Cheney Says U.S. Will Never Ask Permission to Defend Itself," American Forces Press Service, March 17, 2004, http://www .defenselink.mil/news/newsarticle.aspx?id=27050.

3. Text of speech, "Be Not Afraid," National Review Online, July 30, 2003, http://www.nationalreview.com/comment/comment-delay073003.asp.

4. Robert Mnookin, "When Not to Negotiate: A Negotiation Imperialist Reflects on Appropriate Limits," *University of Colorado Law Review* 74 (2003): 1077, 1080.

5. Richard E. Hayes, "Negotiations with Terrorists," in *International Negotiation: Analysis, Approaches, Issues*, ed. Victor A. Kremenyuk (San Francisco: Jossey-Bass, 2002), 424–425.

6. Ibid. Similar results have been identified in studies of negotiations in Colombia; see James Zackrison, "Colombia," in *Combating Terrorism*, ed. Yonah Alexander (Ann Arbor: University of Michigan Press, 2002), 130.

7. Grant Wardlaw, *Political Terrorism* (Cambridge: Cambridge University Press, 1989), 71–72.

8. Harmonie Toros, "'We Don't Negotiate with Terrorists!': Legitimacy and Complexity in Terrorist Conflicts," *Security Dialogue* 39 (2008): 407, 411.

9. U.S. Department of State, "Foreign Terrorist Organizations (FTOs): Fact Sheet" (2008), http://www.america.gov/st/texttrans-english/2008/April/2008041 0111249xjsnommis0.111355.html.

10. Toros, note 8, at 412.

11. Zackrison, note 6, at 147.

12. Jeffrey D. Simon, *The Terrorist Trap*, 2nd ed. (Bloomington: Indiana University Press, 2001), 30.

13. Ibid., at 32.

14. Ibid.

15. See Philip C. Wilcox Jr., "United States," in *Combating Terrorism*, note 6, at 42.

16. Peter R. Neumann, "Negotiating with Terrorists," *Foreign Affairs* 86 (2007): 128, 130.

17. Ibid., at 136.

18. Neumann, note 16.

19. Dean G. Pruitt, "Negotiation with Terrorists," *International Negotiation* 11 (2006): 371, 390.

20. John Lukacs, *The Duel: Hitler vs. Churchill: 10 May–31 July 1940* (London: Bodley Head, 1990); see also Gabriella Blum and Robert H. Mnookin, "When *Not* to Negotiate," in *The Negotiator's Fieldbook*, ed. Andrea Kupfer Schneider and Christopher Honeyman (Washington, DC: American Bar Association, 2006), 107.

21. Guy Olivier Faure, "Negotiating with Terrorists: The Hostage Case," *International Negotiation* 8 (2003): 469, 476.

22. Tom Kuntz, "Aftermath," *New York Times*, September 23, 2001, section 4, 3.

23. White House press briefing, "President to Send Secretary Powell to Middle East," April 4, 2002, http://georgewbush-whitehouse.archives.gov/news/releases/2002/04/20020404-1.html.

24. Faure, note 21, at 475.

25. Michael Ross Fowler, "The Relevance of Principled Negotiation to Hostage Crises," *Harvard Negotiation Law Review* 12 (2007): 251, 261.

26. Richard Clutterbuck, "Negotiating with Terrorists," *Terrorism and Political Violence* 4 (1992): 261, 277: "Moreover, it is only by negotiation that the police and others concerned (e.g., psychologists) can obtain information, make judgments and gain time in which to secure a release or mount a rescue." See also Faure, note 21, at 484; Adam Dolnik and Keith M. Fitzgerald, *Negotiating Hostage Crises with New Hostages* (Westport, CT: Praeger Security International, 2008), 143.

27. Louise Richardson, "Britain and the IRA," in *Democracy and Counterterrorism: Lessons from the Past*, ed. Robert J. Art and Louise Richardson (Washington, DC: United States Institute of Peace, 2007), 95.

28. See suggestion by Erich Rosenbach in Ravi Khanna, "Afghan Government Says It's Ready to Negotiate with Taliban," October 14, 2008, http://www.globalsecurity.org/military/library/news/2008/10/mil-081014-voa05.htm; Toros, note 8, at 414. See also "Six Experts on Negotiating with the Taliban," interview, Council on Foreign Relations, March 20, 2009, http://www.cfr.org/publication/18893/negotiating_with_the_taliban.html.

29. See suggestion by Rosenbach, note 28.

30. Bertram Spector, "Negotiating with Villains Revisited: Research Note," *International Negotiation* (2003): 613, 616.

31. See Dolnik and Fitzgerald, note 26, at 140.

32. Arunabha Bhoumik, "Democratic Responses to Terrorism: A Comparative Study of the United States, Israel and India," *Denver Journal of International Law and Policy* 33 (2005): 285, 344; D. P. Sharma, *Countering Terrorism* (New Delhi: Lancers Books, 1992), 68.

33. Pruitt, note 19, at 374–375.

34. A total of 128 hostages were killed in the crisis: 126 by gas used in the Russian assault and 2 by the terrorists prior to the storming of the theater. See Adam Dolnik and Richard Pilch, "The Moscow Theater Hostage Crisis: The Perpetrators, Their Tactics, and the Russian Response," *International Negotiation* 8 (2003) 577, 585; Fowler, note 25, at 262.

35. Blum and Mnookin, note 20, at 108.

36. Richard E. Hayes, Stacey R. Kaminski, and Steven M. Beres, "Negotiating the Non-negotiable: Dealing with Absolutist Terrorists," *International Negotiation* 8 (2003): 451, 451–467.

37. Ibid., at 457.

38. Emily Pronin, Kathleen Kennedy, and Sarah Butsch, "Bombing Versus Negotiating: How Preferences for Combating Terrorism Are Affected by Perceived Terrorist Rationality," *Basic and Applied Social Psychology* 28 (2006): 385, 385–392.

39. Ibid., at 389–390.

40. Blum and Mnookin, note 20, at 102.

41. See Audrey Kurth Cronin, "How al-Qaida Ends," *International Security* 31 (2006): 25. For example, when members of the IRA agreed to negotiate, a splinter group that called itself the "Real IRA" broke away.

42. United Nations Development Programme, Colombia, "Unfunding the War: A Strict Control of Income Sources," chapter 12 in *Solutions to Escape the Conflict's Impasse*, National Development Report 5 (2003), http://www.pnud/org/co/2003/EnglishVersion/Chapter12.pdf.

43. See Clutterbuck, note 26, at 279 (stating that the result of similar policies in Italy and Argentina was a decrease in the number of kidnappings reported).

44. Ibid., at 5.

45. On the benefits of secret negotiations, see Anthony Wanis-St. John, "Back-Channel Negotiations: International Bargaining in the Shadows," *Negotiation Journal* 22 (2006): 125–126.

46. Ibid., at 138.

47. Ibid., at 136.

48. Dolnik and Pilch, note 34, at 598.

49. Ibid., at 597.

50. See Robert Mnookin and Susan Hackley, "Disconnecting 'Quid' from 'Quo,'" *Los Angeles Times*, Commentary, September 26, 2004.

51. Philip B. Heymann, *Terrorism and America* (Cambridge, MA: MIT Press, 2001), 45.

52. Paul Wilkinson, *Terrorism versus Democracy: The Liberal State Response* (London: Routledge, 2006), 65.

53. Yochi J. Dreazen, Siobhan Gorman, and Jay Solomon, "U.S. Mulls Talks with Taliban in Bid to Quell Afghan Unrest," *Wall Street Journal*, October 28, 2008, http://sec.online.wsj.com/article/ SB122515124350674269.html.

54. As U.S. General John Craddock, NATO's supreme operational commander, noted in expressing support for talks: "I have said over and over again this is not going to be won by military means." "U.S. May Rethink Talking to Taliban," CBS/AP, October 8, 2008, www.cbsnews.com/stories/2008/10/08/terror/main 451185.shtml?source=RSSattr=HOME_4511185; "NATO Question: Is It Time to Talk with Taliban?" Associated Press, October 8, 2008, www.msnbc.msn .com/id/27090845/.

55. See Art and Richardson, "Conclusion," note 27, at 565; Spector, note 30, at 619; Pruitt, note 19, at 374.

8   The Case for Sustained Efforts to Reduce Moral Support for Terrorism

1. "Text: Obama's Speech in Cairo," *New York Times*, June 4, 2009, http://www.nytimes.com/2009/06/04/us/politics/04obama.text.html?_r=1&scp=1&sq=june%204,%202009&st=cse.

2. "How Terrorist Groups End: Implications for Countering al-Qa'ida," Rand Corporation Research Brief (2008), http://www.rand.org/pubs/research _briefs/2008/RAND_RB9351.pdf.

3. Alan B. Krueger and Jitka Malecčková, "Education, Poverty, and Terrorism: Is There a Causal Connection," *Journal of Economic Perspectives* 17, no. 4 (2003): 119–144.

4. Address of President Bush to the Joint Session of Congress, September 20, 2001, http://www.c-span.org/executive/transcript.asp?cat=current_event&code =bush_admin&year=0901. Later in his address, President Bush continued this theme by stating "Americans are asking 'Why do they hate us?' They hate what they see right here in this chamber: a democratically elected government. Their leaders are self-appointed. They hate our freedoms: our freedom of religion, our freedom of speech, our freedom to vote and assemble and disagree with each other."

5. WorldPublicOpinion.org, "Public Opinion in the Islamic World on Terrorism, al Qaeda, and US Policies" (2009), 19, http://www.worldpublicopinion.org/ pipa/pdf/feb09/STARTII_Feb09_rpt.pdf.

6. Pew Research Center, "The Great Divide: How Westerners and Muslims View Each Other" (2006), 12–14 [hereafter, Pew, "Great Divide"]; Pew Research Center, "Global Opinion Trends 2002–2007, A Rising Tide Lifts Mood in the Developing World" (2007), 5 [hereafter Pew, "A Rising Tide"].

7. John L. Esposito and Dalia Mogahed, *Who Speaks for Islam?: What a Billion Muslims Really Think* (New York: Gallup Press, 2007), xii (it must be noted that this was also the most popular criticism Americans gave of the West).

8. WorldPublicOpinion.org, note 4, at 22.

9. Esposito and Mogahed, note 6, at 34.

10. Ibid., at 88 (this distaste for Western morality is significantly more pro-nounced among the politically radicalized). By *politically radicalized* we refer to the 7 percent of respondents who said that 9/11 was "completely justified." The authors identify this group of people as the "political radicals" (69–70).

11. Ibid., at 94.

12. Pew, "A Rising Tide," note 5, at 55.

13. Alan Travis, "MI5 Report Challenges Views on Terrorism in Britain," *The Manchester Guardian*, August 20, 2008, http://www.guardian.co.uk/uk/2008/aug/20/uksecurity.terrorism1.

14. WorldPublicOpinion.org, note 4, at 7.

15. Ibid., at 8.

16. Pew Research Center, "Global Public Opinion in the Bush Years (2001–2008)" (2008), 3 [hereafter Pew, "Bush Years"].

17. WorldPublicOpinion.org, note 4, at 17.

18. Esposito and Mogahed, note 6, at 86–87.

19. WorldPublicOpinion.org, note 4, at 12; see also Esposito and Mogahed, note 4, 87–88.

20. Esposito and Mogahed, note 6, at 61–62.

21. Ibid., at 89.

22. WorldPublicOpinion.org, note 4, at 14.

23. Ibid., at 20.

24. Ibid., at 17–18.

25. Ibid.

26. Ibid., at 16; Esposito and Mogahed, note 6, at 83.

27. WorldPublicOpinion.org, note 4, at 14; Esposito and Mogahed, note 6, at 87.

28. WorldPublicOpinion.org, note 4, at 12.

29. Pew, "Bush Years," note 14, at 4.

30. WorldPublicOpinion.org, note 4, at 30–31.

31. Ibid., at 21.

32. Ibid., at 24.

33. Pew, "Great Divide," note 5, at 22; Pew, "Bush Years," note 14, at 4.

34. Pew, "Great Divide," note 5, at 22; Pew, "Bush Years," note 14, at 4.

35. Esposito and Mogahed, note 6, at 69–70. It must be noted, however, that "the issues that drive radicals are also issues for moderates," it is just a difference

in "prioritization, intensity of feeling, degree of politicization, and alienation" (93).

36. Ibid., at 91–92.

37. Ibid., at 89, 91–92.

38. Ibid., at 84.

39. Ibid., at 90.

40. Ibid., at 89.

41. Ibid. (identifying these two desires as those associated with the politically radicalized). The desire for political independence includes the desire for the United States to "stop interfering, meddling in . . . internal affairs, colonizing, and controlling natural resources." Ibid., at 92. Thus, this belief actually implicates many of the assumptions we tested before, including those regarding U.S. cultural imperialism, military imperialism, our position in the Arab-Israeli conflict, our abuse of power, U.S. economic imperialism, and our support for particular governments in predominantly Muslim countries.

42. WorldPublicOpinion.org, note 4, at 6.

43. Peter Bergen and Paul Cruickshank, "The Unraveling: Al Qaeda's Revolt against bin Laden," *The New Republic*, June 11, 2008.

44. Senator John McCain, "Hone U.S. Message of Freedom," editorial, *Orlando Sentinel*, June 28, 2007.

45. Carnes Lord and Helle C. Dale, *Public Diplomacy and the Cold War: Lessons Learned*, The Heritage Foundation (2007), http://www.heritage.org/Research/nationalSecurity/upload/bg_2070.pdf.

46. For a detailed comparison of the Cold War and the war on terrorism, see Ehsan Ahrari, "Why the Long War Can and Cannot Be Compared to the Cold War," *Comparative Strategy* 26 (2007): 275.

47. John Robert Kelley, "U.S. Public Diplomacy: A Cold War Success Story?," *The Hague Journal of Diplomacy* 2 (2007): 53, 65. See also James Critchlow, "Public Diplomacy during the Cold War," *Journal of Cold War Studies* 6, no. 1 (2006): 75, 81 (describing the objectives of Cold War diplomacy as providing a better understanding of the United States and "encouraging people to consider ideas for positive change").

48. Kelley, note 45, at 65.

49. Ibid.

50. Critchlow, note 45, at 78–79.

51. Kelley, note 45, at 65–66. The United States also employed other forms of media such as print magazines, films, and television.

52. Ibid., at 67, 74–75. On the one hand, Kelley points out that although there is evidence that the broadcasts successfully reached millions of listeners, multivariation and the difficulty of obtaining reliable statistical data prevented the United States from every accurately measuring the impact these campaigns had on the attitudes of Soviet listeners. On the other hand, the massive Soviet investment in blocking technology demonstrates that, at a minimum, we were able to

change state behavior due to the *possibility* that such broadcasts would change attitudes.

53. Ibid., at 63–64.

54. Ibid., at 66.

55. Ibid., at 64.

56. Ibid., at 70.

57. Ibid.

58. Ibid., at 56.

59. Ibid., at 75.

60. Ibid., at 78; see also Critchlow, note 45, 75, 81–83.

61. Ibid., at 73–74.

62. Ibid., at 81; Peter Aspden, *Counterpoint, Selling Democracy? The Past and Future of Western Cultural Relations and Public Diplomacy* (March 2004), 18–19, http://www.interarts.net/descargas/interarts663.pdf.

63. Critchlow, note 45, at 81–82. Indeed, Critchlow points out that eventually programmers began to realize the need to show "respect and a certain sense of humility" in order to get their message accepted by the Soviet public (83).

64. In fact, the United States to some extent has emulated the early rocky days of Cold War public diplomacy as evidenced by the State Department's failed "Shared Initiatives" campaign, which consisted of five advertisements featuring Muslim Americans speaking positively about their life in America. Widely criticized as crude propaganda, Egypt, Lebanon, and Jordan failed to even air the advertisements, and the project died shortly thereafter. See Stephen V. Johnson, "Improving U.S. Public Diplomacy toward the Middle East," Heritage Foundation, Heritage Lectures, no. 838, February 10, 2004, 3, http://www.heritage.org/research/nationalsecurity/hl838.cfm; and Liam Kennedy and Scott Lucas, "Enduring Freedom: Public Diplomacy and U.S. Foreign Policy," *American Quarterly* 57, no. 2 (2005): 309.

65. Lord and Dale, note 43, at 4–7; Aspden, note 58, 18–23.

66. Lord and Dale, note 43, at 4–7.

67. Labeled the "chief instrument of American public diplomacy," USIA was the agency responsible for the previously mentioned public diplomacy tactics. Critchlow, note 45, at 84.

68. To be sure such challenges were faced during the Cold War as well, but USIA's 1999 dissolution, according to some, has dealt a severe blow to American public diplomacy's stature. Critchlow, note 45, at 84–85; Lord and Dale, note 43, at 6.

69. Lord and Dale, note 43, at 2–4, 7.

70. Ibid.

71. Over its first 150 years, Europe's reformation led not to civility or the triumph of reason but to conflict, intolerance, and chaos. If the Reformation led eventually to the Enlightenment, among its most important contributions were

the sheer exhaustion of two centuries of religious bloodshed and the desire to move beyond it. The road from the Reformation to the Enlightenment was long and often convoluted. Indeed, to the extent a reformation suggests a departure from a previous orthodoxy, the Islamic world's reformation may already have happened. During the late nineteenth and early twentieth centuries, thinkers like Muhammad Abduh and Qasim Amin tried to rethink the relationship between classical Islamic structures and the rapidly changing world. Meanwhile, the decline of the Ottoman Empire, the rise of new nationalist ideologies, and the spread of literacy and communications technologies undermined the traditional role of highly trained scholars in interpreting Islamic doctrine.

True, those trends gave rise to liberal, tolerant interpretations, which sought to render longstanding doctrines more compatible with modernity. But they also sparked the intolerant, belligerent movements that gave rise to Osama Bin Laden and his supporters.

That conflict still burns. Perhaps the intolerance and conflicts will eventually exhaust themselves, as arguably happened in Europe. But there is little evidence to believe that this will happen anytime soon—or that the United States can hasten the day. Instead, the United States might be better off removing itself from the line of fire in this conflict by reducing moral support for attacks against U.S. civilians rather than attempting to sponsor a side.

72. *Joint Forces Quarterly*, no. 55 (4th quarter 2009).

Index

Belfer Center for Science and International Affairs

Graham Allison, Director
John F. Kennedy School of Government
Harvard University
79 JFK Street, Cambridge, MA 02138
Tel: (617) 495–1400; Fax: (617) 495–8963
http://belfercenter.ksg.harvard.edu
belfer_center@hks.harvard.edu

The Belfer Center is the hub of the Harvard Kennedy School's research, teaching, and training in international security affairs, environmental and resource issues, and science and technology policy.

The Center has a dual mission: (1) to provide leadership in advancing policy-relevant knowledge about the most important challenges of international security and other critical issues where science, technology, environmental policy, and international affairs intersect; and (2) to prepare future generations of leaders for these arenas. Center researchers not only conduct scholarly research, but also develop prescriptions for policy reform. Faculty and fellows analyze global challenges from nuclear proliferation and terrorism to climate change and energy policy.

The Belfer Center's leadership begins with the recognition of science and technology as driving forces constantly transforming both the challenges we face and the opportunities for problem solving. Building on the vision of founder Paul Doty, the Center addresses serious global concerns by integrating insights and research of social scientists, natural scientists, technologists, and practitioners in government, diplomacy, the military, and business.

The heart of the Belfer Center is its resident research community of more than 150 scholars, including Harvard faculty, researchers, practitioners, and each year a new, international, interdisciplinary group of research fellows. Through publications and policy discussions, workshops, seminars, and conferences, the Center promotes innovative solutions to significant national and international challenges.

The Center's International Security Program, directed by Steven E. Miller, publishes the Belfer Center Studies in International Security, and sponsors and edits the quarterly journal *International Security*.

The Center is supported by an endowment established with funds from Robert and Renée Belfer, the Ford Foundation, and Harvard University, by foundation grants, by individual gifts, and by occasional government contracts.

Belfer Center Studies in International Security

Published by The MIT Press

Sean M. Lynn-Jones and Steven E. Miller, series editors
Karen Motley, executive editor
Belfer Center for Science and International Affairs
John F. Kennedy School of Government, Harvard University

Acharya, Amitav, and Evelyn Goh, eds., *Reassessing Security Cooperation in the Asia-Pacific* (2007)

Agha, Hussein, Shai Feldman, Ahmad Khalidi, and Zeev Schiff, *Track-II Diplomacy: Lessons from the Middle East* (2003)

Allison, Graham T., Owen R. Coté, Jr., Richard A. Falkenrath, and Steven E. Miller, *Avoiding Nuclear Anarchy: Containing the Threat of Loose Russian Nuclear Weapons and Fissile Material* (1996)

Allison, Graham T., and Kalypso Nicolaïdis, eds., *The Greek Paradox: Promise vs. Performance* (1996)

Arbatov, Alexei, Abram Chayes, Antonia Handler Chayes, and Lara Olson, eds., *Managing Conflict in the Former Soviet Union: Russian and American Perspectives* (1997)

Bennett, Andrew, *Condemned to Repetition? The Rise, Fall, and Reprise of Soviet-Russian Military Interventionism, 1973–1996* (1999)

Blackwill, Robert D., and Michael Stürmer, eds., *Allies Divided: Transatlantic Policies for the Greater Middle East* (1997)

Blackwill, Robert D., and Paul Dibb, eds., *America's Asian Alliances* (2000)

Blum, Gabriella, and Philip B. Heymann, *Laws, Outlaws, and Terrorists: Lessons from the War on Terrorism* (2010)

Brom, Shlomo, and Yiftah Shapir, eds., *The Middle East Military Balance 1999–2000* (1999)

Brom, Shlomo, and Yiftah Shapir, eds., *The Middle East Military Balance 2001–2002* (2002)

Brown, Michael E., ed., *The International Dimensions of Internal Conflict* (1996)

Brown, Michael E., and Šumit Ganguly, eds., *Government Policies and Ethnic Relations in Asia and the Pacific* (1997)

Brown, Michael E., and Šumit Ganguly, eds., *Fighting Words: Language Policy and Ethnic Relations in Asia* (2003)

Carter, Ashton B., and John P. White, eds., *Keeping the Edge: Managing Defense for the Future* (2001)

Chenoweth, Erica, and Adria Lawrence, eds., *Rethinking Violence: States and Non-State Actors in Conflict* (2010)

de Nevers, Renée, *Comrades No More: The Seeds of Political Change in Eastern Europe* (2003)

Elman, Colin, and Miriam Fendius Elman, eds., *Bridges and Boundaries: Historians, Political Scientists, and the Study of International Relations* (2001)

Elman, Colin, and Miriam Fendius Elman, eds., *Progress in International Relations Theory: Appraising the Field* (2003)

Elman, Miriam Fendius, ed., *Paths to Peace: Is Democracy the Answer?* (1997)

Falkenrath, Richard A., *Shaping Europe's Military Order: The Origins and Consequences of the CFE Treaty* (1994)

Falkenrath, Richard A., Robert D. Newman, and Bradley A. Thayer, *America's Achilles' Heel: Nuclear, Biological, and Chemical Terrorism and Covert Attack* (1998)

Feaver, Peter D., and Richard H. Kohn, eds., *Soldiers and Civilians: The Civil-Military Gap and American National Security* (2001)

Feldman, Shai, *Nuclear Weapons and Arms Control in the Middle East* (1996)

Feldman, Shai, and Yiftah Shapir, eds., *The Middle East Military Balance 2000–2001* (2001)

Forsberg, Randall, ed., *The Arms Production Dilemma: Contraction and Restraint in the World Combat Aircraft Industry* (1994)

George, Alexander L., and Andrew Bennett, *Case Studies and Theory Development in the Social Sciences* (2005)

Gilroy, Curtis, and Cindy Williams, eds., *Service to Country: Personnel Policy and the Transformation of Western Militaries* (2007)

Hagerty, Devin T., *The Consequences of Nuclear Proliferation: Lessons from South Asia* (1998)

Heymann, Philip B., *Terrorism and America: A Commonsense Strategy for a Democratic Society* (1998)

Heymann, Philip B., *Terrorism, Freedom, and Security: Winning without War* (2003)

Heymann, Philip B., and Juliette N. Kayyem, *Protecting Liberty in an Age of Terror* (2005)

Howitt, Arnold M., and Robyn L. Pangi, eds., *Countering Terrorism: Dimensions of Preparedness* (2003)

Hudson, Valerie M., and Andrea M. den Boer, *Bare Branches: The Security Implications of Asia's Surplus Male Population* (2004)

Kayyem, Juliette N., and Robyn L. Pangi, eds., *First to Arrive: State and Local Responses to Terrorism* (2003)

Kokoshin, Andrei A., *Soviet Strategic Thought, 1917–1991* (1998)

Lederberg, Joshua, ed., *Biological Weapons: Limiting the Threat* (1999)

Mansfield, Edward D., and Jack Snyder, *Electing to Fight: Why Emerging Democracies Go to War* (2005)

Martin, Lenore G., and Dimitris Keridis, eds., *The Future of Turkish Foreign Policy* (2004)

May, Ernest R., and Philip D. Zelikow, eds., *Dealing with Dictators: Dilemmas of U.S. Diplomacy and Intelligence Analysis, 1945–1990* (2007)

Shaffer, Brenda, *Borders and Brethren: Iran and the Challenge of Azerbaijani Identity* (2002)

Shaffer, Brenda, ed., *The Limits of Culture: Islam and Foreign Policy* (2006)

Shields, John M., and William C. Potter, eds., *Dismantling the Cold War: U.S. and NIS Perspectives on the Nunn-Lugar Cooperative Threat Reduction Program* (1997)

Tucker, Jonathan B., ed., *Toxic Terror: Assessing Terrorist Use of Chemical and Biological Weapons* (2000)

Utgoff, Victor A., ed., *The Coming Crisis: Nuclear Proliferation, U.S. Interests, and World Order* (2000)

Williams, Cindy, ed., *Filling the Ranks: Transforming the U.S. Military Personnel System* (2004)

Williams, Cindy, ed., *Holding the Line: U.S. Defense Alternatives for the Early 21st Century* (2001)